# LEGAL
# BLACKSMITH

# LEGAL
# BLACKSMITH

## HOW TO AVOID AND DEFEND SUPPLY CHAIN DISPUTES

**Rosemary Coates & Sarah Rathke**

ISBN: 0692561366
ISBN 13: 9780692561362

# FOREWORD

I have worked in the field of aerospace component engineering and manu-facturing for over 20 years and currently run a business that specializes in manufacturing gas turbine engine control systems. The supply chain relationships that are developed in the aerospace industry are partnerships that have existed for many decades from initial product design until the aircraft is retired from service. Since it is quite often the case that the partnership on any particular product stays in existence for 50+ years, due in part to a unique product life cycle, the contract formed between the partners is paramount to mutual success.

I have written and negotiated numerous long-term contracts with both customers and suppliers and received my first real exposure to the complex world of supply chain disputes in 2012. It is this dispute that brought together Rosemary and Sarah for the first time, and ultimately this book. Throughout the many ensuing months, I got to know Rosemary and Sarah extremely well as we charted our way through the expensive, time-consuming, and unpre-dictable dispute resolution process.

Rosemary is a seasoned global supply chain executive with 25+ years in supply chain, operations, and project management. She has significant inter-national experience spanning a broad range of industries and has worked for extended periods overseas. She is extremely personable, practical, and under-stands how to create effective "win-win" business partnerships that will stand the test of time.

Sarah is a trial lawyer whose practice focuses on complex supply chain disputes working for one of the largest 25 law firms in the world. She is meticulous in her attention to detail and she understands the process of bringing highly engineered products to market. She has been named an Ohio Super Lawyers "Rising Star" eight times, an honor given to the top 2.5 percent of Ohio lawyers age 40 or under. Sarah also provides support to manufacturers outside of litigation concerning supply chain contracts and laws governing supply chain relationships.

I could not think of two more qualified and accomplished individuals to team together to write this book. Both authors have a wealth of experience—both textbook and real life—that if followed will give you a better chance to create a mutually successful relationship. Take it from me: spend the time and energy up front at the beginning of a new program or relationship rather than trying to resolve your issues after the fact through the litigation or dispute resolution process!

Alec Searle

President

Triumph Group

# Authors' Foreword

We had the good fortune of working together on a legal case involving a manufacturer in a dispute with its customer. Over the months of working closely together on this case, we had many discussions about supply chain processes and a typical company's inability to effectively protect itself from legal disputes in its supply chain.

Supply chain legal disputes don't start out as legal disputes. They typically start out as badly written contracts, poor communication with supply chain partners, and an inability to resolve conflicts. While legal battles are sometimes inevitable, most of the time, they can be avoided through planning and an informed approach to the supply chain and associated processes.

As a result of our experience together, we set out to write a book that would explain the best ways to avoid and manage conflict in supply chains. Rosemary brought her 25+ years of experience in supply chain processes and technologies, and Sarah brought her considerable legal focus in the supply chain field. We quickly found a writing rhythm and also found that our writing styles were quite complementary. With the goal of teaching attorneys about supply chain processes and teaching supply chain professionals about the legal aspects of their day-to-day businesses, we designed the approach to this book. Each chapter begins with a process overview and then describes the legal aspects of that process.

For supply chain professionals, if you've never been in a legal battle, you may not know what to watch for. Our goal is to help you understand how to avoid disputes, but if you should find yourself involved in a legal case, our objective is to demonstrate how best to defend your company. We present information that you cannot find in textbooks or seminars. This book is a unique combination and collection of information from both of our fields.

For attorneys involved in supply chain disputes, our goal is to describe the fundamentals of the major supply chain processes. We help you quickly understand the basic structures, issues, and relationships in the supply chain from an operational perspective, and show how these operations fit within the relevant legal precedents.

We did not accomplish the writing of this book alone. We had many advisors and helpers in this effort. Ricky Gurbst and Laura Lowell helped us with executive editing. Diane Vo supported us with copy editing, and Maureen Widmer and Kathy Zalewski assisted us with organization and keeping track of our many drafts. Sandy D'Amico supported us with social media. Ayako Hobbs and Michelle DeVito provided able legal research. We owe the completion of our book to each of these wonderful and hard-working people. Thank you.

But most importantly, we are grateful to each other. Over the course of the year (or so) it took us to write this book, we became friends with a healthy respect for each other's knowledge and commitment to our professions. The process was stressful and demanding, but mostly a lot of fun.

We hope you will find the book interesting and helpful in avoiding and defending supply chain disputes.

Rosemary Coates
Silicon Valley

Sarah Rathke
Cleveland

# TABLE OF CONTENTS

# Acronyms & Initialisms Used

This book uses a number of acronyms and initialisms. For the convenience of the reader, we have included a list here, as well as the chapters in which they first appear:

——

## Terms & Phrases                 Chapter

# Introduction: Thinking Ahead to Avoid Supply Chain Disputes

## Overview

So you want to manufacture something? Making things is once again sexy. The resurgence of manufacturing and newly popular reshoring initiatives have increased public awareness of the importance of having effective procurement and supply chain operations. Procurement and the supply chain were once treated as backwater business functions, and supply chain leaders were usually not represented in the C-suite. Now, the supply chain is commonly understood to be vital to corporate success. New titles such as "Chief Supply Chain Officer" and "Executive Vice President of Supply Chain" are on the rise in forward-thinking organizations. With specialized programs being created at universities all over the country, education in procurement and supply chain is also catching up. Procurement and supply chains finally have professional cachet.

These days, there is so much at stake in the supply chain. Getting a product from concept to market bears almost no resemblance now to what the process looked like one hundred, or even 25, years ago. The notion of inventory-on-hand is virtually dead. Lean, global supply chains and just-in-time manufacturing have become universal. Computer systems record every step and transaction in supply chain operations and enable a comprehensive understanding of the entire supply chain. Supply chains are increasingly international, even in smaller companies. Global communications enable networks of suppliers and buyers to work together 24/7. But supply chains are also increasingly stretched, brittle, and thin as time and money are extracted from every process. Even small problems in the supply chain can shut down production, or even a whole company, in no time at all.

The term "supply chain" used to be defined as sourcing and procurement only. The addition of other functions and processes, however, has significantly broadened its definition to include planning and forecasting, product engineering and development, procurement, inventory management, manufacturing, quality control, warehousing, logistics, distribution, import/export, and field service. Each company may define its supply chain differently, but corporate awareness of the interconnected nature of supply chain functions has broadened, not narrowed, the definition. In this book, we have tried to focus on the broadest definition of supply chain as we could, within the confines of a few hundred pages.

Failing to manage supply chain relationships well can quickly threaten the viability of a company. One of the hot supply chain stories in recent news (at the time of this writing) involved GT Advanced, a New Hampshire company that entered into a supply chain contract with Apple to make synthetic sapphire for use in iPhone screens. According to GT Advanced's court filings, Apple forced GT Advanced into a one-sided contract that did not require Apple to make reasonable minimum purchases. GT Advanced also accused Apple of causing massive project delays and cost increases. Then, when Apple refused to reimburse GT Advanced for these costs, GT Advanced claimed that it was forced to file Chapter 11 bankruptcy. The parties settled, but the relationship suffered permanent damage. Case studies like this are covered extensively in this book, to provide an up-to-date understanding of the impact of supply chains on business.

Supply chains are also increasingly susceptible to events beyond human control. The 2011 earthquake and tsunami that struck Japan and damaged many major producers of computer chips affected computer and automotive companies around the world. Many carmakers were forced to shut down factories in both Japan and elsewhere for months afterward. The 2013 floods in Thailand had similar consequences, and Hurricane Sandy in 2012 crippled retail supply chains preparing for the busy Christmas shopping season. Climatologists predict an increase in weather disasters in the years to come, creating one more challenge for supply chain executives.

In today's world, failures in the supply chain can have dire consequences. Few days in 2014 and 2015 have passed without the media reporting on

General Motors' ignition switch defects, a supply chain debacle caused by the failure to integrate components with each other. The consequences have included recalls, Congressional hearings, and innocent victims.

Supply chain failures affect not only the products we use, but also the food we eat. In China, milk thought to be adulterated at some point in the supply chain caused over 50,000 infant hospitalizations and several deaths in 2008. Not only did the Chinese government compel product recalls, but it also criminally prosecuted more than a dozen milk company executives.

International supply chains are now common and pose unique challenges. The negotiation process and contract laws are different in every country. Multiple countries' laws may apply to different aspects of a supply chain relationship, and companies must scrupulously ensure that they and their supply chain partners comply with anti-corruption (and similar) legislation, data privacy rules, and the corporate social responsibility laws of all countries in which they operate. Public relations are also an issue. Problems with conflict minerals, poor labor practices, and environmental damage have haunted US companies in the recent past. For instance, apparel and footwear companies have earned a reputation for paying low wages and allowing unsafe working conditions.

Visibility across the supply chain is also increasingly important. In many cases, avoiding supply chain disputes can be accomplished by knowing what is going on in the supply chain, but this is not always easy. Supply chain contract provisions that require visibility all the way down the supply chain for critical components are now common—but not as common as they should be. Companies need to know what to track and how to track it. Software can help, but keeping suppliers connected and providing information can be a monumental task.

### *The Purpose and Structure of This Book*
This book is designed to help executive management, supply chain staff, in-house legal professionals, and other attorneys deal with supply chain issues. The chapters progress more or less sequentially through the supply chain relationship phases, beginning with pre-supply chain contract negotiations and moving through handling actual supply chain disputes. Among other things, we discuss product integration issues, procurement, IT support systems,

recalls, warranties, and best practices for putting together a workable supply chain agreement.

Each chapter includes an "Overview" section that discusses the practical- and business-related aspects for each topic, and a "Legal Overview" section that discusses the laws that govern them. Some chapters focus more on business practicalities (like Chapter 14 on information technology), while other chapters focus more on legal issues (like Chapters 19 and 20 on dispute resolution clauses in US supply chain contracts and dispute resolution clauses in non-US supply chain contracts, respectively). For each chapter, we have included a "Lessons Learned" section with a summary of the recommendations we make in each chapter.

We have attempted to be comprehensive but conversational in this book. We presume some familiarity with the basic principles of supply chain management and supply chain law by our readers. Keeping in mind that some of our readers with legal backgrounds may not be intimately familiar with supply chain operations, we have tried to provide explanations of operational functions that can be understood by non-experts. We also recognize that part of our audience consists of supply chain personnel who are not attorneys, so in the sections that discuss the law, we have attempted to provide explanations that can be understood by those with no legal training. We fully understand that some of our readers may not need so many of the basics.

Our main goal, however, is to encourage supply chain personnel to think ahead to avoid supply chain disputes—and to discuss issues that supply chain personnel should think about to maintain harmonious and effective supply chain relationships. Even though supply chain management has come a long way in the past 10 years, corporations are still not expert at ensuring that their supply chain agreements are tailored to their needs, even for major contracts. Supply chain agreements are still too reliant on standard forms that may or may not reflect the interests of the supply chain partners using them. In this book, we identify supply chain issues where standard-form language may not be appropriate, especially for high-value or strategically important contracts.

Supply chain contracts are often substantial business transactions, so when they fall apart, the results can be catastrophic. It is not unusual to see supply chain disputes in which the damages claimed are in the hundreds of millions of dollars or more. Yet often in those cases, the parties paid insufficient attention to their supply chain contracts during the negotiation and formation stage. Think about it—if a company were to conduct a several hundred-million-dollar merger or acquisition, the deal would be teeming with professionals, lawyers, and advisors. Yet in the supply chain context, it is not unusual to have a hundred-million-dollar deal that receives little, if any, legal, executive management, or expert review.

This book seeks to provide a reference to flag important supply chain issues. However, it is important to note that this book does not constitute specific legal advice to any company or industry, or for any particular legal issue or dispute, and that neither author intends to act as any reader's attorney or consultant. Some aspects of the law change rapidly, and accordingly we cannot guarantee that the information in this book will be accurate or up-to-date when any reader decides to read it. Also, the law differs from jurisdiction to jurisdiction, so any particular dispute will be subject to the interpretation of courts in the jurisdiction where a dispute may be adjudicated. Finally, this book is not intended to be a complete statement of the law that applies to supply chain disputes. Indeed, no book can do that. This book should not be used as a substitute for the advice of competent legal counsel and other advisors.

In this book, we intentionally use examples from different industries to illustrate the principles we discuss. Our case studies come from the automotive, aviation, high-tech, fashion, food and beverage, medical, pharmaceutical, and other fields. Although every industry has its own issues and concerns, many supply chain issues are universal.

## Legal Overview

We would like to start with a word on the law that applies to supply chain issues.

There is no fully uniform law that applies to all supply chain disputes. In the United States, supply chain disputes generally consist of breach of contract and related allegations that are almost always governed by state law. Within the US, state law sometimes varies as it applies to supply chain issues (and when this is the case, we try to point it out), but fortunately, the variations are minimal. All states except Louisiana have adopted Article 2 of the Uniform Commercial Code (UCC), which governs contracts for the sale of goods, including supply chain transactions. Therefore, many of our legal discussions in this book will focus on Article 2 of the UCC. Originally published in 1957 as the joint effort of a number of legal organizations and legal scholars, the UCC is its drafters' recommendation of uniform laws to be enacted by the states.

The UCC is not perfect, however, and some states have differing interpretations of different UCC provisions. We discuss some of these ambiguous areas in this book.

Internationally, the law is more complicated. As readers can imagine, supply chain disputes that are governed by Chinese law may have very different outcomes than those governed by New York law, German law, or Mexican law. Fortunately, it is often not necessary in supply chain disputes to work with foreign law. If a supply chain contract between a US and a non-US party does not specify the governing law, the governing law is almost always supplied by an international treaty called the United Nations Convention on Contracts for the International Sale of Goods (CISG), also known as the "Vienna Convention."

Originally enacted in 1980, the CISG has 83 signatories (as of this writing), including most countries involved in international commerce. The purpose of the CISG is much like the purpose of the UCC in that it supplies a uniform body of contract law that applies to international contracts for the sale of goods, which includes most international supply chain contracts. There are some substantive differences between the UCC and the CISG, and where these differences are important, we will discuss them.

The CISG does not necessarily govern all international supply chain contracts, however. If supply chain partners have a forum selection clause in their contracts that selects a particular country's law—say Taiwanese law—to govern the supply chain contract, then that law will govern the contract. A full comparative study of the difference in contract law between countries is beyond the scope and purpose of this book, but where we find important or interesting supply chain anecdotes that involve foreign law, we will share them.

———

Now let's start learning about how to avoid and defend supply chain disputes!

# CHAPTER 1

# THE PRE-CONTRACT PLANNING PHASE

## Overview

The best time to engage in long-term strategic planning with supply chain partners is in the initial sourcing, pre-contract negotiation phase. During this time, supply chain partners can engage in creative, outside-the-box thinking and structure their relationship in the way that creates the most value for both parties. In fact, there is no other time during a supply chain relationship that offers the same opportunity. During the pre-contract planning phase, supply chain partners can identify each other's needs, priorities, and strategic goals, and begin to design a negotiation blueprint based on their findings.

The initial stages of the relationship between supplier and buyer are generally filled with optimism. Both parties are open to exploring new ideas and expanding the deal to ensure maximum value to each side. This is the time when skilled procurement professionals are most likely to think beyond cost and contemplate the value that can be created in a broader deal. But optimism at the outset of a supply chain relationship can cause blindness to issues that may arise down the road. Most experienced procurement and supply chain professionals have experienced this and have learned to be cautiously optimistic and careful moving forward.

There are often several aspects to the pre-contract planning phase of a supply chain relationship. Many supply chain relationships start off with marketing materials. Some supply chain relationships involve Requests for

Information (RFI), Requests for Quotation (RFQ), and Requests for Proposals (RFP). Many also involve a negotiating process between the parties. Good communication is required for success in all aspects of pre-contract planning. Failing to clearly communicate will likely mean that expectations will not be met, which can create frustrations that permeate the relationship for years. On the other hand, good communication can increase the value of a supply chain relationship for each side and will smooth the pathway for optimal working conditions. This is particularly important when a supply chain relationship is likely to last several years or if the supply chain relationship is one that requires intense collaboration.

We cannot stress enough how often we have seen supply chain breakdowns end in litigation as the result of poor communication. Maintaining good communication is well worth the time and effort.

### Creating Effective Marketing Materials

Creating effective marketing materials can be one of the first steps in establishing successful supply chain relationships. By "marketing materials," we do not mean only the brochures that companies distribute at trade shows and fairs. Marketing materials include any generalized statements about a company's products or capabilities that are distributed or available to the public. These could be trade show materials, product descriptions on a company's webpage, white papers, or presentations that a company gives to larger groups. Supplier marketing materials matter in supply chain relationships since they often precipitate relationships and, ultimately, sales. But buyers' marketing materials can be important as well; potential suppliers often consult buyers' marketing materials to determine how best to approach buyers and use them to guide the relationship.

So how do you create effective marketing materials? The answer will depend on your intended audience. There is no one-size-fits-all approach—you need to know your audience. In some industries, such as aerospace, medical products, and pharmaceuticals, quality control and meeting tight tolerances is critical and therefore will likely be the marketing focus. In other industries, such as consumer goods, product attractiveness and durability are key. For many products, cost will be the determining factor.

Often, companies that want to expand their supply chain relationships over-rely on marketing firms to create their marketing materials. Outside marketing services can be helpful, but it is important to realize that marketing consultants often will not have sufficient knowledge about your industry, products, or customers. It is you who must make sure that marketing materials incorporate the information that matters to your target audience. Ideally, this is a collaborative process between you and your marketing professionals.

Also—and we hope this goes without saying—marketing materials must be accurate. This means that you should avoid overstating your products' or your company's capabilities. In any industry, manufacturing firms looking for supply chain relationships should concentrate on marketing what they are actually good at. You may find yourself in projects that are a "stretch" for you—and that does happen—but your marketing should not focus on stretch opportunities.

On the buyer's side, your written materials to potential suppliers (even emails and PowerPoint presentations) should accurately state what your rules and processes are. If you intend to provide suppliers with forecasts, quarterly reviews, and the like, then you should communicate this during the pre-contract phase and follow through. Describe how you intend to do business in enough detail so that there is no ambiguity about your expectations. And remember, both buyer and supplier marketing materials will likely become evidence if a supply chain relationship ends in litigation.

### Creating Effective RFIs, RFQs, and RFPs

In the RFI, RFQ, and RFP stage, buyers publicize their needs to potential suppliers in the hopes of getting competitive and competent bids. Collectively, these requests are called the "RF$\underline{X}$" phase and may include all three types of requests. Any or all three of these RFXs may be used in the procurement process, whether the buyer is dealing with one or multiple suppliers.

RFIs are typically used to solicit input regarding a new idea or change in strategy. This is an "ask" process to obtain confirmation that something is possible and that a supplier is interested in further communication. For example, if a company wants to purchase a large item, such as a new factory or an ocean vessel, the RFI will set the initial stage for development talks. Buyers often issue RFIs when they begin working with a new product or a new technology, or perhaps if they are considering sourcing internationally for the first time. RFIs do not focus on cost, and some do not even request cost information.

RFQs are used primarily to obtain cost information for a defined product and defined scope of work and are best used with commodity, well-defined, and low-risk products where the supplier has little to no discretion in how the product is made. If a supplier's price is acceptable to the buyer, the RFX process may stop after the RFQ and not progress to an RFP. If the lowest-cost bidder meets minimum capabilities, and all other things are equal, the buyer will probably award the project to that bidder. Most procurement departments will then carefully track cost savings/avoidance and evaluate suppliers on the achievement of cost-saving goals.

If the scope of a project is not totally defined or if new information is introduced into the process, an RFP is often the next step after an RFI or RFQ. RFPs are used to define requirements more clearly by requesting that one or more suppliers propose solutions and costs. The focus in evaluating RFP responses is often the prospective suppliers' capabilities or the feasibility of their proposed solutions. Prospective suppliers' proposed solutions typically include their recommended approaches and associated costs.

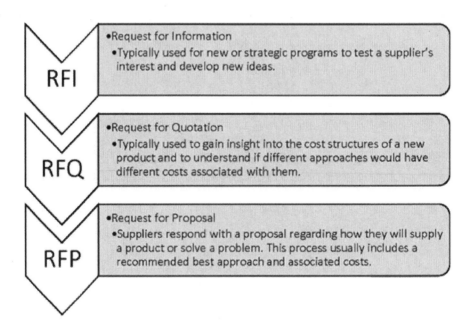

RFI
•Request for Information
 •Typically used for new or strategic programs to test a supplier's interest and develop new ideas.

RFQ
•Request for Quotation
 •Typically used to gain insight into the cost structures of a new product and to understand if different approaches would have different costs associated with them.

RFP
•Request for Proposal
 •Suppliers respond with a proposal regarding how they will supply a product or solve a problem. This process usually includes a recommended best approach and associated costs.

Whichever documents are used (RFI, RFQ, RFP, or a combination), it is usually best to include (1) the rules for responding to the request, including deadlines and any formatting requirements; (2) a description of any qualifications required for the project and a request for bidders to describe their qualifications; (3) a realistic timeline for the project; (4) a detailed description of what is needed from bidders, including performance requirements and technical specifications if possible; (5) any standard terms and conditions that will apply; and (6) the buyer's proposed agreement for bidders to mark up. If the project has any assumptions or constraints, such as upward cost limitations, the RFX should also state these.

Suppliers should be scrupulous in following the rules set forth in buyer RFXs. Most RFX rules are designed to make suppliers' responses easy to evaluate and compare. If it is impossible for some reason to follow an RFX's instructions, a supplier should clearly and succinctly explain why.

All of a buyer's operational constituencies that will be involved with a project (engineering, project management, procurement, manufacturing, IT, finance, and perhaps others) should review RFXs before they are issued to suppliers to ensure that requests capture all of a project's salient characteristics. Ideally, RFXs should be sent only to pre-qualified companies that the buyer has screened and that possess the necessary qualifications to perform the project. The field of RFX recipients should be narrowed to only a few (usually three to five) that could be successful candidates. Bidders should have ample time to respond, and the buyer should give bidders an opportunity to ask questions. This is especially important if the product or service is complex and will take the supplier some development time to form a viable solution. Generally, we advise having only one point of contact for questions from bidders to ensure a consistent message and fair process. In many instances, it is more expeditious to hold one RFX call for all potential bidders to ask questions at the same time.

Even if a buyer's intention is to award the contract to the lowest-cost bidder, it is best to include a statement in the buyer's RFX that reserves the buyer's right to award the contract to the most qualified supplier, regardless of cost. This is standard procedure in certain kinds of government contracts, which often must be awarded to the "lowest cost and best" candidates. It is also a best practice for buyers to reserve the right in their RFXs to withdraw an RFX for any reason.

## Reverse Auctions

When we think of auctions, we usually conjure up images of people bidding higher and higher for a product (e.g., for a work of art or prized gem). But in industrial buying, the reverse sometimes happens through a process called a "reverse auction." In a reverse auction, a buyer defines the services or commodities that it needs, and suppliers place opening bids and then subsequent bids against other suppliers, taking the price lower and lower. Since most procurement functions now operate on business IT systems called enterprise resource planning (ERP) systems, reverse online auctions have become common and popular. Reverse online auction functionality is usually built into the procurement functional modules of ERP software systems. In reverse auctions, suppliers must be careful. If a supplier offers a price in an online auction, it will be required to honor that price when the auction is over.

Hated by suppliers but loved by procurement departments, reverse auctions squeeze the last pennies out of competitive services and commodities. In reverse auctions, the playing field is not level, and buyers clearly have the upper hand. In some situations, buyers use reverse auctions to establish price, but determine other components of a supply chain contract through an RFX process.

## Effective RFX Responses

To respond effectively to an RFX, it is important that a supplier's business development and sales personnel have an accurate and comprehensive understanding of the supplier's products and capabilities. One problem that we see too frequently is that a supplier's sales or business development staff will prepare an RFX response without consulting the technical personnel who will actually do the work. Later, the supplier discovers that the cost assumptions in its bid were incorrect or that the supplier does not have the capability to do the project. The result is increased cost, dissatisfaction, and perhaps failure of the agreement, ending in litigation.

We recommend being conservative in bid responses. Requests that strain the boundaries of what your company is capable of, or cost limitations that test your company's ability to make a satisfactory profit, should be entertained only if senior management has expressly decided that there are legitimate or strategic reasons to pursue this direction. It is also important to be honest and accurate in bid responses, particularly because during contract negotiations many buyers require suppliers to affirm representations made during the RFX process.

If a buyer changes the project requirements or scope during bidding or after bidding is complete, it is important for suppliers to fully evaluate the impact the buyer's changes will have on profit margin, timing, and the supplier's ability to perform successfully. If a buyer change necessitates a change to the terms and conditions of a supply chain agreement, we recommend raising this point as soon as possible. The best practice is for a supplier's RFX response to state that its bid is not binding, and no contract can be formed, until all contract terms are fully defined and negotiated.

Just as buyers should include all constituencies that will be involved in a project when they create RFXs, suppliers should also include all of their constituencies that will be involved in a project (e.g., business development, engineering, contracting, quality, finance, etc.) when they submit RFX responses. Getting feedback from all of the relevant perspectives and interests within a supplier's company helps to ensure the best RFX response.

### Evaluating Bids from Suppliers

Evaluating bids from suppliers is always easier if bids are submitted in a uniform format. This will be straightforward in an RFQ scenario where the primary focus is price. But it is also typical to require formatted responses for at least part of RFPs and RFIs, even if bidders are proposing different technologies or different solutions. Each RFX must be constructed on a case-by-case basis, but finding a way to require suppliers to respond uniformly to at least part of an RFX will save time and effort in comparing bids later.

Buyers should ensure that a cross-functional team reviews bid responses. As with the earlier steps of the RFX process, any constituency involved in the project from the buyer's perspective should be included in the bid review, and should be given a conduit to provide reactions and thoughts. Typically, buyers will design weighted-average scoring processes in order to conduct an objective comparison between bidders. For high-value or strategically important relationships, executive management should be involved in the final review.

On larger projects, buyers will typically conduct site visits and reference checks as part of the RFX process, before awarding a contract. It is all too common, especially in international procurement, for a supplier to submit an impressive bid, only for the buyer later to learn that the supplier's factories or finances are inadequate to support the project. Reference checks are common, and should be completed with a structured questionnaire that will probe for problem areas and expose risk. (See Chapter 7: International Procurement.)

### *Negotiating the Contract*

In some ways, the most important elements for negotiating a supply chain contract are good planning and good manners. Both parties need to come to the table prepared with an understanding of the economics and mechanics of a proposed deal and the ability to appreciate the priorities of both sides. Both sides should also be represented by personnel with authority to compromise and agree to a final, or very nearly final, contract. We advocate developing a blueprint for the negotiation and multiple bundled alternatives to be presented during discussions. This keeps the conversation open and the negotiators thinking about the best overall deal.

Unfortunately, supply chain negotiations often do not happen as scripted. Supply chain partners sometimes fail to dedicate sufficient planning and resources to the negotiating process. The result is negotiations that become adversarial, stretch on longer than necessary, and that sometimes never come to a close. This is a dangerous situation because if supply chain partners begin work on a project before an agreement is finalized, it is very difficult to predict what a court will interpret the terms of the supply chain contract to be. (See Chapter 2: Drafting the Supply Chain Contract.)

In our experience, the best negotiations occur when supply chain partners work diligently to collect information about what is important to each side early in the buying process. This information can be gathered in meetings with stakeholders, through research, and in correspondence during the business development process. The information-gathering culminates in one or more negotiation meetings. At negotiation meetings, it is best for the buyer and/or seller to come with two or three bundled solution and offer alternatives that can be executed if accepted.

We coach our clients to stay away from going line-by-line and negotiating items separately because that approach tends to deteriorate into price concessions. By keeping the commercial aspects of a deal in a bundle, the focus will stay on the overall value. Regardless of what country or culture you are deal-ing with, the bundling method works well and helps to maximize value in the deal. This is not to say that parties cannot ever focus their discussions on a particular contract provision—just that the focus should remain to the great-est extent possible on maximizing overall value.

Finally, in our experience, the contract items that supply chain partners find most frustrating are warranty and indemnification provisions. Once pur-chase price and the technical parameters of the product are determined, these two items are the ones with the most potential impact on the economics of a supply chain contract. We suggest that supply chain partners determine their tolerance for liability internally before going into negotiations with the other side. This will both expedite the negotiating process, and ensure that both companies fully understand how these items will impact the deal value for them.

## Legal Overview

The legal issues involved in the pre-contract phase of supply chain relation-ships generally involve whether statements that supply chain partners make to each other before a contract is finalized are legally binding.

This is an important issue because sometimes supply chain partners be-lieve that their pre-contract statements are merely sales talk, when in fact, in some circumstances, the law will enforce those statements as binding contrac-tual "warranties." To avoid disputes during the pre-contract negotiating phase, it is important for supply chain partners to know when pre-contract state-ments are legally binding. Unfortunately, this is not always easy because the law provides no bright-line rules. Therefore, supply chain partners should take care to ensure that the statements they make to each other are accurate and supportable, especially those that relate to product performance or quality.

### Potentially Binding Marketing Materials

Suppliers make representations on their websites, in marketing brochures, and through sales people about their products. Often, these are vague statements about reliability, suitability in a particular environment, or superiority to com-petitor products. Suppliers sometimes assume that if marketing statements are made in an informal setting or at a preliminary stage of dealing, they are not contractually binding.

*Price Brothers Co. v. Philadelphia Gear Corp.*[1] is the case most often cited for the proposition that informal pre-contract sales statements are not contractually binding. In *Price Brothers*, the buyer sued the supplier to enforce pre-contract statements the supplier made verbally and in sales literature about the capabilities of a pipe-wrapping machine. The court determined that because the buyer was sophisticated and was the party that created the technical specifications for the machine, the supplier's statements were "nonspecific, pre-contract statements," and not binding contractual promises.

However, not all cases are in accord.

In *Confer Plastics, Inc. v. Hunkar Laboratories Inc.*,[2] for instance, the supplier of a manufacturing system submitted a pre-contractual "proposal" to the buyer. In the proposal, the buyer made representations about the supplier's capabilities and the product's ability to increase the buyer's profits. However, the proposal disclaimed all performance warranties. The buyer accepted the proposal without alteration, including the warranty disclaimer. Later, the buyer sued the supplier, claiming that the product did not meet the supplier's pre-contractual representations.

The supplier in *Confer Plastics* argued that its pre-contract statements could not be enforced as binding warranties because the supplier disclaimed all warranties, with no objection from the buyer. The court, however, held that the representations in the supplier's proposal could be construed to be binding warranties, notwithstanding the disclaimer.

Although we think that most courts would decide *Confer Plastics* differently, to play it safe, suppliers should be wary of making representations in their sales materials about product performance if there is any uncertainty as to whether the performance is achievable. Statements about a product's past accomplishments, how the product is constructed, or the supplier's qualifications are safer. Business development personnel should be trained not to speculate or make representations about the suitability of a product in a particular application without consulting with technical staff first. Suppliers that make

---

1   649 F.2d 416, 31 U.C.C. Rep. Serv. (Callaghan) 469 (6th Cir. 1981).
2   964 F.Supp. 73 (W.D. N.Y. 1997).

complex products, or that make products whose performance is impacted by the operating environment, should be especially cautious.

### *Integration Clauses in Supply Chain Contracts*

One way that supply chain partners can minimize the chance that pre-contractual statements will be construed to be binding warranties is by including an integration clause in their contracts. An integration clause (sometimes called a "merger clause") is a contract provision that states that the only binding commitments that exist between the parties are those contained in the final contract. The purpose of an integration clause is to prevent pre-contract statements and representations from becoming part of the contract. A sample integration clause is as follows:

**Integration Clause**

This Agreement encompasses and constitutes the entire agreement between the Parties, and supersedes and takes precedence over all previous understandings, communications, discussions, and representations, whether oral or written.

### *Potentially Binding RFX Documents*

Statements made in RFX documents and responses can also be contractually binding, even if the parties later negotiate a supply chain contract that supersedes the RFX documents.

Sometimes, supply chain partners will incorporate RFX documents into their contracts on purpose. When this is the case, buyer RFXs should explicitly state that any representations made in a supplier's response will become part of the supply chain contract. To the extent that a supplier is unwilling to be bound by its RFX response, the RFX response should expressly say so.

After bidding is complete, buyers will sometimes retroactively ask suppliers to guarantee statements made during the RFX process. Suppliers should be cautious about agreeing to be bound retroactively to any pre-contract statements. If the parameters of the project have changed, if a supplier's bid response contains vague or general language, or if the performance of the supplier's product depends upon the operating environment, a supplier should proceed carefully.

As protection, suppliers sometimes include language in their RFX responses that their bids are conditioned on the project description set forth in the buyer's RFX; if the project changes, the supplier will not be bound to statements made in its RFX response. This is generally an effective strategy, and one that we recommend as a best practice.

As with other pre-contract statements, RFX documents can be contractually binding, even if that is not what the parties intend. When this occurs, it is typically because an RFX or a supplier's response is sufficiently specific that a court will construe it as being a formal "offer" that the other party was invited to "accept" and thus create a binding contract.

The rule under the UCC is that a price quote or other communication that leads the receiving party to reasonably believe that its acceptance will conclude the agreement constitutes a contractual offer, and acceptance of the offer will create a binding contract. Factors that make courts more likely to conclude that an RFX response or price quote is an offer include: (1) if the buyer specifically solicited the RFX response or quote from the supplier, (2) if the buyer provided the supplier with enough information to calculate a price for the product, and (3) if the supplier issued the RFX response or quote to the buyer individually rather than to the public at large.

Suppliers take note, because some or all of these factors are present in most supply chain RFX scenarios! In the supply chain context, buyers often issue RFXs to one or a small number of potential suppliers. Frequently, responding suppliers are asked to and do quote a precise price. And often, supplier responses are directed exclusively to the requesting buyer. Although suppliers may not realize that communications of this nature are enough to create a binding contract, often, they are.

An illustrative (and disturbing) case is *Verasun Fort Dodge, L.L.C. v. Industrial Air Technology Corp.*[3] In *Verasun Fort Dodge*, the buyer issued an RFQ for an industrial fan. The supplier responded with a price quote that stated, "All quotations are for information only and are not an offer by the Seller." Despite the supplier's statement that it was <u>not</u> making a formal offer, and although the court recognized that a price quote is usually only "an invita-

---

3   2008 U.S. Dist. LEXIS 99292 (N.D. Iowa Nov. 25, 2008).

tion for an offer," the court held that the supplier's RFQ response was an offer that became binding when the buyer accepted it. The court acknowledged that many of the terms one would expect to see in a complex supply chain contract were missing from the supplier's quote (like warranty terms), but reasoned that their absence was not fatal because missing terms could be supplied by the UCC's "gap filling provisions."[4]

Does this result seem surprising? We think so, particularly because of the supplier's express statement that it was not making a formal offer. Although we think most courts would reach a different result, suppliers acting with caution should consider including a clause in their bid responses that reserves their right to reject any orders from the buyer, which the court in the *Verasun Fort Dodge* opinion stated would have changed the result in that case.

A case that reaches what we think is the correct result is *Q.C. Onics Ventures, LP v. Johnson Controls, Inc.*[5] In this case, an automotive parts buyer requested quotes from multiple suppliers, and issued a blanket purchase order and terms and conditions to the winning bidder. The buyer's terms and conditions gave the buyer the right to terminate the contract for convenience. Pursuant to that provision, the buyer terminated the contract, and the supplier sued.

The supplier argued that the buyer had no right to terminate the contract because the supplier's bid response was a contractual offer, which the buyer accepted when it chose the supplier. The contract between the parties, therefore, did not include the buyer's right to terminate for convenience or any of the buyer's other terms and conditions. But the court disagreed. According to the court, because the supplier's bid lacked the detailed terms one would expect to find in a fully negotiated supply chain agreement, it was not a contractual offer. The buyer's purchase order, which included detailed and complete commercial terms, was the offer, which the supplier accepted by delivering components. Thus, the parties' supply chain contract allowed the buyer to terminate the contract for convenience.

Another relevant case can be found in *Rich Products Corp. v. Kemutec, Inc.*,[6] which involved the sale of a conveyor for use in manufacturing bak-

---

4   The UCC contains a number of so-called "gap filling terms" like warranty and delivery terms that are used to interpret contracts that fail to include such terms themselves.

5   2006 U.S. Dist. LEXIS 45189 (N.D. Ind. June 21, 2006).

6   66 F.Supp. 2d 937, 41 U.C.C. Rep. Serv. 2d (Callaghan) 23 (E.D. Wisc. 1999).

ery items. The supplier's marketing materials stated that the conveyor could "move mountains of almost anything," including food and fine powders. The supplier confirmed orally to the buyer that its conveyors were used in the bakery industry. The supplier's RFP response also stated that its product had "[e]xcellent experience in handling bakery materials and products." After deciding to purchase the conveyor, the buyer issued a purchase order that it stated was an "offer," subject to additional terms and conditions that were supposed to be attached to the purchase order, but the buyer forgot to attach them. Had the buyer's terms and conditions been included, they would have contained broad warranties on the conveyor. The supplier sent the buyer an "acknowledgement" that included the supplier's terms and conditions and provided a limited warranty on the conveyor.

When the conveyor failed to perform as expected, the buyer sued for breach of the representations in the supplier's RFP response about the conveyor's capabilities. The court held that the supplier's RFP response was sufficiently detailed to constitute an offer, even though the response lacked many of the commercial terms normally found in a fully negotiated supply chain contract. However, because the buyer conditioned its acceptance on the additional terms and conditions that accompanied its purchase order (even though it forgot to send them), the buyer's terms and conditions were a counteroffer, not an acceptance. And because the supplier's acknowledgement contained additional terms, the acknowledgement also constituted a counteroffer, rather than an acceptance. Therefore, the court held that neither party was right as a matter of law, and a jury would have to decide whether and to what extent the supplier's pre-contract representations were part of the parties' agreement.

Confused yet? We are not surprised. The negotiating history in *Rich Products* is a model of how not to structure a supply chain relationship. Needless to say, this confusing bid process added significant expense and uncertainty to the transaction that both parties likely wish they had avoided.

———

## Lessons Learned

When working together to negotiate a supply chain contract, prospective supply chain partners should:

- Discuss important issues at the start of the relationship and seek to maximize business opportunities
- Clearly communicate expectations
- Ensure that marketing materials and RFX documents are accurate and speak to the needs of the audience
- Include an integration clause stating that the executed agreement constitutes the total agreement between the parties, and any prior statements or representations are not part of the contract
- Ensure that all constituencies involved in a supply chain project are also involved in creating and evaluating RFX documents
- Be conservative in RFX responses
- Make sure that all RFX submissions reflect any changes made to a project
- Be prepared for negotiating sessions, and negotiate contracts as unified packages rather than line-by-line
- Be conscious that pre-contractual statements made during the RFX process may be binding

# CHAPTER 2

# DRAFTING THE SUPPLY CHAIN CONTRACT

## Overview

By the end of the RFX process, the buyer will have determined to go forward with the project, settled on its technical specifications, and selected one or more suppliers. The buyer and supplier will have established a price each of them can live with. A timeline will have been established to ensure that all stages of the project are on track. All that is left to do will be to memorialize the agreement in writing. The hard part is over, right?

Absolutely wrong. Drafting the contract is a critical moment in the supply chain relationship that requires foresight, discipline, and precision. The supply chain agreement forms the basis of every aspect of the supply chain relationship going forward. While it is theoretically possible to address new issues and renegotiate contract provisions later in the relationship, in reality, this rarely happens. Nevertheless, companies often fail to give supply chain contracts the attention they require during the drafting phase, and end up paying the price later.

Just think about it. If an American manufacturing company planned to enter into a merger or acquisitions deal valued at, say, $100 million, the transaction would be crawling with consultants and lawyers. Negotiations would be conducted formally with full due diligence, and the parties would insist on a formal signing and closing before transferring whatever was being acquired. Yet, parties rarely proceed with the same care when drafting supply chain contracts of equal or greater value, even though supply chain relationships sometimes last decades!

Even today, many companies enter into multi-million-dollar supply chain agreements without dedicating much attention to the terms of these contracts. Supply chain agreements are considered to be "boilerplate," based on pre-existing forms, and are often coupled with technical specifications written by engineers without meaningful executive or legal review. Even when supply chain agreements are strategically important or involve non-standard features, many are nevertheless consummated using only purchase orders and standard terms and conditions. As the famous UCC commentators James J. White and Robert S. Summers once described, "It is a sad fact that many sales contracts are not fully bargained, not carefully drafted, and not understandingly signed or otherwise acknowledged by both parties. Often, here is what happens: underlings of seller and buyer each sit in their offices with a telephone and a stack of form contracts."[7]

## *Boilerplate Supply Chain Contracts*

Fortunately, twenty-first century supply chain contracts are beginning to come out of this legal backwater, and many companies have started to develop and share best practices. What companies are learning is that there is no such thing as boilerplate supply chain terms that apply with equal logic to all supply chain relationships, especially those that involve anything more complex than commodity parts. The circumstances of each deal are usually important, and the wisdom of contract terms varies from deal to deal. Companies today that have complex supply chain networks are increasingly relying on fully negotiated long-term agreements, rather than standard purchase orders or terms and conditions.

In parallel, the purchasing profession has gone through a major transformation over the past 15 to 20 years. Today's procurement professionals are well educated (many new MBAs start in procurement), tech-savvy, and willing to work cross-functionally with their company's legal department to negotiate and draft supply chain contracts. They have probably taken a class or two in business law and recognize the need for robust and well-tailored contracts.

Of course, forms and standard terms and conditions can save time for busy purchasing departments in commodity transactions, but relying on them too much risks conflict and confusion that translates negatively to the company's

7   James J. White & Robert S. Summers, *Uniform Commercial Code*, vol. 1, 54 (Thompson West, 5th ed. 2002).

bottom line. Both suppliers and buyers can become so eager to begin work that they do not take the care they should to protect their interests and to plan for contingencies.

Buyers often assume that their purchasing power means they can pressure suppliers to accept buyer terms, and that buyer terms will always prevail. Here's another quote from White and Summers: "Under the present state of the law we believe that there is no language that a lawyer can put on a form that will always assure the client of forming a contract on the client's own terms."[8] Both parties to supply chain agreements need to engage meaningfully in the contract negotiation and drafting process.

Buyers need to understand that it is often counterproductive to force terms on suppliers if those terms lead to performance issues and damage the relationship, and that it is usually better to negotiate a deal that guarantees a viable program. Similarly, suppliers need to understand that it is counterproductive to take on a new program that is difficult or impossible to perform, and that it is usually better to direct resources towards programs that are achievable and profitable in the long term. Butting up against sales quotas and quarter-end pressure, sales people often feel the need to close a deal to please senior managers. But this is when senior managers must step in to protect the company, no matter what week of the quarter or year it is.

The number one goal of supply chain contracts is certainty. If the expectations for both parties are clearly established, supply chain partners are generally able to avoid disputes. A second goal is mutual success. If one supply chain partner suffers economically, both will suffer eventually—it is the nature of commercial dealing. A supply chain partner losing money will often find ways to cut corners, sacrificing quality, reliability, or technical compliance. At the very least, a losing partner will start looking for ways out of the relationship. This is a destructive dynamic.

## Rules for Drafting Supply Chain Contracts

Drafting successful supply chain contracts is about more than just the contract terms. There is a procedural component as well. How you negotiate is almost as important as what you negotiate.

---

8  James J. White & Robert S. Summers, *Uniform Commercial Code*, vol. 1, 82 (Thompson West, 5th ed. 2002).

An important preliminary consideration in negotiating new supply chain contracts is whether information exchange that occurs during negotiations should be confidential. Confidentiality is a best practice if supply chain partners will be sharing sensitive trade secret, proprietary, or business information with each other. Executing a confidentiality agreement at the beginning of supply chain contract negotiations allows the buyer to disclose proprietary information about its program and allows potential suppliers to disclose sensitive information about their costs and capabilities, which enables further negotiations. Not all supply chain contracts require confidentiality or involve proprietary or sensitive data, but many do.

A sample confidentiality clause is below. A confidentiality agreement can be much longer and may include provisions governing the protection of third-party information, the destruction of confidential information that is no longer needed, dispute resolution and so forth, but the following language can be used to provide the basic confidentiality protections.

**Non-Disclosure of Confidential Information**
"Confidential Information" means any information, technical data, research, inventions, processes, engineering, techniques, trade secrets, financial information and/or business information, or opportunities disclosed by either Party in any form whatsoever.

Each Party hereto desires to receive Confidential Information of the other Party for the purpose of considering and negotiating a business. Each Party agrees not to use Confidential Information for any purpose except considering and negotiating an ongoing business relationship. Each Party agrees not to copy, infringe, or reverse engineer any Confidential Information provided by the other Party and agrees not to disclose any Confidential Information to any third parties without the prior written consent of the other Party. If the Parties are unable or unwilling or determine for any reason not to enter into an ongoing business relationship, each Party agrees to return or destroy all Confidential Material provided by the other Party.

After confidentiality is established, supply chain partners can exchange information, conduct due diligence, and draft the more substantive portions of the supply chain contract.

The first rule for substantive contract negotiations is that both parties must involve each of their key constituencies in the process. We often see contracts in which the finance department establishes pricing, the purchasing department sets the commercial terms, and the engineering department negotiates technical specifications, all independently of one another. The problem is that these functions are not truly independent. Technical specifications influence what a product should cost. Product pricing informs the wisdom of agreeing to other commercial terms. Depending on technical requirements, commercial terms may or may not be tenable. Failing to coordinate these functions on the supplier's side can create a contract that the supplier is unable to perform. Failing to coordinate these functions on the buyer's side can result in a program that is not commercially viable or that does not meet market demand.

The second rule for drafting successful supply chain contracts is that supply chain parties should negotiate their agreement to completion before beginning work on a project. Partially negotiated supply chain agreements provide fertile ground for confusion and conflict. Moreover, both parties have less leverage in negotiations if they sink resources into a project before the agreement is fully drafted. Having the discipline to resist beginning work before the contract is executed also provides a powerful incentive to dedicate the resources needed to finalize a sound agreement.

The third rule for drafting successful supply chain contracts is that there is no such thing as too much communication. Parties frequently raise issues and concerns during the drafting process. Each issue and concern should be addressed. Ambiguity may seem expedient to get a deal done, but in reality, it rarely is. Prompt and thorough communication prevents minor misunderstandings from becoming major ones. Unaddressed issues invariably cause delay and conflict.

The fourth rule for drafting successful supply chain contracts is that each party should take the time to ensure, internally, that it is willing and able to perform each proposed term and condition. Often, supply chain partners use "compliance charts" to do this, in which each department involved in the contract (engineering, purchasing, etc.) will check "yes" or "no" to the proposed terms on a term-by-term basis. If the compliance chart yields any negative responses, these should be investigated and addressed before proceeding. Supply chain partners may be willing to comply with difficult provisions if they get concessions on other terms. But this must be actively determined. It should not happen by default or because of inattention.

### Supply Chain Contracts in Development Programs

Supply chain contracts for development programs pose the highest degree of difficulty. Whether the supplier is creating new technology, adopting existing technology to a new application, making a product in a new way, or trying to achieve a manufacturing efficiency never before achieved, the contracting process has to accommodate the fact that, for development programs, success might not happen, might not be on schedule, and might not be achievable within the contemplated cost structure.

We deal more fully with the special problem of development programs in Chapter 3. But for now, suffice it to say, the challenges of contract drafting are exponentially greater in development programs.

## Legal Overview

Supply chain relationships become confusing and contentious when the parties' legal rights and duties are unclear. Rights and duties should be spelled out with precision in supply chain agreements. Unfortunately, this does not always happen. When supply chain partners fail to pay sufficient attention to detail, fail to grant negotiators sufficient authority to compromise, or fail to negotiate the supply chain agreement to completion before beginning performance, they risk uncertainty and conflict. To avoid disputes, supply chain partners need to take the time to thoughtfully negotiate sensible and well-tailored agreements.

### Prioritizing Contract Documents

For complex supply chain relationships, the contract between the parties may not be set forth in a single document. Rather, the contract may be expressed in several documents that complement each other. These might include (1) a primary agreement (sometimes called a "Long-Term Agreement"), which sets forth the principal commercial terms; (2) one or more purchase orders that establish product quantities and delivery schedules; (3) terms and conditions taken from either the buyer or supplier's standard forms and adjusted as needed; (4) a schedule setting interim and production deadlines; and (5) technical specifications, drawings, and/or samples. Sometimes, supply chain contracts will incorporate RFX documents as well.

It is important to carefully analyze all of a supply chain contract's constituent documents to ensure that they do not contain provisions that conflict with each other. It is disappointingly common to find conflicting deadlines, dispute resolution provisions, or (worse) performance requirements in supply chain contract documents. Internally conflicting contract provisions are often the result of when different business functions have drafted different parts of the agreement without coordinating with each other. It is helpful to appoint one person or a small group of people to perform a final contract review, part of which should be to ensure that the contract documents are internally consistent.

Each of the documents that constitute the contract should be identified in the primary supplier agreement in an "Order of Precedence" paragraph. The Order of Precedence paragraph establishes which documents take priority in the event of a conflict. It can also help resolve disputes when a supply chain contract has internally conflicting terms. A sample Order of Precedence paragraph is below:

### Order of Precedence

The Agreement between the Parties is composed of the following contract documents, which are to be interpreted together as one Agreement. In the event there is an irreconcilable conflict between them, the following order of precedence applies: (1) this Supplier Agreement, (2) any PO(s) issued by Buyer and accepted by Supplier, (3) Specifications and Drawings, (4) Buyer's standard terms and conditions, and (5) the Statement of Work.

## *Drafting and Executing Supply Chain Agreements*

The biggest task in drafting a supply chain contract is to ensure that you address all of the substantive terms of the relationship in writing.

In the United States, establishing a supply chain agreement in writing is required by law—sort of. Article 2 of the UCC requires a "signed writing" in order for contracts for the sale of goods over $500 to be legally enforceable.[9] This requirement, however, is not robust, since the UCC does not require the signed writing to contain all of the agreement's terms. On the contrary, the only term the UCC requires to be included in the signed writing is order quantity (which we think is arbitrary). The remaining terms may be unaddressed, agreed to verbally, or filled in by a court if a dispute arises.

The UCC's requirement that the writing be "signed" is limited too, since the UCC defines "signed" to include "any symbol executed or adopted by a party with present intention to authenticate a writing."[10] Thus, a typed name, letterhead, the sender's email, or company logo have all been held to be sufficient evidence of signature. Moreover, between businesses (referred to as "merchants" in the UCC), the "signed writing" requirement is relaxed even further, and a proposed contract may be enforceable against a business that receives it if it does not object within 10 days.[11] For international supply chain agreements, the CISG (Convention on Contracts for the International Sale of Goods) does not require contracts to be signed or in writing. The law of individual countries may vary and should be investigated before proceeding.

Even though the law may not require all terms of a supply chain agreement to be in writing, fully documenting all supply chain agreements is the best practice. To add clarity and avoid disputes, supply chain contracts should be fully negotiated and memorialized before work on any project begins.

When supply chain partners go wrong during contract negotiations, it is generally in one of two ways. Either the parties exchange forms and templates, with neither party really agreeing to the other's terms—and begin performing. Or the parties begin negotiating with one another but do not fully reach agreement—and begin performing. Both scenarios cause confusion and conflict.

In the United States, both scenarios are addressed by UCC 2-207 (the notorious "Battle of the Forms" provision that causes post-traumatic stress in anyone who attended law school). The source of the trauma is, frankly, that UCC 2-207 is arbitrary and counterintuitive, not least because courts do not always interpret it consistently. Negotiating a complete supply chain contract before beginning work will help you avoid UCC 2-207.

---

9   UCC § 2-201(1).

10   UCC § 1-201(b)(39).

11   UCC § 2-201(2).

## The Battle of the Forms

An all-too-common supply chain failure occurs when (1) a buyer sends its standard purchase forms to a supplier, which contains terms and conditions; (2) the supplier sends its standard acknowledgment back to the buyer, which contains different terms and conditions; (3) the parties begin work on the project; and (4) a dispute arises. The question of whose terms prevail in this scenario is one that often goes to litigation, and is the classic "Battle of the Forms" under UCC 2-207. Unfortunately, the law provides few clear answers as to who wins.

Buyers often assume that their terms and conditions prevail in the event of a conflict with a supplier's terms, but under UCC 2-207, the reality is more complicated. In fact, under UCC 2-207, the supplier's terms can and do prevail, even if they conflict with a buyer's terms. The rule under UCC 2-207 is that the first-transmitted terms (say, the buyer's) become part of the contract if they are not objected to, and if the second party does not propose conflicting terms. If the second party (say, the supplier) responds with additional or conflicting terms, they may become part of the contract as well.

Terms that are merely "additional" (and not conflicting) in a second transmission will become part of the contract unless they "materially alter" the transaction.[12] Additional terms that courts have held do not "materially alter" a transaction, and thus become part of the contract, include reasonable interest charges on late payments, requiring complaints to be made in a timely manner, and force majeure clauses. On the other hand, additional terms that courts have held do "materially alter" a transaction, and therefore will not become part of the contract, include warranty disclaimers, clauses allowing cancellation if prompt payment is not made, clauses requiring payment of attorneys' fees, indemnification clauses, and clauses requiring warranty claims to be made in a very short period of time. Arbitration clauses, forum or choice of law clauses, and liability limitations have been found to be material alterations by some courts and non-material by others. The case law is inconsistent.

UCC 2-207 is unhelpfully silent on what happens with supplier terms and conditions that "conflict with" a buyer's terms and conditions, and are not merely "additional" (for example, if one party's terms include warranties, but the other party's terms disclaim all warranties). Courts have reached

---

12    UCC § 2-207(2).

inconsistent results. The majority of courts follow the "knock-out rule," in which conflicting terms knock each other out, and the court then inserts "gap fillers," which are default terms contained in the UCC. UCC gap fillers may or may not be appropriate to a particular supply chain relationship, but likely will not be what either party wanted. Some courts treat conflicting terms as counter-proposals, and drop both out of the contract. Still other courts hold that the second-transmitted term becomes part of the contract if it does not "materially alter" the transaction, mirroring the rule that applies to "additional" terms.

UCC 2-207 does not apply if the either party expressly conditions its willingness to contract on the other party's unconditional acceptance of its terms. Indeed, both buyer and supplier standard forms often contain language to the effect that, "Acceptance is limited to the terms and conditions contained herein." If either party insists that contract formation is contingent upon its terms, then, under the UCC, no contract is formed until the parties reach agreement. However, if supply chain partners begin performing, despite not reaching complete agreement, they face the problem described in the next section—the problem of partially negotiated agreements.

### *Partially Negotiated Agreements*

UCC 2-207 also comes into play when supply chain partners begin performing before they fully negotiate a supply chain agreement. UCC 2-207(3) provides that conduct by both parties that "recognizes the existence of a contract" is sufficient to establish a contract, even if the parties have not fully agreed on all terms. In such cases, the terms of the contract are deemed under UCC 2-207 to be those "on which the writings of the parties agree, together with any supplementary terms incorporated under any provisions of this Act."[13]

Businesspeople will immediately recognize why this is a problem. Imagine being mid-negotiation with a supply chain partner, and one or both of you has begun work on the project. You have tentatively agreed to some of the commercial terms, but not all of them. Perhaps you have exchanged redline drafts. Suddenly, a dispute arises that becomes intractable. If a court gets involved,

---

13   UCC § 2-207(3).

the "contract" becomes frozen at the state of your negotiations at that particular point in time.

This may work in academia, where UCC 2-207(3) was drafted, but in the real world it is hazardous and arbitrary. In the real world, it is common during contract negotiations to re-open or revisit previously agreed-upon terms to achieve agreement on other terms. Until a supply chain contract is finalized, business people understand that all terms are eligible for revision, and none are written in stone. Having to resort to UCC 2-207(3) to resolve disputes that arise because supply chain partners began work before finalizing their contract is a bad practice, and one that is not likely to result in terms that accurately reflect the intent of the parties.

### *Integration Clauses*

In Chapter 1, we discussed the importance of integration clauses, and how they help prevent pre-contractual communications from inadvertently becoming contractually binding. We reiterate the importance of integration clauses in this chapter. An integration clause is an important part of any fully negotiated supply chain agreement because it limits the rights and duties of supply chain partners to those contained in the agreement, and nowhere else. This promotes certainty and helps avoid supply chain disputes.

### *Non-US Law Versus US Law*

You can forget almost everything you just read if your supply chain contract is not governed by US law. Virtually every other legal system has its own battle-of-the-forms rules. Some countries, such as Germany and the UK, follow the "mirror image rule," which provides that no contract is formed until the parties achieve perfect agreement. Some countries, such as the Netherlands, follow a "first shot rule" that provides that the terms that prevail are those contained in the first-transmitted forms. Other countries, such as France, hold that in the event of conflicting terms, the terms that are included in the contract are only those on which the parties agree.

The CISG more or less follows the mirror image rule, under which an acceptance that "contains additions, limitations, or other modifications is a rejection of the offer and constitutes a counter-offer."[14] The CISG allows some leeway for additional terms in a second transmission that "do not materially alter the terms of the offer."[15] If supply chain partners begin performance before finalizing their agreement, the CISG follows the "last shot rule," under which the final communication forms the terms of the contract, which the other party is construed to have accepted by performance. However, courts interpreting the CISG are no more consistent than courts interpreting the UCC. Some CISG decisions employ the knock-out rule, and a few have adopted the terms in the first-transmitted form.

In short, because there is no way to predict how courts will handle contract interpretation when a contract has not been negotiated to completion, the best course is to finalize supply chain agreements before performing. Internally, companies should forbid work on new programs whose terms have not been finalized. Strict executive oversight should be provided in cases where either party wishes to begin performance sooner.

─────

## Lessons Learned

Supply chain partners drafting supply chain agreements should be certain to:

- Negotiate fully integrated agreements before beginning performance
- Include all key constituencies (engineering, purchasing, quality, etc.) in contract negotiations
- Communicate frequently with supply chain partners
- Thoughtfully evaluate all potential contract terms
- Be particularly cautious with development contracts
- Provide for confidentiality when appropriate
- Carefully review all forms transmitted during the contracting process

─────

14   CISG Art. 19(1).
15   CISG Art. 19(2).

# CHAPTER 3

# New Product Design and Development Contracts

## Overview

Any new product, whether it is an improvement on an aging product or something entirely new and different, starts with engineering and product development. Engineering and development groups in manufacturing organizations gather information and input from other internal departments, such as sales, marketing, field service, customer service, and external groups, including customers and competitors. This information about customer preferences and market direction is then used to design and develop new products.

We are accustomed to seeing the words "new" and "improved" on consumer goods and food product packaging. These changes and improvements to products are the result of product development engineering. The same is true of industrial products. Input is gathered from internal and external sources and a product is changed or developed or something brand new is created. The typical goals are increased customer satisfaction, more efficient design, etc.

Sometimes, a customer will ask a supplier to develop a totally new or different product to meet a specific need. The new product may be a part of an overall design change or some new concept. This is where things can get complicated. One of the thorniest problems from a supply chain perspective is dealing with development programs and new product design. Product development engineers work closely with customers to estimate development costs and design products that integrate into overall designs. Ideally, everyone in the supply chain hopes for and works to achieve the success of new programs. But things can and do go wrong.

The design of a highly engineered product, such as an automotive or aerospace part, is likely to go through an "engineering gates" process. This is a common technique where at each major development milestone—from design through first article production—a review process is applied. At each "gate" there is a series of engineering reviews and management sign-offs. Gating enforces design-principle adherence and gives management an opportunity to verify the strategic direction of the development. For example, if a new product is designed for operation underwater versus an old product that was designed for land, the design process may include up to 10 engineering gates that track progress. The first gate may be at the blueprint design completion, the second gate may be at component design completion, the third may be at vendor/supplier selection and pricing, etc., through gate 10, the final sign-off. At each gate, costs may be reviewed internally and reported to the buyer. As the design progresses, supply chain partners may need to renegotiate their contract in the event costs are higher than expected or if there is design delay.

## New Product Design Development

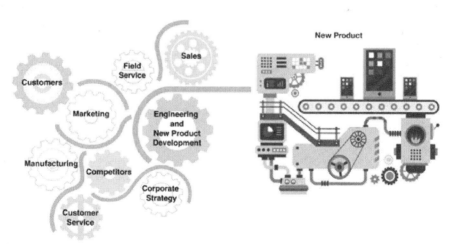

It is often difficult to establish production price, appropriate warranty coverage, and technical parameters for a new product before it is fully developed.

Uncertainty as to how new product development will affect later commercial terms is an issue that flows all the way through the supply chain and is exacerbated when components need to be integrated with one another. (See Chapter 4: Product Integration.) Although supply chain partners try very hard to follow product development schedules and milestones, perfect compliance is not always possible, especially if the development process spans several years. Business conditions change and so do supply chain partners. Production costs that an engineering department estimated 10 years ago are likely to evolve over time.

Another complication in development programs is that supply chain partners are often uncertain whether the market will accept the new product. Even if the new product is an improvement on existing technology, as long as the existing technology is not failing, there is a risk that customers may reject the new and untested option. Remember Microsoft Zune? Sony's MD Player? Betamax? These new products flopped as innovations because they just did not catch on with customers.

Consequently, development contracts put a high level of stress on supply chain relationships. This stress is amplified when supply chain partners have not worked together before, which is common in development projects that are competitively bid. Other factors increase the degree of difficulty as well, such as when international suppliers are used, when the product is highly technical, and when there are tight project deadlines.

The supply chain is at its best in development programs when supply chain relationships are effectively managed and communications are open. Over the life of a development project, there are going to be iterations and changes. All product changes should be communicated to the supply chain, and supply chain partners should be given an opportunity to respond. If project changes are significant, they should be approved formally by all affected parties via engineering change orders (ECOs). This is critical (and sometimes legally required) in highly regulated industries such as medical devices and aerospace. Project changes often impact production costs, and communication should flow freely about cost changes as well. We have seen development projects that spanned many years undergo no changes to the contract pricing, even though there were significant design changes. When this happens, one or more of the supply chain partners usually ends up losing money.

Project management is also a critical factor. Project managers on a development project sit squarely between product engineering and the customer. They are responsible for satisfying both parties by keeping track of progress and costs, as well as being responsive to customer needs and concerns. The best project managers communicate well and regularly, and follow up promptly on open items. However, project management can also be a failure point in development contracts. There is often high turnover in project management groups, and therefore a constant stream of new project managers going through the learning curve. We have also seen project managers who are good at documenting details, but ineffective at truly managing issues.

### *Failure Alert: How an Ineffective Project Manager Can Sink a Project*

One of our clients manufactured industrial equipment used in oil and gas production around the world. These development contracts typically took longer than five years to perform, and our client's components usually required integration with multiple other components. These programs were not scheduled to become profitable for our client until development was complete and the equipment was operational in the field.

The project manager was great at capturing and distributing the minutes from the weekly status calls, but consistently failed to drill down into the root causes of issues. She did not feel it was her responsibility to address engineering problems or logistics problems inside her own company, so she simply passed information to the product development and logistics staff and hoped for the best. When the product was ready to be delivered to a remote site in Russia, the company discovered that the product was not properly engineered for the harsh winter environment. In addition, the delivery site was so remote that special equipment had to be brought in at great expense to make the final delivery. The relationship between the parties broke down over time because these issues were never fully communicated, managed, or resolved by the project manager and the project ended up in a legal dispute.

The lesson here is twofold: first, communication is key, and second, there is a difference between checking items off a project manager's list, and really attending to issues that the project manager has reason to know will affect the project, the supply chain relationship, and the bottom line.

## Legal Overview

In addition to the operational challenges posed by development programs, there are significant legal challenges as well. The biggest legal challenge occurs when supply chain partners attempt to negotiate the legal rights and duties that will govern the production phase of their relationship before development is complete. Until a new product is meaningfully developed, there are often too many operational unknowns for the parties to agree comfortably on final contract terms. Operational unknowns affect price, warranty, reliability, quality, and other technical parameters in the supply chain contract.

Often, the desire to negotiate development and production terms simultaneously is the result of pressure imposed by buyers, customers further up the supply chain, or a sense that "this is how we always do it." But prematurely committing to production terms before development has occurred can be economically hazardous. Buyers often expect that suppliers' production pricing is set so that the suppliers can recoup their development costs. Consequently, buyers may be unwilling to renegotiate production pricing, even if development turns out to be more costly than the parties expected. Taking this one step further, in some industries like aerospace, many upstream buyers expect that development and original equipment production will occur at a loss, with profits to be made in aftermarket sales only. Betting on this assumption often causes problems.

While we know that negotiating production contract terms before development is complete is common and often the default, in our experience it is not the best practice. We see frequent supply chain disputes during the production phase emerge as the result of festering issues that originated during development. Often, supply chain contract terms do not take into account problems encountered during development. Usually the result is that suppliers are (or feel) undercompensated.

While it may seem like undercompensated suppliers would be a good outcome for buyers, in reality this is usually not the case. Disgruntled suppliers who are not meeting their margins on a program are not likely to dedicate the necessary resources to making the program work, will be inattentive to issues that arise, and will be less accommodating of any necessary changes. The consequences of economically challenged suppliers will inevitably be increased costs for buyers. And, of course, economically challenged suppliers will most likely look for every opportunity to get out of unprofitable or underprofitable programs. Furthermore, buyers may also benefit from deferring the negotiation of production-phase terms until after development, since there may be unanticipated cost <u>savings</u> during development.

### *Negotiating Development and Production Contract Terms Separately*

Supply chain partners who separate development and production contract phases do so using a variety of structures. Some dual-phase supply chain contracts are structured so that if the supplier meets the buyer's specifications by the end of development (and sometimes by a certain date), the buyer is obliged to purchase its requirements of the new product from the supplier, with full production terms to be negotiated at that point. Sometimes supply chain partners agree to negotiate production terms after the first prototype is approved, after beta products are approved, or at some other benchmark.

In other situations, the buyer agrees to pay the supplier on a cost-plus basis upon the achievement of specified milestones (sometimes with incentive bonuses for achieving milestones by a certain date). Or, for new products that require development work by both the buyer and supplier, supply chain partners sometimes use "co-development agreements" in which each party bears its own development expenses. If development is successful, the supply chain contract will then require the parties to enter into a production contract with terms to be negotiated at that point. Some research and development contracts require the buyer to pay the supplier based on time billed by the hour, which can morph into or be combined with a cost-plus development contract as progress is made.

A more complicated development structure that is sometimes used gives the development-phase supplier the first right to bid on and accept the production contract if the development-stage supplier can establish competitive pricing (within 10 percent, for example, of other potential suppliers).

If production terms must be established before development is complete, supply chain partners can still leave themselves an opportunity to renegotiate production terms. In these circumstances, the supply chain contract can be written to allow one or both parties the right to a price or other contract adjustment upon a showing of undue hardship or good cause. The effectiveness of this type of contract provision relies heavily on contract partners' good faith with one another, but in some situations, it does work.

### *Other Development Contract Considerations*

In addition to dividing the development and production phases of the supply chain contract, development programs involve other unique legal considerations as well.

**Timing:** For some development projects, timing is important. When deadlines are critical, the development contract should provide for project milestones (the more specific the better), with a provision that "time is of the essence." To accommodate the possibility of changed circumstances, the development supply chain contract can include a provision allowing milestones to be changed upon the mutual agreement of the parties. Supply chain partners can also include a short period (one week to three months) in which a party that encounters delays is allowed to cure any failure to meet contract milestones.

**Specification Changes:** For some development projects, technical specifications may evolve during development. Even products with tight tolerances, such as medical devices and aerospace components, often allow some deviation from the originally assumed technical parameters. If evolving technical parameters are a possibility, supply chain partners can include a clause in their contract providing that the parties may mutually agree to any specification changes, or, if appropriate, that the buyer can change specifications in its discretion. If the latter approach is chosen, it may be appropriate for the supply chain contract to provide the supplier with the right to an equitable price adjustment in the event that specification changes impact the supplier's costs.

**Component Integration Issues:** If supply chain partners anticipate that integrating a supplier's product with other components in the end-product will be complicated, the development contract should clearly specify the supply chain partners' respective product integration responsibilities. (See Chapter 4: Product Integration.)

**Warranties:** Suppliers working on development products should be cautious about extending warranties. If a warranty is extended, it likely makes sense to limit the buyer's remedy to repair, replacement of the defective part, or refund of the buyer's purchase price. All implied warranties should be conspicuously disclaimed.

**Damages:** In addition to warranty considerations, it probably makes sense for development supply chain contracts to bar recovery of consequential damages, which are damages (such as lost profits) that are not the direct and immediate consequence of a breach of the development contract.

**Term and Termination:** It may be appropriate for development supply chain contracts to include milestone deadlines that, if not met, will cause the agreement to terminate automatically. Alternatively, it may be appropriate for development supply chain contracts to provide for short, automatically renewing terms (such as three or six months) in which the parties can terminate after giving notice. To accommodate the possibility that the market for a development product may not emerge, supply chain partners also might want to allow termination for convenience at any time.

**Product Upgrades:** If it is possible that the product being developed will require upgrades over time, a development supply chain contract can specify the conditions in which the buyer has the right to demand upgrades, and the circumstances in which the supplier may demand a price adjustment for upgrades.

**Intellectual Property:** If a development project will produce intellectual property rights, the supply chain contract should specify to whom the intellectual property rights belong and whether the other party has licensing rights or must make royalty payments.

### Taking Market Reaction into Consideration

Often, development projects seek to replace existing technology with an unproven technology that supply chain partners hope will be an improvement. In such cases, there is always a possibility that the market will reject the new technology in favor of what has been tried and true. Until the new technology is proven, many customers may prefer to hold onto what has worked in the past. Taking market reaction into account is often vitally important in ensuring the success of a new product.

Supply chain partners facing uncertain market reaction must achieve a careful balance. On the one hand, the supplier has an interest in requiring the buyer to use its product in all of the applications the buyer sells to the market. On the other hand, if the buyer has competitors still using the old technology, and if the market does not accept the new product, then neither supply chain partner sells anything.

One solution may be to include a provision in the supply chain contract obliging the buyer to purchase only as much of the supplier's product as the buyer's customers demand, which in turn may be augmented by objective measures defining customer demand levels. The development contract can also require the buyer to use best efforts or commercially reasonable efforts to promote the new product. The supply chain contract may allow the supplier to sell the newly developed technology to other customers to accelerate its acceptance in the market.

### The Law That Governs Development Contracts

Up to this point, this book has been discussing supply chain contracts as being governed by Article 2 of the UCC, which in the United States applies to contracts for the sale of goods over $500. UCC Article 2 may not be the governing law for development contracts, however. Development contracts that primarily involve design, research and development, engineering, or consulting services will be governed by state common law instead of the UCC since they are principally contracts for services rather than contracts for the sale of goods.

There are several meaningful differences between the common law of most states and the UCC. For instance, under the UCC, in the event of a breach, an aggrieved buyer may be entitled to "cover" damages, meaning the buyer's cost of securing substitute goods. But at least some courts have held that cover damages are not available under state common law.[16] In addition, the UCC includes implied warranties of merchantability and of fitness for a particular purpose that provide rights and protections to buyers that the common law does not recognize.[17] Furthermore, the common law of contracts is less uniform between the states than the UCC is. In many states, the statute of limitations is longer for common-law breach of contract claims than it is for breach of contract claims under the UCC.[18] Paradoxically, this means that

---

16  *See, e.g., Navcom Technology, Inc. v. OKI Electric Industry Co., Ltd.*, 2014 U.S. Dist. LEXIS 32159, 83 U.C.C. Rep. Serv. 2d (Callaghan) 86 (N.D. Calif. Mar. 11, 2014).

17  *See, e.g., Systems America, Inc. v. Rockwell Software, Inc.*, 2007 U.S. Dist. LEXIS 8483, 61 U.C.C. Rep. Serv. 2d (Callaghan) 933 (N.D. Calif. Jan. 26, 2007).

18  *See, e.g., Dahlmann v. Sulcus Hospitality Technologies Corp.*, 63 F.Supp.2d 772 (E.D. Mich. 1999).

supply chain partners may have far longer to sue for breaches of development contracts than they do for production phase contracts.

There are factors and indicators that influence whether a development contract is governed by the common law or by the UCC. If a development contract contemplates purchase orders, delivery terms, and defined product characteristics, and especially if the buyer's payments to the supplier are characterized as payments for goods rather than services, courts are more likely to apply the UCC. In contrast, development contracts that contemplate payments in exchange for design work, intellectual property development, engineering services, or achieving development benchmarks are more likely to be governed by the common law.

For international development projects, the CISG is similar to the UCC in that it applies only to contracts for the sale of goods. Much like the UCC, the CISG applies unless "the preponderant part" of the contract is for labor or services.[19] Therefore, as in the United States, international development contracts may fall outside of the CISG and will be governed by the domestic law of whichever country has the most significant relationship with the parties and the project. To avoid unpleasant surprises, it is especially important for international development supply chain contracts to include a choice of law clause specifying the governing law. (See Chapter 7: International Procurement.)

———

**Lessons Learned**

When working with development projects and new designs, supply chain partners should:

- Extensively research the need for a new product through market research, competitor research, and a thorough internal evaluation of costs and benefits
- Empower project management personnel with the authority to investigate and fully address problems that arise during development, and ensure that the project manager is not simply checking off boxes

---

19   CISG Art. 3.

- Understand that development is a process, and one that will likely involve changes to the supply chain partners' original plans, timelines, and expectations
- Be fully open about changes in technical parameters, cost, and anything else likely to affect the success of the development program
- Avoid negotiating production contract terms before development is complete—or at least leave room for production contract terms to be renegotiated to address issues encountered during development
- Disclaim warranties in development contracts
- Understand that the UCC may not govern development contracts, and for international developmental contracts especially, include a choice of law provision to avoid unfamiliar foreign law

# CHAPTER 4

# PRODUCT INTEGRATION

## Overview

From mining, drilling, growing, or harvesting raw materials, all the way to assembling finished products, it is rare to find any company that is fully vertically integrated. Instead, products today are made by complicated networks of partners, suppliers, and customers who buy, sell, and interact with one another to produce finished products and deliver them to the right place at the right time. The products we use are collaborations and integrations of parts from multiple suppliers. Someone must be responsible for making these parts work together.

Manufacturing companies face enormous challenges when engineering products that incorporate multiple suppliers' parts and services. The integration process may involve supplier components, a company's own components, and industrial processes such as coating and polishing. Highly engineered products increase the complexity and challenge of product integration because every integration point has the potential to fail. Add software and the potential failure points multiply exponentially.

In consumer goods, fashion, automobiles, and high tech, fast-paced product development requires fast-paced integration. Take your smart phone, for example. While Apple and Samsung are busy developing the features and functions for the next smart phone release, their semiconductor vendors, camera makers, and software vendors are also developing the new and improved next generation of products to function as Apple and Samsung require. Apple and Samsung rely on their supply chain partners, but they must also ensure successful integration for phones to work as expected.

High-tech smart phones are just one example in which rapid product introduction and integration happens. Fast-fashion companies such as Zara, Forever 21, and H&M design their own styles and use global sourcing for garment production. Garment factories use fabric sourced elsewhere, together with notions and embellishments such as buttons, buckles, zippers, and embroidered emblems. These components are integrated to produce finished garments. The life cycle of garments is shortened considerably for fast-fashion companies compared with traditional fashion. Fast-fashion companies that are successful quickly move on to the next style with little or no leftover inventory.

The fashion business is completely dependent on supply chain integration points working perfectly. If timing is off due to integration problems or late vendor shipments, the result will be markdowns, overstocks, past-season inventory, and revenue losses. Fashion companies must monitor their suppliers carefully and take immediate action if something goes wrong with the product integration process. If fabric, zippers, or buttons are not at the right sewing factory at the right time, garments cannot be produced. To be successful, contracts between supply chain partners in the production of garments are typically written with tight specifications and penalties for late deliveries and quality issues.

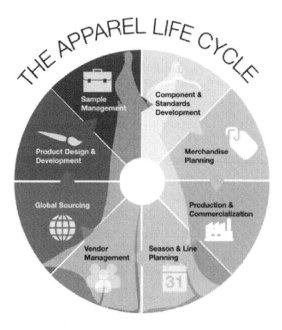

Similarly, the processed food we buy at the grocery store also contains components such as preservatives, dyes, and other ingredients that must be combined in exact quantities. Without the right ingredients, consumer food products cannot be produced. If ingredients are incorrect or spoiled, the product's taste will suffer, or worse, the product may be dangerous to humans. Once again, tightly controlling supply chain partners through detailed contracts and service agreements helps keep integration failures to a minimum.

### Globalization

International sourcing and the globalization of supply chains amplify integration challenges. If a supplier is overseas, there will be communication delays and perhaps difficulties making corrections. There are likely to be language and cultural barriers too. In China, for example, instructions are taken very literally. If you have not called out detailed step-by-step instructions for all manufacturing processes, you may not get the production results that you want. (See Chapter 7: International Procurement.)

### Dealing with Supplier Integration Points

Potential integration failure points are a constant hazard. Because of the degree to which integration failures plague manufacturing operations, we always recommend to our clients that a cross-functional group within the company work to identify all potential integration failure points before going into production and before entering into binding agreements with suppliers. Companies should include representatives from engineering, sales, manufacturing, and procurement in their product integration strategies. To maximize success in integrating complex products, companies need to clearly identify and define integration points, performance expectations, and the party or parties responsible for making integration work. Companies should also identify the protocol for supply chain partners to follow when integration points fail. Contract provisions that address supply chain partners' integration responsibilities should become a part of supply chain contracts or purchase orders between buyers and suppliers.

Typically, buyers are responsible for providing specifications and making sure that supplier products function properly in the integrated end product. But when a product is highly engineered, the development process may require both the buyer and suppliers to participate and engage in product integration activities. All product integration expectations should be clearly articulated and documented in the contract documents. Frank and detailed discussions about integration expectations will keep you out of the courtroom.

### Highly Engineered Products

Complex, highly engineered products often include both hardware and software. For these products, the potential for failure points is multiplied. Electronic servers are a good example. Not only do servers include hardware such as circuit boards, screens, cases, cables, and racks, but most of the hardware pieces also have individual software that makes the hardware run. The hardware and software must work together. When something goes wrong, it can be extremely difficult to pinpoint which component is the cause.

Figure 1. The High-Tech Ecosystem

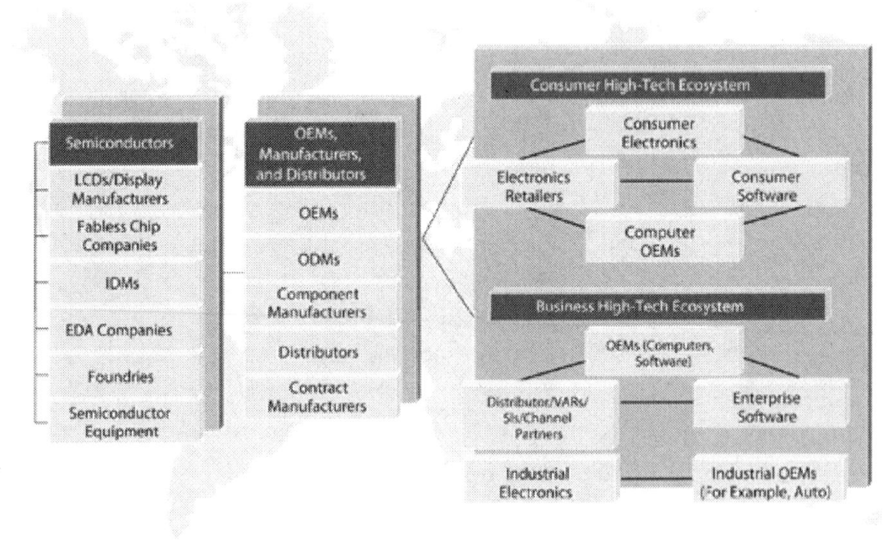

Source: Cisco IBSG High-Tech Manufacturing Practice, 2009

## *Integration of Software*

Integrating software systems, such as connecting Enterprise Resource Planning (ERP) systems to warehouse management systems or connecting financial systems to eCommerce programs, face substantial integration challenges. With software, every integration point has a potential for failure. The more integration points the software has, the more risky its architecture becomes.

Today, major software packages, such as SAP, Oracle, Microsoft, and Salesforce.com, have open integration points that ease the difficulty of deploying multiple software packages. Still, the overall systems architecture must be well defined and detailed for implementation. This is not a trivial task. In addition, every time software has a major upgrade or the architecture is disturbed to add new features, all of the integration points need to be retested for validity. The cycle of implementation, integration, upgrade/fix, test, and reimplementation is ongoing.

Most companies use software consultants to deploy new systems and major upgrades. To avoid integration failures and other software disasters, be sure the consulting team includes only experienced consultants and project managers. (See Chapter 14: Information Technology.)

## *Failure Alert: They Blamed Each Other*

An electro-mechanical parts supplier got into a dispute with its customer. The supplier's highly engineered parts included hardware and software that had to be integrated with the customer's machine controls. Although the supplier's parts always passed the supplier's quality inspections, they sometimes failed when installed in the customer's machinery. The supplier suspected that the failures were due to the customer's software integration, but could not convince the customer to take responsibility for investigating the problem, even though the supplier and the customer had an amicable relationship. The supply chain contract between the parties did not include integration testing procedures, responsibilities, or conflict resolution procedures. Over time, each party blamed the other, and they ended up in a complicated and prolonged legal dispute.

## Legal Overview

Supply chain contracts often fail to spell out who bears responsibility for integrating the components required to create the end product. Suppliers may assume that parties "up the chain" should and will bear integration responsibility. When suppliers are delivering products made according to detailed and precise specifications drafted by the buyer, this assumption is probably correct. But sometimes buyer instructions are not specific and leave room for suppliers to exercise judgment in determining how to make their components work in the end product. In such cases, product integration may be more of a shared responsibility. The wording of the supply chain agreement is important.

Supply chain contracts sometimes contain provisions that make suppliers liable for product integration failures, but suppliers do not always realize it until it is too late. These stealth provisions often do not address product integration responsibilities directly. Instead, the often come in the form of general warranty, reliability, quality, or performance provisions that are phrased in a way that makes suppliers responsible for the performance of the finished product. Suppliers need to pay attention during drafting to ensure that they have not inadvertently agreed to broad product integration duties that are beyond their expertise or control.

Consider the following reliability provision that governs the supply of components in a helicopter engine:

### Component Reliability Requirement

On a fleet-wide basis, Supplier shall ensure that its Components do not require removal, maintenance, service, or repair more frequently than one instance per 8,000 fleet operating hours. In the event that the Components are removed more often, Supplier shall institute a program, approved by the Buyer, for the purpose of improving its reliability statistics to the required level.

As written, this component reliability provision places responsibility for all failures of the supplier's component on the supplier, whether failures are caused by the supplier's product, interfacing components, the environment in which the component is used, or any other reason. This allocation of responsibility may not square with the reality of the supply chain relationship. If not, this kind of provision provides fertile ground for disputes.

Provisions like this component reliability requirement are often buried deep within technical specifications, and are reviewed by a company's engineers but usually not by executive management, legal counsel, or even the business lead, and therefore can escape attention.

It is possible to draft contract provisions that allocate product integration responsibilities appropriately, however. Sample clauses that apply when (1) the buyer bears integration responsibilities and (2) responsibility is split between the buyer and the supplier are as follows:

### Product Integration

*Buyer is solely responsible:* Buyer shall be responsible for all product integration tasks required in connection with manufacturing the End Product.

-or-

*Shared responsibility:* Supplier shall be responsible for product integration to the extent identified in the "Testing" obligations set forth in the Specifications. Buyer shall be responsible for all other product integration tasks required in connection with manufacturing the End Product.

It is important to address product integration responsibilities in the supply chain contract because contract law provides the only avenue for redress between supply chain partners in the event that supplier components damage the end product or other components, or vice versa. This is the result of the "economic loss doctrine" that is widely adopted in the United States and internationally.

The economic loss doctrine provides that commercial parties cannot recover economic damages from each other that are caused by the failure of a product under any non-contract legal cause of action. Supply chain partners cannot sue each other in negligence, strict liability, or other tort theory to redress product integration failures. The purpose behind the economic loss doctrine is, as one case stated, that "it encourages the party best suited to assess the risk of economic loss, usually the purchaser, to assume, allocate, or insure against that risk."[20]

---

20  *Gentek Building Products, Inc. v. Sherwin-Williams Co.*, 2005 U.S. Dist. LEXIS 45312, *36 (N.D. Ohio Feb. 22, 2005).

## *Failure Alert: GM Ignition Switch Recall*

In 2014, GM and its supplier and former subsidiary Delphi became the center of a legal and media firestorm concerning alleged defects in ignition switches supplied by Delphi for GM vehicles. Reportedly, when installed, Delphi's ignition switches did not provide enough torque to remain in the "on" position if accidentally bumped, resulting in accidents. A fact that has been reported about the supply chain relationship between GM and Delphi is that during development, GM approved Delphi's prototype switches, even though both Delphi and GM knew they did not meet GM's specifications.

GM and Delphi have not publicly described how liability for the damages caused by this issue will be allocated between them. However, the controversy surrounding the GM ignition switch defects shows why product integration should be expressly addressed in supply chain agreements.

## *Indemnification for Damages to Third Parties*

Product integration failures can also cause injuries to consumers. Sometimes, injuries are caused by the finished product, sometimes by a particular component, and sometimes by the way a component is integrated into the finished product. These injuries often result in product liability, consumer, and other tort lawsuits against manufacturers.

Determining suppliers' and buyers' liability when a product causes personal injury can be difficult and contentious. The law governing allocation of fault between two or more entities that may be jointly at fault varies widely from state to state. Internationally, each country has its own rules. Some US states have adopted a judicially-created doctrine called the "component part manufacturer defense." Under the component part manufacturer defense, a supplier of a component that is not itself defective will not be liable for third-party injuries unless the supplier "substantially participated" in integrating the component into the end product.

However, the component part manufacturer defense has not been adopted consistently within the United States or internationally. Therefore, to avoid disputes about responsibility for personal injuries that occur as a result of product failure, supply chain partners should include indemnification provisions in their agreements. We recommend indemnification clauses as a best practice that creates clear expectations, and therefore avoids disputes.

There is no such thing as a standard or boilerplate indemnification clause, contrary to popular belief. Indemnification clauses vary as widely as the relationships between supply chain partners. Historically, US courts were hostile to indemnification clauses, viewing them as an unfair attempt to avoid the consequences of one's own wrongdoing. Today, however, indemnification clauses are common and accepted. Indemnification clauses allow supply chain partners to agree how they will allocate responsibility for personal injury or other claims before these claims are made, which helps avoid litigation between supply chain partners when injuries occur. Many courts still would not allow indemnification for a party's own intentional or recklessly wrongful acts, however.

To be effective, an indemnification clause needs to specify which party will be liable for third-party claims, in what circumstances, and for how much. It is generally best for indemnification clauses to set liability in a way that matches what the supply chain partners' actual level of fault likely would be, to the extent this can be predicted in advance. An indemnification clause that holds a party liable for damages grossly beyond its likely level of fault will probably meet with resistance if enforced. An example of an indemnification clause that is probably too sweeping is as follows:

### Overly Broad Indemnification Clause
Supplier shall indemnify Buyer, as well as Buyer's employees, agents, representatives, directors, and corporate affiliates, from any and all liabilities, damages, costs, expenses, awards, and settlements to third parties arising out of or in connection with Supplier's acts, omissions, conduct, negligence, wrongful conduct, or the Component provided by Supplier.

This indemnification clause provides a complete indemnification right against the supplier for damages "arising out of or in connection with" the supplier's product, regardless of the degree to which the supplier contributed to the damages in question. This indemnification clause may be legally enforceable, but, in our experience, if it does not reflect the supplier's actual degree of responsibility, the supplier is likely to resist it. A more tailored indemnification clause that contains mutual indemnities is as follows:

### Tailored, Mutual Indemnification Clause

Supplier shall fully indemnify Buyer, as well as Buyer's employees, agents, representatives, directors, and corporate affiliates, from liabilities, damages, costs, expenses, awards, and settlements to third parties, including but not limited to attorneys' fees, arising out of or in connection with Supplier's negligence or any breach by Seller of this Agreement *in an amount proportionate to the Supplier's responsibility for such liabilities, damages, costs, expenses, awards, and settlements.*

Likewise, Buyer shall fully indemnify Seller, as well as Seller's employees, agents, representatives, directors, and corporate affiliates, from liabilities, damages, costs, expenses, awards, and settlements to third parties, including but not limited to attorneys' fees, arising out of or in connection with Buyer's negligence or any breach by Buyer of this Agreement *in an amount proportionate to the Buyer's responsibility for such liabilities, damages, costs, expenses, awards, and settlements.*

When supply chain partners agree to indemnification, it is also wise to include a contract provision that entitles the indemnifying party to any information the other party has that would provide notice that a defect or problem exists. All too often, supply chain partners do not share information with each other that would enable them to conduct prompt and effective root cause investigations and implement corrective actions that could mitigate claims and damages quickly.

Indemnification clauses should also clearly state whether attorneys' fees and expenses are to be included in the costs being indemnified. In addition, indemnification clauses should state that they will survive the termination of the agreement. Finally, supply chain partners should be aware that indemnification liabilities are often not covered by commercial general liability (CGL) insurance policies because many insurers take the position that they will not cover liabilities that their insureds voluntarily assumed.

———

**Lessons Learned**

When integrating components into an end product, supply chain partners should:

- Identify and document all potential failure points and determine how they will be addressed
- Take special care with products that involve software, as they are likely to have more potential failure points
- Take special care to monitor the integration process with international suppliers, and make sure that communication with international partners about integration responsibilities is clear and consistent
- Specify clearly in the supply chain agreement which supply chain partner is responsible for product integration tasks
- Include indemnification clauses in supply chain agreements that allocate responsibility for injuries to third parties
- Expressly state whether attorneys' fees and expenses are included in the costs being indemnified
- State in the supply chain agreement that the indemnification clause will survive the termination of the agreement

# CHAPTER 5

# FORECASTING AND PLANNING

## Overview

Forecasting is the process of determining the quantity and mix of products a company should produce to meet customer demand. This is a delicate balancing process, being careful to predict just the right amount to manufacture . . . not too much and not too little. The key is to predict the level of production that will satisfy customers without causing too much inventory to remain on the shelf or in a warehouse, or that must be sold at a deep discount. Failing to accurately forecast demand and then producing too much or too little can be financially catastrophic.

To complicate matters, supply chain partners rely on each other's forecasts to plan their own production and services. A US buyer places orders with Chinese factories based on the buyer's sales forecast. The Chinese manufacturer relies on the buyer's forecast to schedule production time and order raw materials from its suppliers who also depend on forecasts. The logistics provider and transportation carrier rely on cargo forecasts to schedule vessels and aircraft. Even US Customs and Border Protection (CBP) relies on passenger forecasts to schedule immigration and customs agents. Supply chain partners are dependent on one another for accurate forecasts to plan their operations.

Forecasting typically requires sophisticated mathematical modeling best done by computer software programs designed for this task. (See Chapter 14: Information Technology.) The algorithms used for the software-modeling take into account sales forecasts, marketplace variables, and information about competitors, and extend even to things like weather forecasts, which may affect demand for whatever the manufacturer is producing. (We have all seen pictures of empty grocery store shelves just before a hurricane or snowstorm.)

But even with sophisticated computer modeling, forecasts are often wrong. For example, fast food restaurants plan for demand over the course of a year. If there is a warm-weather weekend in the middle of January, a restaurant may run out of food because people tend to eat out more often in nice weather. We know of one hamburger chain that ran out of paper wrappers for hamburgers during a surprise warm-weather weekend and therefore could not sell burgers to customers. Several restaurants in the chain had to shut down because they ran out of food and supplies. The estimated loss of revenue was nearly $100,000.

Other events can also trigger swings in demand. After September 11, 2001, for example, the demand for networking equipment increased as companies scrambled to install redundant networking systems in alternative locations. Because equipment manufacturers were unprepared for the increase in demand, many customers had to wait six to nine months to get their orders filled. When unexpected events trigger changes in demand, it can be tough for business to respond.

There can be huge profit-and-loss consequences if forecasts are not accurate. Generally, manufacturers will prepare 12-month rolling forecasts that are updated regularly with current information, and adjusted as facts become clearer and orders materialize. In our experience, forecast accuracy for most manufacturing companies is between 40-50 percent accurate 12 months before production starts and 80-90 percent accurate 30-60 days before production starts. As the production day gets closer, forecast accuracy improves because companies have more visibility as to actual orders.

Forecast accuracy statistics vary from industry to industry. Forecasting heavy machinery demand, like farm equipment, is based on comparatively stable indicators. Forecasting fashion industry trends is a whole other story, often fickle and difficult to predict. When evaluating forecast accuracy and making business decisions based on forecasts, we always make sure to compare companies within the same industry.

## *Cash-Flow Planning*

Accuracy in forecasting also affects cash-flow planning and working capital requirements. In parallel with the forecasting needs of the supply chain and procurement functions, the finance team needs forecast information to plan for working capital requirements. If a forecast is not accurate, this will adversely affect the management of the business' cash-flow needs. Most CFOs and controllers stay in close contact with the forecasting and planning process to make sure the right amount of cash is available for operations.

## *Sales and Operations Planning (S&OP)*

In addition to forecasting, most companies also engage in sales and operations planning, commonly known as "S&OP." In this process, leaders from sales, manufacturing, purchasing, and finance get together to decide what to build based on the preferences and strategies of the company. For example, a furniture manufacturer may decide to build 100 chairs and 50 sofas, or 50 chairs and 75 sofas, or 100 chairs, 50 tables, and 50 sofas, and so forth. Each plan is based on the optimization and constraints of the plant, labor, raw materials, etc. Each option produces different financial margins and different financial outcomes. Depending on the company's strategy, certain options may be more attractive than others. In the furniture example, if the company is trying to expand its table line, it may choose to sub-optimize financial margins during the table ramp-up period.

S&OP is a compromise process in which everyone ultimately agrees on a plan. The sales department agrees to sell what can be produced, production agrees to produce the products that will achieve business goals within a certain schedule, and finance agrees to the margins and revenues in the plan. If the S&OP working group does not reach agreement, then the decision regarding what will be produced rests with one or more senior executive officers.

## *The Limitations of Computerized Forecasting Tools*

Often, the computerized analytical tools used for forecasting are treated as the definitive truth that must be followed. This is not the best practice. Best-practice companies use computer analytics to generate a preliminary plan, but include the experience and expertise of human beings to make adjustments.

Typically, sales people are overly optimistic and forecast more than can be sold to ensure that there are no stock-outs or delays in delivering products to customers. Of course, production planners know this, and may make downward adjustments to sales projections. Finance may make additional downward adjustments to protect the company's working capital requirements, which triggers another set of upward adjustments by production planners and purchasing. All of this adjusting can cause swings in the operating plan. Ultimately, what gets produced rests on the shoulders and common sense of a group of people called production planners.

### Production Planning

Production planning is the process of taking a forecast and planning what items will be produced and when. But it is not so simple. Even in non-eventful conditions, the process is complex and involves production, inventory, scheduling, and purchasing. Sales staff and/or executives may also prioritize orders to favor the most important or strategic customers, or customers with special requests, all of which will change production plans. If there are issues with production machinery, engineering changes, product recalls, quality issues, or a hundred other things, production planners have to adjust the plan on the fly.

Planners start with a proposed production schedule. They then review inventory to determine what parts are on hand and what materials and supplies need to be purchased. If some materials are long-lead-time items, production may have to be postponed until all raw materials are on hand. Coordinating schedules and expediting orders with purchasing are first among the planner's tasks and are usually hot topics for the morning "war room" meetings where production people talk about the day's production plan.

Engineering may change a product's manufacturing or design, and as a result, production planners have to review bills of materials (BoMs) for changes, additions, and deletions. If a change is related to a recall or a safety issue, production planners may have to stop production immediately until the issue is resolved. Planners may need to make further adjustments if other issues arise, such as machine shop downtime, supplier issues, or labor issues.

The planning process is in constant flux to achieve the optimal use of factories and to provide the best service to customers. Production planners are in the center of all this, making sense out of a lot of rapidly changing variables.

### *Failure Alert: Building a Plant Based on a Forecast*

A supplier to a high-tech company had a five-year relationship with its customer, a company that was both profitable and growing. Each year, the customer sent the supplier a production forecast with the caveat that it was just a forecast and nothing more. Nevertheless, the supplier used the forecast to project its own production of parts in sufficient quantities to assure on-time deliveries with no stock-outs.

Because one of the buyer's forecasts projected that the buyer would soon double its growth, the supplier took the forecast to the bank to ask for a construction loan for a new factory. All went well for about six months, and the new factory construction was well underway. Then, business conditions changed for the high-tech company, and sales fell by nearly 50 percent, resulting in orders to the supplier falling by 50 percent. Consequently, the supplier was forced to stop construction on the factory.

Claiming that it reasonably relied on its customer's forecast, the supplier sued the high-tech company for breach of contract. The high-tech company argued that the forecast was just an estimate that could not be relied upon to be accurate. The case was resolved in favor of the customer.

## Legal Overview

Forecasting and planning can create supply chain disputes if these tasks are not done properly. When disputes arise, it is often because one party believes that a forecast provided by the other party is legally binding, but the other party claims that it is a non-binding estimate—as in the case study about the supplier that built a new factory based on its customer's business projections. Avoiding this ambiguity is the key to avoiding supply chain disputes about forecasting and planning.

From a legal perspective, forecasts tend to be used in connection with two types of supply chain contracts, blanket purchase orders and requirements contracts, because these documents do not state exact order quantities. Blanket purchase orders are purchasing documents that state all or most of the terms and conditions of a buyer's order, with order quantities to be determined as needed. Requirements contracts are agreements in which the supplier agrees to supply all of a buyer's requirements for a product. For both blanket purchase orders and requirements contracts, forecasts are tools for anticipating production needs. Sometimes forecasts are intended to be binding, and sometimes they are not. Whichever approach is used, supply chain partners need to be clear about what they are doing.

For requirements contracts, forecasts have special legal significance. Under the UCC, buyers in requirements contracts cannot demand a "quantity unreasonably disproportionate to any stated estimate."[21] By law, buyers in requirements contracts must use good faith efforts to provide accurate forecasts. Courts have held that attempts to stockpile products beyond a buyer's actual requirements—whether in anticipation of a contract ending or a price increase—constitute bad faith.[22]

Simply stating that a forecast is a "forecast" may not be sufficiently clear to determine whether the forecast is binding or non-binding if a dispute about the forecast ends up in court. Stating that a forecast contains the "anticipated requirements" of a buyer or that the forecasted quantities are "approximate" is clearer, and courts have held that forecasts using these words are not binding.[23] The best practice, however, is to be as clear as possible. If a forecast is not intended to be binding, it is best if both the forecasts and the underlying supply chain contract state explicitly that the forecast is not binding and is intended for planning purposes only. Suggested language is as follows:

### Periodic Forecasts Not Binding

Buyer agrees to provide Supplier with periodic forecasts every three months, estimating its anticipated needs for the Product over the following 12-month period. The purpose of these forecasts is to enable Supplier to manage its inventory, supply chain, and lead times, but such forecasts are not binding on Buyer. Buyer will use good faith efforts to estimate its needs for Product accurately. Supplier understands and agrees that Supplier bears the risk of order quantities that differ, even if materially, from forecasts provided by Buyer.

Courts are inconsistent in how they interpret forecasts that are ambiguous as to whether they are binding. Courts are more likely to hold that an ambiguous

---

21   UCC § 2-306(1).

22   *See, e.g., Enzo Biochem, Inc. v. Affymetrix, Inc.*, 2013 U.S. Dist. LEXIS 18599 (S.D.N.Y. Dec. 6, 2013)

23   *See, e.g., Brooklyn Bagel Boys, Inc. v. Earthgrains Refrigerated Dough Products, Inc.*, 1999 U.S. Dist. LEXIS 11229, *18 (N.D. Ill. July 19, 1999); *see also Bayer Clothing Group, Inc. v. Sears, Roebuck & Co.*, 2008 U.S. Dist. LEXIS 59679 (N.D. Ill. Aug. 7, 2008); *BRC Rubber & Plastics, Inc. v. Continental Carbon Co.*, 876 F.Supp.2d 1042 (N.D. Ind. 2012).

forecast is binding if a supplier set its product price based on the forecast, if a product is custom-made for the buyer, or if the buyer knew the supplier requires substantial lead-time for production. On the other hand, if a supplier did not set its product price based on a buyer's forecast, if a product is not custom-made, and if lead-time is not a significant issue, courts are more likely to hold that an ambiguous forecast is not binding.

An illustrative case is *Detroit Radiant Products Company v. BSH Home Appliances Corporation.*[24] BSH, the buyer, requested a price quote from the supplier for custom stove burners based on an "estimated" 30,000-unit order. After the supplier responded, the buyer requested an updated price quote based on an order of *precisely* 30,000 units. The supplier's updated quote showed that its price was calculated to recoup its engineering costs for the customized product over the course of the 30,000-unit order. The buyer then issued purchase orders for 31,000 burners to be delivered at specific intervals over a period of several years. The buyer attempted to terminate the contract after purchasing only a fraction of the anticipated 31,000 burners, however. The court held that because the goods were specially manufactured for the buyer, and because the buyer knew that the product price was calculated based on anticipated order quantity, the buyer's forecast was binding.

Another case in which an ambiguous forecast was held to be binding is *Scovill Fasteners, Inc. v. Northern Metals, Inc.,*[25] which involved a contract for the purchase of metal. In its RFQ, the buyer promised to provide quarterly forecasts "to allow suppliers to obtain necessary stock." The buyer also knew that the supplier required lead-time for orders because the supplier procured raw materials from overseas. Ultimately, the buyer sued, and claimed that it was entitled to damages based on purchase quantities that exceeded the buyer's forecasts. Appropriately, the court limited the buyer's damages to the amount of purchases the buyer forecasted to the supplier, reasoning that because the buyer knew that the supplier relied on the forecasts, the buyer's forecasts were binding, and additional damages were not legally supported.

––––––

24    473 F.3d 623, 61 U.C.C. Rep. Serv. 2d (Callaghan) 701 (6th Cir. 2007).

25    303 Ga. App. 246, 692 S.E.2d 840, 71 U.C.C. Rep. Serv. 2d (Callaghan) 263 (Ga. App. 2010).

## Lessons Learned

Buyers and suppliers using forecasts to plan for production should:

- Coordinate their forecasting efforts as much as possible
- Understand that there are limits to what forecasting models can predict, and that unexpected events can still occur
- Include human analysis in forecasting
- Know all relevant industry-specific forecasting variables
- Be clear about whether forecasts are binding or non-binding
- Be cautious about relying on non-binding forecasts

# CHAPTER 6

# PROCUREMENT

## Overview

In supply chains, the term "procurement" describes the process of obtaining goods or services from the outside world. "Procurement" is often used interchangeably with "purchasing," but for most companies this would not be correct. The procurement department for most companies includes sourcing, purchasing, and supplier management, and, in some cases, product-cost estimating, production planning, and supplier quality. More recently, procurement has become an integral part of manufacturing operations and accounts payable and plays a critical support role to engineering, quality assurance, and customer contracts.

Compared with other supply chain functions, the procurement function has undergone drastic change over the past 25 years, so much so that a 1980s-era buyer would no longer recognize most procurement processes and may not be qualified to be a buyer today. Buyers are now typically called "commodity managers" or "procurement managers," have a bachelor's degree or MBA, and use systems tools to execute sourcing and buying processes. Not only are buyers now better educated, they are typically skilled in negotiation techniques and use ERP (Enterprise Resource Planning) systems to process and keep track of buying transactions.

## *History of Procurement*

History of Procurement

| 1980s | 1990s | 2000s | 2010s |
|---|---|---|---|
| • Arms length business relationship (our-side vs your side)<br>• Very basic software with purchasing systems that automate POs<br>• Use of learning-curve theory to drive down pricing year over year<br>• $1000 govt toilet seats, $75 ashtrays because these required "R&D<br>• Personal relationships with vendors - off the books | • Win-win approach to negotiation<br>• Emergence of purchasing modules in ERP systems<br>• Title changes from buyer and purchasing agent to procurement manager<br>• Use of consultants to help with spend analysis<br>• Increased acknowledgement of procurement as a part of the broader supply chain | • Adding value to negotiations through bigger, more complex buys<br>• Non-production spend analysis and solutions<br>• Control over maverick buys through software<br>• China sourcing (low cost country sourcing and production)<br>• Coordination across the Supply Chain<br>• Extensive use of on-line auctions | • Significantly more automation and electronic interchange with suppliers<br>• Extensive use of data<br>• Global business environment, global sourcing<br>• More complexity<br>• Professional procurement staff with more education, training and systems savvy<br>• Procurement is part of core supply chain |

Procurement organizations are typically organized under a vice president of supply chain or vice president of operations, with some dotted-line reporting responsibility to finance. Procurement holds the purse strings of the company and is responsible for somewhere between 40-60 percent (sometimes higher) of the cost of producing a product. Not only is the finance department interested in controlling these expenditures, finance is also interested in monitoring and controlling the investment in inventory and making sure that what is purchased is enough to sustain the production schedule without over-investing in raw materials. The finance and accounting departments also set payment schedules, sometimes extending supplier payments out as long as possible to optimize working capital. It is not unusual for a purchase order to indicate "Net30" payment terms, but for accounting to actually pay Net45 or Net60.

### *Procurement Organizations*

Most procurement organizations have two primary functions: sourcing and purchasing. In addition, procurement organizations also have data collection functions that track supplier activity and expenditures. Procurement typically reports to the head of the business group that also manages manufacturing and logistics. In smaller organizations, procurement may report to finance to allow finance to control procurement's large expenditure of company funds. The typical steps in the procurement function are represented in the diagram below.

## *Sourcing*

The sourcing function within procurement refers to the process of finding, evaluating, and engaging suppliers of goods and services. Sourcing is the initial step in acquiring goods and services, and generally involves researching suppliers and their capabilities, communicating with suppliers regarding their interest in doing business, and evaluating the potential match with the buyer's organization. Once suppliers are identified and qualified, they may be asked to provide sample products or production of first articles, which are then tested for quality. During the sourcing process, the procurement department will check suppliers' references and financial standing, as well as any past history with the buyer.

The supplier may also be asked to participate in the buying organization's RFQ, RFI, or RFP processes. (These processes are discussed in Chapter 1: The Pre-Contract Planning Phase.) Information received from the RFX process is used to analyze, compare, and select suppliers.

## *Purchasing*

The purchasing process comes after sourcing, and may be performed by the same or different people in the procurement organization. In some organizations, procurement managers or commodity managers perform both sourcing and the purchasing/buying functions, while other organizations treat the buying function as an administrative task that follows the supplier sourcing and selection process.

Purchasing entails finalizing and documenting the details of supplier contacts and the final negotiation of supplier terms and pricing. In recent years, buyers have received more training in negotiation and often know to include important non-commercial items in a contract to make the transaction more valuable overall. Things like access to additional opportunities, providing references, quarterly business reviews, use of electronic data interchange (EDI), beta test sites for new software, equipment training, etc., are likely to be included in the deal. This adds complexity and sometimes risk to transactions.

The vast majority of purchases are completed using purchase orders (POs) with standard terms and conditions that are tailored very little, if at all, to the transaction before both parties sign off. Many POs are generic and may even be available for download from the Internet. POs constitute legally binding contracts that should be periodically reviewed by legal staff as business conditions change. For large or strategically important purchases (say, for example, the purchase of an airliner or manufacturing plant, or a highly technical development contract), POs should be more individually tailored. Terms and conditions need to be reviewed and customized for every important deal. For high-value or strategic purchases, we recommend executing individually tailored long-term agreements, rather than simply relying on POs. (See Chapter 2: Drafting the Supply Chain Contract.)

Besides performing the two major functions of sourcing and purchasing, the procurement process generally follows these basic steps:

1. **Product Design Requirements and Supplier Quotations**: As company engineers design and develop new products, procurement will identify suppliers and quote raw materials and component prices to complete the cost estimate.
2. **Production Forecasting**: As sales forecasts are developed, procurement will place orders for long-lead-time items (which ideally may be cancelled if orders do not materialize).
3. **Production Planning and Requisitioning**: Once production is planned for the factory, procurement will receive requisitions to order raw materials, components, sub-assemblies, and whatever else is needed.
4. **Sourcing and Qualifying Suppliers**: This is an ongoing effort in procurement to identify and develop new and existing suppliers and to determine their fit for the company's needs. The supplier qualification process often identifies alternative suppliers and second-source suppliers.
5. **Purchasing**: Purchasing involves the release of POs and long-term contracts to suppliers once suppliers have been identified and qualified.
6. **Supplier Quality Management**: Once suppliers have begun to supply product, procurement performs ongoing quality testing,

management, and product correction. This usually involves keeping statistics on supplier quality performance.

7. **Supplier Management**: Procurement typically manages relationships with suppliers and monitors supplier performance. This usually involves keeping statistics regarding on-time deliveries, invoice accuracy, and quality.

8. **Accounts Payable**: Procurement reviews supplier invoices for accuracy and approves supplier invoices for payment by the accounting department.

These basic process steps are found in most procurement organizations, and may be supplemented by sub-processes such as data collection, continuous training, and systems support.

### *Direct and Indirect Procurement*

Purchases of goods and services that relate directly to the manufacturing process constitute "direct" procurement. Direct procurement includes purchasing things like raw materials for manufacturing, sub-assemblies, and manufacturing services, such as metal finishing and painting. Typically, these items have general ledger accounts associated with each category. Tracking direct procurement purchases allows companies to collect and track cost-accounting information. Companies can also monitor and analyze part cost and deviations from standard costs for project control.

"Indirect procurement" is the sourcing and purchasing of goods and services that are required by the company, but that are not directly related to manufacturing the products that a company makes and sells. This includes things like office supplies, office furniture, and electricity. Typically, purchasing departments initiate these purchases through a requisitioning process. These purchases will then be associated with a general ledger account. A typical indirect procurement process is depicted in the diagram below.

### Managing Inventory

The management and timing of inventory is a complex process that is executed jointly by the production planning and purchasing departments, and powerfully impacts a company's financial functions. Production planning releases requisitions for raw materials that are timed to support production schedules, especially for long-lead-time items. Purchasing places orders that are timed to meet the company's production schedules, and must achieve a careful balance between not acquiring materials too early and not allowing stock-outs or production stoppage because parts are not in-house. Delivery windows and terms are usually made part of supplier contracts, making suppliers partners with buyers in managing inventory and delivering "just in time" for production. Companies' finance functions manage working capital so that investment in inventory occurs as needed, and so that capital is not tied up needlessly in raw materials, work in progress, or finished goods.

Because of these complexities and because of imperfect supplier compliance with schedules, companies will always need to track inventory and carefully manage overages. In addition, most purchasing departments have an expediting function to make sure suppliers deliver on time and as expected. As business conditions change, buyers will always need flexibility to be able to alter supplier schedules.

In the special case of outsourcing production to contract manufacturers (CMs), third-party vendors that perform manufacturing functions for other companies, CM purchasing departments may buy the same part for multiple customers. When this is the case, a CM may be able to aggregate and requisition some of its supplies across customers, which may entitle the CM to discount for volume. Sometimes, CMs buy components directly, and sometimes on consignment for their customers. Thus, CM procurement is even more complex than it is for ordinary purchases.

### Procurement Systems and Metrics

Today, procurement departments operate many different systems to assist with their functions. Transactions are recorded in these systems and are traceable, providing an audit and evidence trail.

The primary procurement system is usually the business ERP (enterprise resource management) system that connects and supports processes across functions. ERP systems can generate purchase requisitions based on production plans, support the issuance of POs and other contracts, record the receipt of materials from suppliers, and issue payments for supplier invoices. If a company has implemented additional ERP procurement functionality, there may be a host of other supported activities as well, such as supplier quality tracking, online auctions, RFX issuance, purchase history, and purchase price variance.

Sometimes, even with extended functionality, ERP systems are not enough. Some of the smaller or tier 2-3 ERP systems do not possess all of the functions that companies require. In other instances, companies' business requirements are so unique that special functions are required. In either case, procurement may add specialty systems and point solutions for supplier portals, indirect purchases, and data management. In addition, procurement always uses spreadsheets to track important procurement data.

Regardless of the systems or combinations of systems used in procurement functions, these systems should all be capable of tracing the activity of the procurement department and the activities of the buying staff over time. Carefully tracking and managing supplier information can help prevent supply chain disputes before they start.

### Case Study: Justifying a Price Increase

A supplier found itself in a dispute with its customer that claimed that the supplier's price increases were unjustified. The supplier, however, was able to prove that its price increases were directly tied to raw material and logistics price hikes, which were legitimate causes for price increases under the parties' contract. By reviewing the purchase-price history of key components over time, and logistics cost increases due to bunker fuel surcharges, the supplier's cost increases were in fact well supported. This information was available in the supplier's ERP system and in spreadsheets in its logistics department.

In order to defend its price increase, the supplier also had to demonstrate that it capably managed and negotiated with its own suppliers to keep prices down. The supplier's procurement functions had written business procedures, records of meeting presentations, and notes from supplier negotiation sessions as documentation.

All of the evidence in procurement pointed to good internal controls, compliance with best practices, and justification for the supplier's cost increase, which led to a favorable legal outcome for the supplier.

## Legal Overview

Now let's talk about POs and other procurement documents that buyers issue to suppliers to obtain products. POs, long-term agreements, terms and conditions, and other procurement documents are the legal instruments that set forth the rights and obligations of supply chain partners, which means that they are critically important.

For ordinary, commodity products, buyers make most of their purchases through POs. POs typically set forth price, order quantity, shipping and delivery terms, and payment terms, and contain information designed to track orders in both parties' ERP systems. But like any supplier contract, POs can include any information the parties want. Sometimes POs look like full-blown long-term agreements with warranty provisions, material and process standards, and the like. Sometimes, POs are simply one-page forms with the bare minimum of information, such as order quantity, price, and delivery date. POs can augment a long-term agreement that has already been negotiated, or they can function as stand-alone agreements. POs and other procurement documents are contractually binding once a supplier accepts them.

In Chapter 2, when we discussed drafting supply chain contracts, we recommended that supply chain partners not rely on POs alone to purchase components that are complex, strategically important, or that involve high-dollar transactions. Instead, we recommended that supply chain partners negotiate thoughtful and tailored long-term agreements for these purchases. But even when supply chain partners negotiate more comprehensive agreements, POs or similar procurement documents may be used to schedule orders and deliveries, completing the long-term agreements.

In the supply chain world, POs generally come in one of four varieties:

- "Standard POs" are commonly used for one-time or idiosyncratic purchases where order quantity and price are known.
- "Planning POs" contemplate multiple shipments on different dates, which may be flexible.
- "Blanket POs" usually set forth price, delivery terms, and payment terms, but not quantity; the buyer issues periodic "releases" against the blanket PO for specific purchases.
- "Development POs" set forth deliverables or scheduling items for pre-production development or testing programs.

Most ERP systems can create each of these PO types. Often, suppliers will have electronic portals into which buyers can enter PO information electronically. Ambiguity is rarely a problem with POs, but to the extent that POs can be crafted to avoid or minimize supply chain disputes, being clear and unambiguous is a major requirement.

### Vetting Procurement Documents

Who within an organization should receive copies of POs and other procurement documents? The answer is, ideally, anyone who will be involved in the underlying transaction.

In many companies, procurement documents are not circulated outside the procurement department. This is unfortunate because project engineers, quality, reliability, and business development personnel would benefit from understanding the procurement aspect of the supply chain relationship. Obviously, no one wants engineers to be excessively distracted from the task of engineering, but mistakes are often made when engineers and other technical personnel do not have a complete understanding of the commercial aspects of the company's supply chain.

At the very least, project engineers and others should be given training as to what POs and other procurement documents look like, what their essential terms contain, and what the legal implications of important terms are.

### Accepting Procurement Documents

When disputes arise concerning POs, it is often because a supplier claims that it did not accept in part or in total the terms set forth in a buyer's PO—but the supplier nevertheless delivers product in response to the PO. In this situation, the terms of the buyer's PO will most likely prevail, since under the UCC, a supplier is generally deemed to have accepted a PO when it begins performance.[26]

---

26   UCC § 2-206(1)(b) ("Unless otherwise unambiguously indicated by the language or circumstances . . . an order or other offer to buy goods for prompt or current shipment shall be construed as inviting acceptance either by a prompt promise to ship or by the prompt or current shipment of conforming or non-conforming goods . . . ").

There are exceptions to this rule, however. If a supplier objects to a PO term or insists on alternate terms before beginning performance, the buyer's PO may not control the transaction. (The legal principles governing these scenarios are discussed in Chapter 2: Drafting the Supply Chain Contract.) Ambiguities as to what contract terms have been accepted create conflict. Therefore, it is generally a good idea to create an agreed-upon method for suppliers to accept or dispute PO terms. Some POs require suppliers to indicate acceptance affirmatively each time a PO is placed. But some supply chain partners find this cumbersome, and instead give the supplier a specified time to object to PO terms, after which time a PO is deemed to have been accepted. We think either approach works just fine.

### The Importance of Order Quantity

To avoid costly and unnecessary supply chain disputes, it is important that procurement departments understand how to draft POs and other procurement documents in a way that ensures they are enforceable. For US supply chain partners, this involves ensuring that procurement documents always include a valid order "quantity" term—meaning that they need to specify the quantity of the product being ordered.

Whoever said, "It's quality, not quantity, that counts," never met the drafters of the UCC. Under the UCC's "statute of frauds," a written quantity term is required for a supply chain contract to be enforceable. Weirdly, order quantity is the only term that the UCC requires to be in writing. All other contract terms may be left open and can be determined later. Why the UCC places special importance on order quantity is a mystery, and we think arbitrary, but that is the way it is.

The UCC's quantity term requirement is often badly suited to supply chain needs. There are many occasions in which it makes sense for supply chain partners to negotiate a framework agreement that governs the terms of orders that will be placed in specific quantities later. Specific quantity needs over the long term—and sometimes even over the short term—are not always known or knowable. Under the UCC, however, agreements that do not include a quantity term are unenforceable, even if the parties intended to create a binding contract.

## The Origin of the UCC's Quantity Term Requirement

Before we discuss how courts have interpreted the UCC's quantity term requirement, we would like to take a closer look at the UCC itself. The UCC's quantity term requirement is attributed to UCC 2-201(1), the UCC's "statute of frauds," which states,

> Except as otherwise provided in this section a contract for the sale of goods for the price of $500 or more is not enforceable by way of action or defense unless there is some writing sufficient to indicate that a contract for sale has been made between the parties and signed by the party against whom enforcement is sought or by his authorized agent or broker. A writing is not insufficient because it omits or incorrectly states a term agreed upon but the contract is not enforceable under this paragraph beyond the quantity of goods shown in such a writing.[27]

As some courts and commentators have pointed out, the plain language of this UCC provision does not mandate a written quantity term. It states only that contracts for the sale of goods over $500 are not enforceable beyond the quantity of goods identified in the contract. However, Comment 1 to UCC 2-201, which provides official interpretation, states, "The only term which must appear [in a contract for the sale of goods over $500] is the quantity term which need not be accurately stated but recovery is limited to the amount stated." The comment expressly distinguishes quantity from other contract terms: "The price, time, and place of payment or delivery, the general quality of the goods, or any particular warranties may all be omitted."

An exception to the UCC's rule that supply chain contracts must set forth the precise quantity of goods being ordered exists for so-called "requirements contracts," where the quantity being purchased is all of the buyer's requirements. Requirements contracts are addressed explicitly in UCC 2-306 (which we discuss in Chapter 5 on forecasting and planning). Under UCC 2-306, requirements contracts are valid and enforceable so long as the buyer's requirements are established "in good faith." Requirements contracts do not need to include a specific quantity term to be enforceable, although

---

27 UCC 2-201(1).

requirements contracts do need to state expressly that they are requirements contracts. Many courts also require that requirements contracts expressly state that there is "exclusive" relationship between the buyer and supplier, meaning that the buyer cannot purchase the product in question from any other supplier.

### Supply Chain Agreements That Lack a Quantity Term

There have been many instances in which courts have struck down detailed supply chain contracts because they did not include a written quantity term. It is difficult to believe that in real time, the sophisticated parties to these supply chain agreements did not intend to enter into binding contracts, albeit without written quantity terms, but courts nevertheless are very serious about the UCC's quantity term requirement.

In *Merritt-Campbell, Inc. v. RxP Products, Inc.*,[28] for example, a buyer and supplier entered into an agreement to buy a fuel additive. The agreement was signed and fully integrated and contained provisions governing price, delivery, confidentiality, and other commercial terms, but no quantity term. The buyer issued two POs pursuant to the negotiated agreement, but the supplier rejected them. The buyer therefore filed suit. The court held that the contract was unenforceable because it did not specify order quantity. The buyer argued that the contract was a requirements contract, but the court held that without express language identifying it as a requirements contract, it was not enforceable.

Similarly, in *Crown Battery Manufacturing Co. v. Club Car, Inc.*,[29] the parties negotiated and signed an agreement for the sale of batteries that did not include a quantity term. The agreement contemplated that the buyer would place periodic orders of batteries through POs, but the supplier would manufacture no fewer than 12,000 batteries per week, with the buyer to have the right of first refusal. A quality dispute arose between the parties, which caused the buyer to reduce its orders. The supplier sued, claiming that the agreement was a requirements contract, and argued that "this type of commercial arrangement is commonplace in the supply chain partners' industry." The court nevertheless held that the agreement was unenforceable because it did not

---

28   164 F.3d 957, 37 U.C.C. Rep. Serv. 2d (Callaghan) 565 (5ᵗʰ Cir. 1999).

29   2014 U.S. Dist. LEXIS 18907, 83 U.C.C. Rep. Serv. 2d (Callaghan) 1 (N.D. Ohio Feb. 14, 2014).

contain a written quantity term. The court also held that the agreement was not a valid requirements contract because it did not state that the supply chain relationship was "exclusive."

Some courts, though a slim minority, recognize that it is arbitrary to require a quantity term in a commercial agreement between sophisticated parties. A notable decision is *Advent Systems Limited v. Unisys Corporation*,[30] which addressed a distribution agreement for computer equipment. The supplier argued that the agreement was invalid because it did not contain a quantity term, and that it was not a valid requirements contract because it was not exclusive. The court acknowledged the many cases that have held that agreements for the sale of goods must contain a written quantity term to be enforceable. However, it noted that the "statute of frauds has been frequently criticized as a means for creating rather than preventing fraud," and cautioned that courts must be "careful in construing its provisions so that undesirable rigidity does not result in injustice." The court then determined that "[t]he detailed nature of the document" left "no doubt that the parties intended to create a contract," even though it did not contain a written quantity term.

Nowhere has the difficulty with the UCC's quantity term rule been more evident than in Michigan, home to much of the US automotive industry. In the auto industry, it is common for buyers to issue blanket POs that contain most of the contract's commercial terms, but not quantity and delivery date, and then issue "releases" for particular quantities of products, as they are needed. There is little doubt that supply chain partners who structure their relationships this way intend to create binding contracts, even though they do not specify quantity. Therefore, Michigan cases have engaged in heroic efforts to find these arrangements enforceable, notwithstanding the UCC's quantity term requirement.

In 2007, a Michigan US district court in *Johnson Controls, Inc. v. TRW Vehicle Safety Systems, Inc.*[31] was confronted with blanket POs for the sale of automotive seat assembly components. The blanket POs stated price and other commercial terms, but not quantity. The quantity column in the blanket POs simply stated "AS REL," an abbreviation for "as released." Recognizing

---

30    925 F.2d 670, 13 U.C.C. Rep. Serv. 2d (Callaghan) 669 (3d Cir. 1991).

31    491 F.Supp.2d 707, 62 U.C.C. Rep. Serv. 2d (Callaghan) 863 (E.D. Mich. 2007).

that this contract structure was common in automotive supply chains, the court held that the blanket POs were enforceable, even though they did not specify quantity and even though they were not requirements contracts. The court held that the term "AS REL" gave "some indication that [the buyer] intended to purchase and TRW intended to sell some quantity of parts. This is all the statute of frauds requires."

In 2008, another Michigan US district court reached a similar result in *GRM Corporation v. Miniature Precision Components, Inc.*,[32] which involved blanket POs for the sale of automotive thermostats used in Chrysler vehicles. As in *Johnson Controls*, the blanket POs did not specify quantity, but comprehensively set forth other commercial terms. Even though the blanket POs did not state that they were requirements contracts, the court found that requirements contracts is in fact what they were. Because the buyer was not free, per Chrysler's guidelines, to replace the supplier with another supplier, the court held that the relationship was an exclusive requirements contract that was enforceable under the UCC.

In 2012, a third Michigan US district court decided *Eberspaecher North America, Inc. v. Nelson Global Products, Inc.*,[33] which addressed a blanket PO for the sale of exhaust components that contained no quantity term. The PO stated that it was a requirements contract, but defined "requirements" as "those quantities ordered by Buyer from time to time[.]" Even though this definition did not oblige the buyer to purchase its requirements exclusively from the supplier, the court held that it was "precise enough to satisfy the statute of frauds."

Interestingly, cases outside the automotive context in Michigan have not always reached the same result. In *MacSteel, Inc. v. Eramet North America*,[34] for example, a Michigan US district court held that a contract for the sale of chemicals was unenforceable because it did not contain a quantity term. The parties negotiated a six-month PO for a specified amount of chemicals. The PO stated that the buyer had the option to renew the contract on the same

---

32  2008 U.S. Dist. LEXIS 1128, 64 U.C.C. Rep. Serv. 2d (Callaghan) 797 (E.D. Mich. Jan. 8, 2008).

33  2012 U.S. Dist. LEXIS 136214, 78 U.C.C. Rep. Serv. 2d (Callaghan) 771 (E.D. Mich. Sept. 23, 2012).

34  2006 U.S. Dist. LEXIS 83339, 61 U.C.C. Rep. Serv. 2d (Callaghan) 385 (E.D. Mich. Nov. 16, 2006).

terms for an "additional" six-month period. The court held that the contract's six-month option period was not enforceable because the term "additional" did not contribute a valid quantity term.

## Order Quantity in International Supply Chain Contracts

The statute of frauds and its quantity term requirement is an invention of English law, and although England has long abandoned it, it remains in the United States through the UCC. Most other countries that are meaningfully involved in international commerce, however, have abandoned the requirement that any particular contract terms be in writing, including order quantity.

The CISG (the Convention on the International Sale of Goods) that governs most commercial contracts between the United States and non-US companies, has no statute of frauds and thus no quantity term requirement.[35] However, the CISG allows contracting states "whose legislation requires contracts of sale to be concluded in or evidenced by writing" to impose this rule on CISG-governed contracts that involves parties from those states.[36] Several states have officially invoked this provision, although the United States has not. The UNIDROIT Principles of International Commercial Contracts (UNIDROIT Principles), which contains additional commercial terms that parties to international contracts often adopt in their agreements, also has no statute of frauds or quantity term requirement.[37]

## Avoiding the Order Quantity Rule

The UCC's quantity term requirement is at odds with the supply chain needs of many buyers and suppliers. Supply chain partners often need a way to draft enforceable contracts without committing to precise order quantities. The law in the United States provides no easy answers. Here, we attempt to provide our best guidance.

If you cannot commit to a definite order quantity, and you also cannot commit to a requirements contract for all of a particular product, we suggest defining order quantity as the requirements needed to satisfy a particular program or part of a business. For example, the order quantity in a contract

---

35   CISG, Art. 11.
36   CISG, Art. 96.
37   UNIDROIT Principles, Art. 1.2.

to purchase sheet metal screws might be phrased as "all of Buyer's require-ments for ABC Construction Project needed for roofing," or "all of Buyer's requirements except for Buyer's top 10 programs by sales volume," or "all of Buyer's requirements for XYZ Washers." A requirements contract need not be for the entire requirements of a business to be enforceable. But using the term "requirements," and then carefully defining what the requirements consist of, should be sufficient for a supply chain agreement to be enforceable.

This approach was validated in *Corning Inc. v. VWR International, Inc.*,[38] which involved a contract for ceramics products. The contract was a "memoran-dum of agreement" that the court defined as "semi-exclusive." The buyer agreed to buy its requirements of the supplier's product, but only for certain customers. The language used in the contract was, "VRW will catalog inventory and sell only Corning's Pyrex reusable glass product line, except as warranted by Tier II custom-ers, to the exclusion of other non-Corning brands, including private label reusable glass." The court held that this language sufficiently established a requirements contract that complied with the statute of frauds: "[T]he memorandum can be construed as requiring VWR to purchase its requirements of reusable glass for all customers, except Tier II customers, exclusively from Corning . . . . Accordingly, the agreement is sufficiently exclusive to establish a requirements contract."

Another solution may be to identify the minimum amount of product the buyer is willing to purchase, but allow the buyer to modify this quantity as needed. It is common for supply chain agreements to allow the buyer to modify order quantities without the supplier's agreement, although in some cases, the supplier retains the right to petition for an equitable adjustment of the contract price in the event a quantity adjustment creates financial hard-ship. If a dispute arises, however, courts may refuse to enforce the contract beyond the minimum quantity specified.

Supply chain partners can also provide that their supply chain agreements are governed by the CISG or by the UNIDROIT Principles, neither of which have a quantity term requirement. However, be warned: these rules differ from the UCC in several respects apart from the statute of frauds, and supply chain parties must make sure they fully understand these differences.

---

38  2007 U.S. Dist. LEXIS 18611, 62 U.C.C. Rep. Serv. 2d (Callaghan) 448 (W.D.N.Y. Mar. 16, 2007).

## Lessons Learned

When engaging in procurement activities, supply chain partners should:

- Draft POs and other procurement documents carefully and without ambiguity
- Be aware that POs create binding contracts
- Ensure that engineers and other staff outside procurement understand how POs and other procurement documents are structured
- Negotiate a mechanism for suppliers to accept or reject PO terms
- For US supply chain contracts, ensure that procurement documents and other supply chain agreements specify order quantity, either by stating a specific quantity, or as a function of the buyer's requirements

# CHAPTER 7

# INTERNATIONAL PROCUREMENT

## Overview

In some ways, the use of the Internet and global sourcing have made life easier for procurement departments, and in other ways, these developments have made procurement much more complicated. Now, buyers have the whole world in which to source lowest-cost, highest-value products. But dealing with international suppliers can be a daunting task.

Most purchasing departments have years of experience working with domestic suppliers, and their processes for locating, qualifying, and contracting with suppliers are well established. International procurement introduces significantly more complexity and is typically reserved for more senior buyers and commodity managers. The overlay of cultures, differences in expectations and laws, and communications issues require the experience and finesse of seasoned professionals. Processes by country may vary widely, as may the interpretation and application of manufacturing and quality standards. These differences provide fertile ground for misunderstandings and complicated legal disputes.

### Investigating International Suppliers

Just like domestic sourcing, international buyers locate potential suppliers through online searches, industry organizations, trade shows, and direct sales calls. In addition, particularly for China sourcing, supplier aggregation websites have been successful in assisting manufacturers connect with potential buyers. Websites such as Alibaba.com, GlobalSources.com, and 360Buy.com are often the first stop for buyers trying to find international sources. These sites allow buyers to search for suppliers by product, such as for plastics, pipe fittings, industrial cameras, electronic components, toys, apparel, etc.

Another way that international buyers find foreign suppliers is through trade associations that provide recommendations or lists of members. If a buyer is sourcing automotive parts in Mexico, for example, it might contact the Mexican Automotive Industry Association (AMIA) for information about suppliers.

Many foreign manufacturers also have US sales representatives or organizations. When this is the case, deals can often be negotiated in the United States by the registered US branches of foreign suppliers. Even though these suppliers' operations are foreign, US sales people and coordinators manage US customer orders. If a US buyer does get into a dispute with a foreign supplier that has a US sales force, it may be easier to pursue legal action against that supplier in the United States.

Once a foreign manufacturer has been identified, an intensive qualification process usually follows. Most procurement and purchasing departments have written procedures for qualifying suppliers.

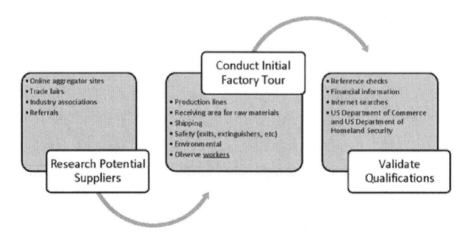

The qualification process starts with contacting the international manufacturer. Sometimes, the initial contact will be made by email or phone, but more often, a buyer will attend a trade show and will connect with foreign manufacturers there. The Canton Fair (also called China Import and Export

Fair), which takes place over two weeks in the spring and fall in Guangzhou, China, is the largest trade show in the world. At the Canton Fair, buyers can set up initial meetings with foreign manufacturers, trading companies, or manufactures' representatives. Other trade fairs around the world specialize in specific industries, such as toys or apparel, and are initial connection points for buyers and sellers.

After initial contact with a foreign supplier, it is usually best to schedule a factory visit. It is common and prudent to physically meet at the supplier's factory to discuss pricing and delivery schedules and to tour the factory floor. Unfortunately, foreign visitors don't always get to see all of a foreign supplier's operations. Very often, visitors are guided to showrooms or conference rooms and special production lines that are set up for visitor demonstrations only. Buyers should ask to see full production lines in operation to validate production and working conditions.

When we are working with clients to develop global factories and suppliers, we recommend brainstorming about what to see and ask about during factory visits. Generally, the first visit to an international supplier is a friendly overview and observation tour. Once a contract is finalized and production has started, a second, more intense audit is conducted, which should include a financial review, employee interviews, and a more intense factory audit to detect unwanted practices and conditions, such as noncompliance with child labor laws or sanitary standards. Develop a list of questions and points to observe, and organize a checklist by production area to observe on supplier tours. Ask suppliers in advance who will be with you during tours and meetings. Make sure you have actual factory management in attendance, not just sales or manufacturing representatives.

Here are some questions we advise our clients to ask, by subject area, when planning international supplier factory tours:

- **Culture**: Observe the boss and how he or she interacts with workers. The boss always flavors the workplace environment and makes a big difference in the work ethic, turnover, and retention of employees. Observe how the workers treat the boss. Are they friendly and interactive or sullen and non-reactive?
- **Equipment**: Observe the equipment and cleanliness of the plant. If a factory is messy and dirty, manufacturing is also likely to be sloppy

and lack attention to detail. Equipment age may or may not be an issue. If machines are well maintained and regularly calibrated, their age is probably not a problem.

- **Quality**: Ask about quality processes and ask to see how the supplier records and charts quality. What quality methodology is the supplier using? Is the supplier's quality system based on statistics? Think about how you can audit quality later if you decide to do business with this supplier.

- **IT Processes**: Ask about business IT systems. Does the supplier use Oracle, Microsoft, or SAP software, or something else? Is the software deployed for the whole company (finance, sales, and operations) or just for accounting? What reports can be generated from the ERP (enterprise resource management) system? How are ERP reports used to drive continuous quality improvement? Is the supplier using other manufacturing software for statistical process control and continuous improvement?

- **Environmental Protection**: What steps is the supplier taking to protect the environment? How is the supplier disposing of waste? What waste capture systems are in place? Is the supplier addressing air and water pollution in accordance with local laws and regulations? How is the supplier controlling and reporting environmental programs and impacts? What do the local and national governments require in terms of reporting?

- **Compliance**: What steps is the supplier taking to verify employee age and eligibility for work? How does the supplier comply with local regulations? How is compliance reported? What is the process for taking corrective action?

- **Operations**: Make sure you plan to tour the operations while people are working. Some manufacturing plants have different hours of operation and long lunch breaks. Make sure you see workers in action and observe products coming off the line. Are components fastened correctly? Are electronic components straight? Is there flux on the boards? Are parts cleaned? Are threads clipped from seams correctly? Is each garment checked for quality? If you are conducting a factory audit, make sure you ask to see your products in production, not some other company's products. Determine appropriate questions for your industry.

- **Subcontractors**: Verify that the materials from the supplier's suppliers and subcontractors meet your quality standards. Many legal cases have been initiated because a supplier lost control over its subcontractors and something went wrong. If you recall the Mattel Toys lead paint problem, Mattel thought it had control over the manufacturing processes, only to find out that painting had been subcontracted to other vendors. If a subcontractor is involved, buyers should tour subcontractor plants too.
- **Packaging and Warehousing**: Check packaging and warehousing. Make sure that these operations are done on site and they meet international shipping standards. Ask to see a packaged order and examine the quality of the packaging materials. Are the warehousing, packing, and shipping areas neat, clean, and dry?

### *References and Ownership Structure*

The next step in qualifying international suppliers is to check references, if possible. If an international factory is producing products for other Western companies, buyers should ask for references from other customers, and should call some of them regarding their experience with the supplier. Buyers should prepare detailed questionnaires for supplier reference calls, including questions such as:

- What is your experience with this supplier's quality?
- What is your experience with this supplier's on-time delivery performance?
- Is the supplier's billing accurate? Do invoices ever require adjustments?
- Is the supplier's export/import and shipping documentation accurate?
- Have you visited the supplier's factories? Did you discover any problems or issues?
- Did the supplier resolve all issues in a timely fashion?
- Did you ever have to take corrective action with this supplier?
- On a scale of 1-10, how would you rate this supplier against others in the same category?

Reference-check data should become part of the permanent supplier files, especially if it is used to justify the decision to select a particular supplier.

US buyers should also investigate the ownership and export orientation of foreign suppliers. It is important to determine if foreign factories are wholly or partially owned by a foreign government. In China, the best values in manufacturing are in factories that build for both the domestic and export marketplaces. These factories are likely to have lower cost structures than all-export factories, but will also have experience with international quality standards. Factories that are export-only factories and state-owned enterprises (SOEs) are more expensive, but require less supervision over time and tend to be more reliable. Chinese export-only factories are typically foreign-owned by citizens of Hong Kong, Taiwan, Singapore, Korea, or Japan. Factory ownership can, however, complicate matters if you have a legal dispute.

### Financial Due Diligence

The next step in qualifying foreign suppliers is usually to conduct financial due diligence. If a supplier is publically traded on an international stock exchange, financial information should be readily available. Most purchasing departments work with colleagues in the finance department to examine and validate international suppliers' financial statements. Cost accounting and other financial processes differ by country, so someone with international accounting experience should be engaged to interpret the numbers. Small, privately held, and state-owned companies will probably not publish or grant access to financial information. Still, we always encourage buyers to ask for it.

The financial stability of suppliers is of key importance to your relationship. Suppliers' financial information should be validated at regular intervals, at least once per year, because you may find early warning signs of failure in the numbers. Most purchasing departments have a standard approach for reviewing suppliers' financial profiles.

### Triangulating the Data

Triangulation is the process of verifying information by comparing two or three different data points or by using two or three different methods. We recommend that buyers triangulate the information about supplier capabilities, performance, and financial viability that they gather during the qualification process.

To triangulate supplier information, buyers should verify business operations through site visits, reference checks, and checking online websites, rankings, and other information.

Before entering into a contract, best practices include:

- Visiting the factory and auditing the processes
- Checking references
- Reviewing supplier websites and online news sources
- Asking for and analyzing financial data
- Requesting personnel data to verify age and eligibility of workers
- Testing sample products

Once you are satisfied with the due diligence and the sample products, it is time to negotiate a contract.

### Negotiating Contracts with International Suppliers

If you are dealing with a European supplier, you can expect the formal contracting process to be similar to negotiating a formal contract or PO (purchase order) in the United States. Of course, there are some differences that could be significant, such as European cost-accounting standards and the application of value-added tax (VAT). If cost accounting is important to your commercial relationship, the language of the contract must be clear about the approach.

Negotiating and contracting with suppliers in the rest of the world will be significantly different than it is in the United States. In China, negotiations are likely to extend beyond the time you have allowed, which can be frustrating for Westerners. Western negotiations are fast, direct, and succinct, and tend to discuss and close one sequential item after another. Then, the agreement is memorialized in a legal contract or PO and business begins. In China, the negotiation process is completely different. The negotiating style is indirect and lengthy, and often confuses Westerners.

It is not unusual for a Chinese negotiating leader to let you think he or she is authorized to make decisions, but in reality, does not. Sometimes, you may learn that the person with whom you have been negotiating is not even an employee of the Chinese manufacturer, but rather an "agent" of some sort. Affiliation can be hard to determine. You must clarify who is in the decision-making and signatory role, and this may be someone not in attendance at your meetings. The Chinese delegation may bring many people along to negotiations to take notes, provide research, and observe every detail of you and your team's facial expressions, reactions, and manner. If the Chinese delegation detects that you are getting impatient, this information will be used to their advantage.

Chinese negotiations are typically patient, meandering, and vague. Even though you may think you have closed on a topic and moved on, the topic may well be opened again with new points raised. In China, nothing is finalized until everything is finalized. Furthermore, when a contract is signed, there is still room for confusion. Westerners view the signing of a contract as the formal end goal of negotiations. Chinese view the signing of the contract as the starting place for what needs to get done. This is why Western supply chain professionals are often frustrated by reinterpretation of terms and conditions they thought were set.

Negotiations and contracting practices vary in other parts of the world too. Americans may believe that our way of doing business is superior to the ways of other cultures. This attitude will not lead to successful negotiations in the Middle East or other regions where it is important to build trust and integrity, and where they do not view Western ways as superior. Culturally direct and indirect communications practices may complicate deals. The greater the cultural differences, the more likely misunderstandings are.

### Managing Contracts with International Suppliers

Once a contract with an international supplier is signed, the process of managing the supplier relationship begins. Again, the complexity of cross-cultural communications, time zones, and different approaches to doing business can cause conflicts and legal battles. To avoid these conflicts, expectations should be carefully documented and agreed to (sometimes over and over until all parties have a clear understanding) during the negotiation and contracting processes. Buyers should not assume that international suppliers have understood all instructions. Buyers who deal with international suppliers must take extra care to ensure that contract requirements are being followed.

In most procurement organizations, the contract management process includes the following activities:

- Weekly or monthly calls to verify progress toward manufacturing completion and ongoing delivery of parts
- Ensuring that quality standards are being met by requiring quality data, by performing quality audits, or both
- Testing products at international laboratories (such as Bureau Veritas or SPS), after all engineering changes, production changes, and raw materials changes, and for finished products
- Monitoring product changes, delays, and expedites through ERP data
- Addressing invoice disputes and delayed payments through open communication with the supplier

In addition, in the case of long-term suppliers, high-value contracts, or strategic sources, the buyer should visit the supplier's manufacturing sites at least quarterly.

### *Failure Report: Chinese Construction Products*

A real-world example of how important it is to monitor and manage the performance of international suppliers involves Chinese construction materials used in US home construction that have been alleged in litigation to be chemically contaminated. Among the issues in the product supply chain was the fact that the US buyer required the Chinese manufacturer to include American Society for Testing and Materials (ASTM) certificates with all of its shipments—a standard requirement used to verify physical characteristics like strength, combustibility, and chemical content. Most domestic manufacturers understand that when a certificate like this is required, this means the supplier must actually conduct the testing and certify the results prior to shipping.

At least one Chinese supplier, however, interpreted the requirement for a completed certificate literally. It produced a certificate, but did not actually test the products! As a result, the products did not meet the ASTM or building code requirements in the United States and presented a potential danger to homeowners where they were used. This US importer and Chinese supplier ended up in a highly visible legal battle.

## *Shipping Documentation from International Suppliers*

Importing into the United States can be a challenging process requiring the assistance of a licensed US Customs broker. To get products cleared through US Customs, the importer of record must file a US Customs entry with the Department of Homeland Security. This entry summary (USA CF7501), together with a packing list, commercial invoice, and any required certificates (Food and Drug Administration verification, lead test results, etc.) must be submitted to US Customs, together with the payment of duty, taxes, and fees. Filing a US Customs entry is very much like filing a tax return with supporting forms and receipts. Importers are required to file entry information electronically, often before shipments leave their foreign port of embarkation. (See Chapter 11: Importing and Exporting.)

These import and filing requirements are part of the international procurement process and must be part of the responsibilities assigned to the supplier in the contract. Suppliers should complete all documentation required for international shipping as a normal part of their business.

## Legal Overview

International supply chain relationships are especially likely to generate disputes due to differences in negotiating style, contract performance norms, and communication between US buyers and international suppliers. A textbook example of what can go wrong when US companies do not pay careful enough attention to their international counterparties during the contract formation period is presented in *Orteck International, Inc. v. Transpacific Tire & Wheel, Inc.*[39]

Orteck, a US tire distributor, wanted to be (and believed that it was) the exclusive US supplier for tires made by Chinese manufacturer GITI China. Orteck's vice president of purchasing initially met with GITI China at GITI China's location in Shanghai in the fall of 2001. At a trade show later that year, the parties again met and negotiated and, Orteck believed, finalized their agreement. Although the parties did not draft a written contract, a few days after the trade show, Orteck's EVP wrote an email to other Orteck personnel, copying GITI China, stating his understanding of the deal was that "Orteck will market the Kiayan Radial Truck tires in USA and Canada. We will take

---

39   704 F.Supp. 2d 499 (D. Md. 2010).

their entire production and [GITI] agreed not to offer the tire to anyone else in USA or Canada." GITI China's response objected only to Orteck's inclusion of Canada in the agreement, stating that GITI China would allow Orteck to sell the tires exclusively "in USA but not Canada. Pls take note." GITI China never objected to Orteck being an exclusive distributor.

Orteck personnel travelled to GITI China several more times, where again, Orteck's purchasing vice president believed that GITI China confirmed the parties' exclusive distributor agreement. Soon, however, things began to unravel. On one China trip, GITI China told Orteck that it was changing the name of the tires. GITI China then wrote Orteck that it was limiting the quantity of tires available to Orteck, and stated that GITI China planned to allow other US distributors besides Orteck to sell GITI China's tires as well. Ultimately, GITI China used Orteck's customer list—which Orteck provided to GITI China as proof of sales network—and began selling to Orteck's customers directly. Not surprisingly, Orteck filed suit.

In a decision that could have easily gone the other way, the US district court held against Orteck on the basis of the Maryland statute of frauds, a legal doctrine that requires agreements to be memorialized in writing. (See Chapter 6: Procurement.) Although many courts would have held that the emails exchanged between the parties were sufficient to establish the required writing,[40] the *Orteck* court held that because the specific quantity of tires to be sold was not stated in those emails, no valid contract existed. The lesson here is, in international supply chain contracts it is never safe to assume you have a deal until all formal documents are fully and formally executed.

### *Apparent Agency Issues*

Another frequent legal problem in international supply chain contracts is the issue of "apparent agency"—determining whether the person you are dealing

---

40    *See, e.g., FFP Marketing Co. v. Medallion Co.*, 2001 U.S. App. LEXIS 30631, *6 (5th Cir. Dec. 19, 2001) (contract for the parties' "requirements" does not violate the statute of frauds requirement that quantity be stated in writing); *Advent Systems Ltd. v. Unisys Corp.*, 925 F.2d 670, 678 (3d Cir. 1991) (same); *O.N. Jonas Co., Inc. v. Badische Corp.*, 706 F.2d 1161, 1165 (11th Cir. 1983) (same); *Crown Battery Manufacturing Co. v. Club Car, Inc.*, 2014 U.S. Dist. LEXIS 18907, *8 (N.D. Ohio Feb. 14, 2014) (same); *Eberspaecher North America, Inc. v. Nelson Global Products, Inc.*, 2012 U.S. Dist. LEXIS 136214, *15-16 (E.D. Mich. Sept. 23, 2012) (same); *AGA Shareholders, LLC v. CKS Auto, Inc.*, 589 F.Supp.2d 1175, 1184 (D. Ariz. 2008) (same).

with truly has the authority to negotiate or make a deal. Apparent agency was one of the problems presented in *Weihai Textile Group Import & Export Co., Ltd. v. Level 8 Apparel, LLC.*[41]

*Weihaie Textile Group* involved a contract between US clothing buyers, on the one hand, and a Chinese manufacturer, on the other. The parties disputed whether a Chinese national whom the US buyers believed was an employee of the Chinese manufacturer was in fact authorized to accept POs placed by the US companies. Although the Chinese national had been directly affiliated with the Chinese manufacturer at one time, the Chinese manufacturer asserted that when the US companies placed their POs, he was authorized to act as a go-between only, but not to accept or reject POs. The court denied summary judgment to the Chinese manufacturer on the issue of whether the contested POs had been validly accepted, allowing the US companies' claims to proceed to trial. This case underscores the importance of knowing whom you are dealing with, and ensuring that they are authorized to bind the company they purport to represent. Beware of dealing with low-level employees or people of ambiguous employment status.

### Failure Alert: But The Buyer Did Everything Right

Even if you do everything right in international procurement, things can go wrong. In *Superwood Co. Ltd. v. Slam Brands, Inc.,*[42] a US furniture designer was sued by its Chinese manufacturer for failing to pay invoices. In its defense, the US buyer claimed that quality defects justified its refusal to pay. The contract, which was fully negotiated and executed, required that "each product shall be delivered with an agreed-upon quality level." The parties cooperated extensively before production began to establish agreed-upon quality standards. Samples and drawings showing the agreed-upon quality standards were left at the Chinese plant. The US buyer continuously employed quality personnel to check the products in various states of production.

Nevertheless, soon after the contract was signed, things started to go wrong. Somehow evading the US quality personnel, the Chinese manufacturer substituted inferior quality components and engaged in numerous

---

41   2014 U.S. Dist. LEXIS 53688 (S.D.N.Y. Mar. 28, 2014).

42   2013 U.S. Dist. LEXIS 116239 (W.D. Wash. Aug. 15, 2013); 2013 U.S. Dist. LEXIS 161855 (W.D. Wash. Nov. 13, 2013).

process shortcuts, resulting in many consumer complaints and quality issues. Ultimately, the US court held that the US buyer's refusal to pay was justified, but not before the owner of the US buyer was forced to sell the company to a third party due to financial troubles caused by these quality issues.

### Choice of Law Clauses in International Supplier Contracts

Choosing the law that applies to international supplier contracts is important to prevent (and prevail in) any legal disputes that arise. US companies understandably prefer that US law governs the contract. (All states, except Louisiana, have adopted some version of Article 2 of the Uniform Commercial Code.) Domestic law is obviously more familiar to US companies, and its adoption makes legal disputes easier to handle for US attorneys.

Non-US supply chain parties may prefer that their countries' law governs, however. This can be problematic because many legal systems in developing nations (for example, China) were not established for the purpose of protecting or enforcing individual rights. They were established primarily to define the powers of the state. Laws in these countries often provide little recourse in disputes between private parties. Therefore, it is best to adopt a governing law that has developed private contract principles.

A lot of international contracts adopt UK law to govern contract performance and dispute resolution. The reasoning for this is more historical than sensible. To many, UK law seems reliable and neutral. There are some aspects of UK contract law, however, that might be surprising to outsiders. For instance, UK law puts an extremely high premium on the contract's language, and can be unreasonably stubborn in refusing to allow context to supply meaning to contractual terms. UK law also does not recognize defenses that are valid under US law, like frustration, impracticability, and force majeure. This may be good or bad, but it is something that should be consciously understood.

If an international contract does not specify the governing law, the governing law is usually supplied by the CISG (the United Nations Convention on Contracts for the International Sale of Goods), also known as the "Vienna Convention." Originally enacted in 1980, the CISG has 83 signatories as of this writing, including most countries involved in international commerce. The United States, most of Europe, China, and Mexico are CISG signatories. The UK and several Asian countries increasingly involved in US supply chain relationships (like Hong Kong, Malaysia, Thailand, and Vietnam), however, are not. Companies in non-signatory states can nevertheless adopt the CISG into their supply chain contracts. The choice will then be enforced by US courts, although it may or may not be given perfect recognition if a lawsuit is brought in a non-US court.

For contracts governed by the CISG, the law is much like the UCC in the United States, but there are some notable differences. Under the CISG, for instance, oral contracts for the sale of goods are valid and enforceable, and in most cases would not be invalidated by "statute of frauds" principles. But some CISG countries have expressly reserved the right to enforce statute of frauds principles (for example, China did, for a time). Consequently, it is important to assess possible exceptions. Also, under the CISG, contracts may be modified orally—often not the case under US law. In addition, under US law, an acceptance containing different or additional terms is sufficient to create a contract. Under the CISG, however, a non-identical acceptance operates as a rejection, and no contract is formed. The CISG is also more lenient than the UCC about the language that can be used to disclaim warranties.

If parties from CISG countries wish to opt out of the CISG in favor of another country's law, they may do so. But there is considerable precedent from the courts of several countries that the language accomplishing this must be very, very clear. The best practice is to choose the law the supply chain parties agree upon, disclaim any conflicts or choice of law provisions, and specifically disclaim the CISG.

### Counterfeiting and International Supplier Relationships

It is an unfortunate and well-known reality of international supply chain contracts that counterfeiting sometimes happens as a result of international supply chain relationships. Counterfeiting happens in all industries, including electronics, apparel, pharmaceuticals, and others. Some high-end fashion brands report that there are more counterfeits made every year than genuine goods. Counterfeiting is illegal and prosecutable by trademark and patent holders. But it still happens—rampantly in some parts of the world.

In the United States, counterfeiting is illegal under the Lanham Act,[43] which allows injured parties to make *ex parte* (without notifying the other side) applications to US courts to seize counterfeit goods. However, the Lanham Act is often of little use against international defendants who do not have sufficient US presence to establish personal jurisdiction. When a counterfeiter cannot be sued in US court, the International Trade Commission provides a mechanism by asserting *in rem* jurisdiction over counterfeit goods. This bars counterfeit goods from being imported into the United States and imposes penalties on counterfeiters through special, expedited proceedings. Trademark owners can also register their trademarks with US Customs, which will seize goods entering the United States that may be counterfeit, pending review of the goods by the trademark owner.

The Internet makes prosecuting anti-counterfeiting actions under US law both more and less complicated. On one hand, Internet activity is often anonymous and difficult to track. On the other hand, if Internet sales are made into the United States, it is often easier to establish jurisdiction over counterfeiters and collect on their assets. The interesting 2010 Southern District of New York decisions in *The North Face Apparel Corp. v. Fujian Sharing Import & Export, Ltd.*[44] provide guidance for US companies seeking to shut down Internet counterfeiting abroad.

In these cases, The North Face and others sued a number of Chinese businesses for manufacturing counterfeit items. After the Chinese defendants failed to appear, the court granted a default judgment of $78 million to the US companies, plus a permanent injunction against any future acts of counterfeiting. Because the Chinese defendants utilized payment services such as PayPal that were accessible in the United States, the court was able to freeze and capture at least part of the judgment. To combat the fact that the Chinese defendants, when caught, would simply shut down their websites and open new ones, the court also entered a contempt order that allowed the plaintiffs to shut down infringing websites as they arose without requiring them to seek court approval each time. This strategy was revolutionary at the time, but now provides a useful playbook for other companies seeking to curb counterfeit Internet operations abroad.

---

43   15 U.S.C. § 1051, *et seq.*

44   Case No. 10-cv-1630, opinions dated Sept. 13, 2010 and June 24, 2011.

Of course, US law is not the only law that prohibits counterfeiting. Almost all countries, including China, provide legal protection for trade-marked goods. Several international treaties address this also, most recently the Anti-Counterfeiting Trade Agreement (ACTA), signed in 2011 by the United States, Japan, Korea, Australia, Canada, Morocco, New Zealand, and Singapore (and pending signature in the EU, Mexico, and Switzerland). The problem is typically on the enforcement side. Every year, the US Trade Representative publishes a "priority watch list" and a "watch list" of countries where intellectual property protection is low. China, India, Russia, Argentina, Thailand, Brazil, Vietnam, Mexico, and Canada are perennially on those lists.

International suppliers are a prolific source of counterfeit goods, unfortu-nately. To prevent counterfeiting within the supply chain, you should be sure to conduct adequate due diligence of your potential foreign suppliers, as we recommended earlier in this chapter. Consult with other US companies that have also used a supplier, do financial due diligence, and run at any hint of impropriety.

You should also insist on a contract provision that prevents suppliers from manufacturing products without authorization. The contract should require your suppliers to secure trademarked or patented materials and should re-quire them to report any known or suspected instances of improper activity. A sample clause is below:

### Required Measures to Prevent Counterfeit Activity

Supplier will ensure that its employees, subcontractors, and other agents do not take any actions that if conducted in the United States would constitute a violation of Buyer's intellectual property rights un-der US law. Supplier shall be strictly liable for any such violations committed by its employees, subcontractors, and/or other agents, and will fully indemnify Buyer for all costs and expenses, including reason-able attorneys' fees, of prosecuting such violations and/or enforcing Buyer's intellectual property rights. Supplier shall secure all intellectu-al property of Buyer at Supplier's facility and limit access to only those personnel necessary to perform under this Agreement. Supplier must promptly report, within 48 hours, any instances in which it suspects Buyer's intellectual property rights have been violated, whether or not the violation is believed to have been caused by Supplier's employees, subcontractors, or other agents, or by unrelated third parties. Any subcontracting agreement entered into by Supplier to perform this Agreement must be approved in writing by Buyer.

You should ensure that all trademarks are registered in countries where trade-marked products are sold, manufactured, or shipped to or through, and record all registered trademarks with these country's customs authorities. Like the United States, nearly all countries have registration systems that are used to help enforce intellectual property rights. Trademarks can be registered one country at a time or all at once through the World Intellectual Property Organization (WIPO), which covers up to 187 contracting states.

Finally, you should implement an effective anti-counterfeiting monitoring program. Intellectual property rights that are not enforced and asserted can be waived. Monitoring may seem expensive, but lost profits due to counterfeit sales are costly too. Third-party vendors can help provide these services.

### Ensuring Compliance with Anti-Corruption Laws

The subject of international procurement would not be complete without discussing anti-corruption laws.

Today, many countries have laws that prohibit individuals and businesses from paying bribes to foreign officials to obtain or retain business. The first such law was the US Foreign Corrupt Practices Act (FCPA).[45] Enacted in 1977 after a federal investigation revealed instances of foreign bribery by US companies, the FCPA applies to all US citizens, business entities, or issuers of US securities, and any foreign persons or entities with a business presence in the United States. The FCPA prohibits payments, offers to pay, or authorizations to pay bribes to foreign officials. The FCPA also requires all publicly listed companies in the United States to maintain records and internal controls sufficient to track corrupt payments.

The FCPA contains an exception for so-called "facilitating" or "grease" payments, which are payments made to "expedite or to secure the performance of a routine governmental action." But there is significant peril in making these types of payments. The FCPA is no longer the only anti-corruption statute on the

---

45    15 U.S.C. § 78dd-1, *et seq.*

books. In 1997, the Organization for Economic Cooperation and Development (OECD), a non-governmental organization composed of the world's most prominent market economy democracies, promulgated the Convention on Combating Bribery of Foreign Public Officials in International Business Transactions. The so-called OECD Anti-Bribery Convention requires its signatories to enact anti-corruption legislation, and has been signed by 40 countries to date, most of which have enacted implementing legislation. Unlike the FCPA, the OECD Anti-Bribery Convention does not allow facilitating or grease payments.

In addition, in 2010, the UK enacted the farthest sweeping anti-corruption legislation in the world, called the UK Anti-Bribery Act. The UK legislation applies to *any* payment of a bribe, not just those to foreign officials. In addition, the UK Anti-Bribery Act does not include any exception for facilitating payments. The UK Anti-Bribery Act also makes illegal the "failure to prevent bribery," meaning the failure to control and monitor anyone and everyone working on the company's behalf. There is, however, a defense to this provision if the company has "adequate procedures" in place to prevent agents and employees from engaging in corrupt behavior. The bottom line for international companies is that they should avoid conduct that is illegal under any nation's laws.

The supply chain relationship comes into play with anti-corruption legislation because companies can be held liable for corrupt payments made by their supply chain partners on their behalf and for failing to monitor supply chain partners' conduct. Red flags that increase the chance that a US company will be held liable for its international supply chain partners' conduct include: (1) if the US company is doing business with suppliers in countries known for corrupt activity, (2) if the international supplier appears underqualified to perform the tasks for which is has been retained, (3) if the payment needs of the international supplier are erratic or unexplainable, and (4) if the international supplier has known interactions with foreign officials.

Freight forwarding and logistics providers acting on behalf of US companies are often a supply chain vulnerability from a corruption standpoint, and have been caught in several well known cases. One prominent case involved Panalpina World Transport (Holdings) Ltd., a Swiss freight forwarder that admitted to bribing numerous foreign customs officials in countries around the world to expedite its clients' exports. Thus, to comply with anti-corruption laws, companies need to monitor their international supply chain partners.

International suppliers may resent being monitored, and without a contractual obligation to cooperate, may ignore requests for information and assurances of compliant conduct. Therefore, to avoid disputes about compliance with anti-corruption laws, international supply chain contracts should include several provisions. The first should require international suppliers to warrant that they are in compliance with all applicable anti-corruption legislation and that they will remain in compliance throughout the life of the contract. The second should require international suppliers to enact anti-corruption codes of conduct—commonplace now for companies with international operations. Another good practice, if it can be negotiated, is to require international suppliers to allow third-party auditing of their books and records to ensure compliance with anti-corruption laws.

Sample language is set forth as follows:

**Compliance with Anti-Corruption Laws**

(1) Supplier represents and warrants that it complies with the US Foreign Corrupt Practices Act (FCPA), the UK Anti-Bribery Act, and all other applicable anti-corruption laws in all countries in which Supplier operates. Supplier further represents and warrants that it will remain in compliance with all applicable anti-corruption laws to and until the termination of this Agreement and the parties' business relationship.

(2) Supplier represents and warrants that it has a robust anti-corruption Code of Conduct and procedures designed to ensure compliance with all applicable anti-corruption laws. Supplier further represents that its employees, agents, and subcontractors have been given copies of its anti-corruption Code of Conduct, and have received instruction at least one time per year on the procedures and requirements contained therein.

(3) Supplier shall, at the request of Buyer, allow unrestricted access to its corporate books and records for the purpose of conducting an independent third-party audit to ensure compliance with all applicable anti-corruption laws.

———

## Lessons Learned

When dealing with international supply chain relationships, US companies should:

- Ensure that the most experienced buyers handle international suppliers
- Conduct extensive diligence on international suppliers, including financial diligence, and follow up with other companies that have worked with the international supplier
- Inspect international factories and working conditions as closely as possible
- Ensure that foreign negotiators are authorized to bind the supplier
- Resist the urge to display impatience when negotiating with international suppliers
- Finalize and formally execute all contract documents before beginning work
- Actively manage the performance of international suppliers, on-site and in person if possible
- Insist on contract provisions that protect intellectual property rights and vigorously monitor possible counterfeiting activity
- Ensure supplier compliance with anti-corruption laws

# CHAPTER 8

# MANUFACTURING

## Overview

Manufacturing is at the heart of the supply chain. No matter what part of the supply chain you are dealing with, it is interdependent with the manufacturing process.

Some companies manufacture their products themselves, while other companies buy partially manufactured sub-assemblies from suppliers and perform final assembly and testing. Still other companies, such as Apple and Nike, completely outsource manufacturing to CMs (contract manufacturers). High-tech companies often use specialty CMs called "electronic manufacturing services" (EMS), which provide design, manufacturing, and testing services for electronic goods.

No matter if a company manufactures its own products or outsources production in whole or in part, manufacturing has significantly changed in recent years. Over the past few decades, manufacturing environments have made great strides. Gone are the dirty, dark, and smelly factories of the 1950s and 1960s. Today's manufacturing in America is much more likely to be clean, high-tech, automated, and full of robots. The skills required for workers involved in manufacturing have drastically changed too. Today's manufacturing workers are likely to have enough engineering skills to reprogram a simple robot, set up a numerically controlled machine, operate computer programs, and read quality reports to adjust production. These workers are likely to be part of "lean manufacturing" teams that work to solve quality and efficiency problems.

## *New Techniques and Methodologies*

Several successful ideas and techniques have been introduced in manufacturing over the past 25 years that focus on improving the manufacturing process. We have seen the rise of "the Toyota Way," "quality circles," "theory of constraints," "total quality management," "lean manufacturing," "Six Sigma," and many other new techniques and methodologies. The goals of each of these systems are simplifying processes, improving visibility and quality, and making manufacturing more efficient. The results have been impressive, making American manufacturers some of the most productive in the world.

## *The Toyota Way*

The Toyota Way was originally designed to set forth Toyota's manufacturing philosophy, describing the values and business methods Toyota employees should embrace to create the best and most efficient manufacturing environment. The Toyota Way is supported by two pillars: "Continuous Improvement" and "Respect for People." All Toyota Way improvement activities are supposed to support one or both of these pillars.

The Toyota Way is never satisfied with the current state of the manufacturing environment and is always searching for ways to improve. The Toyota Way methodology sets forth steps for achieving ongoing operational improvement, described in the following diagram:

### *Lean Manufacturing/Six Sigma*

Lean manufacturing and Six Sigma are the most popular and most common methodologies used in manufacturing. Both lean manufacturing and Six Sigma involve eliminating non-value-added activities that waste time and resources. Lean manufacturing also focuses on improving quality and on-time delivery and driving down costs. In fact, lean methods have been so successful that they are now commonly applied to all business processes, such as accounting, customer service, IT, and other functions.

Lean manufacturing is built on five principles: (1) specifying what creates value from the customer's perspective, (2) identifying the steps in the manufacturing process, (3) making those processes as seamless as possible, (4) making only what is requested by the customer, and (5) continually removing waste from the process. The main idea behind lean manufacturing is to compress the time period from customer order, through the supply chain, to receiving payment. To achieve results, small working teams are assembled and trained to identify and eliminate waste in their areas by identifying improvements that can be made to production processes. These teams find thousands, even millions, of dollars in savings through improved efficiency.

Conventional supply chains and businesses are often encumbered by operational inefficiencies. In lean manufacturing, these are known and categorized as the "seven wastes." The seven wastes are: (1) poor quality, (2) overproduction, (3) excess inventory, (4) transportation and logistics inefficiencies, (5) long processing times, (6) idle time, and (7) unnecessary operator motion. The seven wastes are depicted in the following diagram:

Lean tools and techniques have been proven to eliminate waste, layer after layer. Lean methods are often described in training classes and literature as like peeling an onion—you shed the biggest outer layers first, but there are always more layers and opportunities to eliminate waste. Much of lean manufacturing is common sense, although when teams start to focus on improvement and simplification, all sorts of waste are revealed. When lean methods become part of everyday business activities, business processes become more efficient and responsive.

## The Theory of Constraints

The theory of constraints (TOC) is a methodology that identifies the most important "limiting factors" or "constraints" that stand in the way of achieving a company's goals, then systematically works to eliminate these constraints. The TOC was first developed by Eliyahu M. Goldratt, an Israeli physicist who became a business management guru. His well-known and practiced TOC manufacturing theory views any system as most likely limited by a small number of constraints. However, the TOC adopts the idiom, "a chain is no stronger than its weakest link," and views processes and organizations as vulnerable because the weakest person or procedural step can damage or break the organization's success.

Here is a comparison of lean manufacturing and the TOC. The techniques involved in the two approaches are often combined by team leaders who understand and have experience with both lean manufacturing and the TOC.

| Methodology | Lean Manufacturing | Theory of Constraints (TOC) |
|---|---|---|
| Goal | Increase profitability by improved efficiency and adding value from a customer's perspective | Increased profitability by increasing throughput |
| Measurements/ Metrics | <ul><li>Cost Reduction</li><li>Lead-time reduction</li><li>On-time delivery</li><li>Value-added percentage</li></ul> | <ul><li>Throughput</li><li>Inventory reduction</li><li>On-time delivery</li><li>Operating expenses</li></ul> |
| Target for Change | Eliminating waste, adding value for complete processes | Constraints and weak links in processes |
| Implementation | Process reengineering, focusing on constraint points | Process reengineering, focusing on eliminating waste |
| Timing | Some immediate results, 3-5 years for sustaining results | Some immediate results, 3-5 years for sustaining results |
| Organization | Small teams, trained in techniques, led by senior lean consultant | Management/operations team focused on cause/ effect relationships |

### Contract Manufacturing

Many companies use CMs (contract manufacturers) to manufacture products that the companies develop and design. CMs are most often used by companies that view themselves as product designers and creators, but have little or no interest or capacity for manufacturing. Some of the most famous world brands, such as Apple, Nike, and HP, do not manufacture their own products. Instead, they employ the world's largest CMs, such as Foxconn, Flextronics, Jabil, and Li & Fung.

The benefits and risks of using CMs include:

- **Cost Savings**: Companies save capital because they do not have to invest in manufacturing facilities and equipment. Companies may also save on labor costs, particularly when using CMs in low-cost countries, such as China, India, Vietnam, Indonesia, and others.
- **Long-Term and Flexible Arrangements**: CM agreements may last many years, yet be flexible enough to ramp up when demand is high and ramp down when demand is low. Because CMs usually serve multiple customers, capacity is spread across all customers' demand, allowing more flexibility in planning.
- **Advanced Skills**: CMs often have advanced manufacturing skills and equipment and are more likely to use the latest techniques for maximum efficiency.
- **Focus on Manufacturing**: Companies and brands that use CMs are often better able to focus on their core competencies.
- **Economies of Scale**: Since CMs usually have multiple customers, they can often acquire raw materials at a reduced cost by benefiting from economies of scale in procurement.

However, there are also risks associated with using CMs, which include:

- **Lack of Control**: Control of manufacturing is in the hands of the CM, making adjustments more difficult to execute.
- **Poor Relationships**: As with all supply chain relationships, relationships with CMs can become contentious, which can result in poor quality, needless distractions, and sometimes legal disputes.
- **Quality Issues**: Quality specifications and testing should be clearly spelled out in CM contracts, and companies using CMs should verify that all parties agree on what constitutes compliance.

- **Scheduling and Capacity Changes**: If a company does not make up a large portion of a CM's business, it may find that production of its products is rescheduled to accommodate larger or more profitable customers.
- **Intellectual Property (IP) Theft**: IP theft is a constant risk when using CMs in some foreign countries, such as China. Companies can protect themselves against IP theft by building components or sub-assemblies in different locations and performing final assembly in another location. Employees hired by CMs should be thoroughly screened.

The terms and conditions that govern relationships with CMs are important. (See Chapter 7: International Procurement.) It is critical to include detailed instructions in the contract governing how products should be made and what raw materials must be used. Without specific instructions, CMs are known to substitute processes or materials, which can result in sub-standard quality, or even unsafe products. This has been a common problem with Chinese manufacturing, and because of this, CMs should always be managed diligently.

### Automation Trends: 3D Printing

Automating production lines improve productivity and reduce cost. A major automation innovation during recent years has been 3D printing, which has driven significant productivity improvements in manufacturing. 3D printing, also known as "additive manufacturing," involves combining layers of material to make, or "print," three-dimensional objects. Just about anything can now be made using 3D printing, but 3D printing's most practical use is making unique items that are not conducive to mass production. For example, dentures and medical implants such as hip joints are one-of-a-kind items that are perfect candidates for 3D printing.

3D printing also has applications in product development, rapid prototyping, and specialized manufacturing. 3D-printable models are created with computer-aided design (CAD) software, 3D scanners, or even with a plain digital camera and photogrammetry (software that makes measurements from photos).

## *Automation Trends: Five-Axis Milling*

Five-axis milling is another automation technique that manufacturers use to drive product improvements and reduce costs. Five-axis milling machines are currently the most advanced computer numeric controlled (CNC) milling machines in factory machine shops. Like other milling machines, five-axis machines create parts out of metal by cutting away excess material, either by water jet, cutting, or lasers. Unlike traditional three-axis milling machines, however, five-axis machines allow the material being worked to be rotated along two additional axes for further machining. Using five-axis milling, an experienced machinist can produce extremely complicated geometries with precision. Five-axis milling drastically reduces processing time and improves quality.

Many industries today, especially high-tech, precision optical equipment, medical devices, satellites, and aerospace, use five-axis machining to speed the manufacturing process and increase repeatable accuracy. The ability to machine complex shapes, undercuts, and difficult angles in a single setup reduces tooling costs and labor time, resulting in better precision, lower cost, and improved parts conformity.

## *Automation Trends: Robotics*

Robots also automate production and have been in use in manufacturing for a long time. However, traditional robotic machines were large, expensive, and potentially dangerous around humans. Recent developments in the engineering and science of robots have made them smaller, less expensive, and easier to use. Some even have faces, like "Baxter," the famous small robot that works side by side with humans and requires no sophisticated software programming.

No matter what type of robot is used in manufacturing, they all have three basic similarities: (1) they use some type of mechanical construction for the tasks they perform, (2) they incorporate electrical components for movement, sensing, and operation, and (3) they require some level of computer programming to function.

Along with 3D printing and five-axis milling, the use of robotics in manufacturing improves productivity and efficiency and reduces costs. These technologies represent the pathway to global competitiveness in American manufacturing.

## Legal Overview

Following specified manufacturing processes can be legally important in supply chain relationships. For complex products especially, buyers often care about how a supplier's components are made in addition to what the components can do. For example, with chemical products, the manufacturing process can affect how chemical compounds interact, which can have health and safety implications for pharmaceutical, cosmetic, and food products. For high-tech and mechanical products, the manufacturing process can affect durability, quality, and reliability. Consequently, many supply chain contracts make adhering to certain manufacturing standards or procedures a requirement.

### *Manufacturing Clauses in Supply Chain Agreements*

If a supplier's manufacturing process is important to the buyer or to the functionality of the end product, it is vital that the required process be incorporated into the supply chain contract and made a binding requirement. Without a contract requirement, there is no way to ensure that suppliers will use approved manufacturing processes. Buyers should consider whether manufacturing processes are important at the outset of their supply chain relationships. If suppliers are given discretion in their manufacturing processes when they should not be, quality problems and supply chain disputes are inevitable.

Manufacturing requirements that are set forth in supply chain contracts are enforced by courts. For example, in *Tokyo Ohka Kogyo America, Inc. v. Huntsman Propylene Oxide LLC*,[46] a buyer that made compounds for semiconductors alleged that its chemical supplier changed its manufacturing process without notice to the buyer, in violation of the parties' supply chain agreement. Because the parties' contract required the supplier to maintain a consistent manufacturing process and notify the buyer of any process changes, the court granted summary judgment in favor of the buyer.

Some buyers control manufacturing by requiring that suppliers' processes adhere to industry standards. It is common for supply chain agreements to incorporate and adopt standards that promote good practices in manufacturing that are promulgated by third-party organizations, such as the American Society for Testing and Materials (ASTM), the American Society for Quality

---

46   35 F.Supp.3d 1316, 84 U.C.C. Rep. Serv. 2d (Callaghan) 307 (D. Ore. 2014).

(ASQ), the International Organization for Standardization (ISO), and others, into their supply chain agreements. In *Global Petromarine v. G.T. Sales & Manufacturing, Inc.*,[47] for instance, a supply chain contract for the purchase of oil transportation hoses required a hose supplier to manufacture its products according to an international standard promulgated by the Oil Companies International Marine Forum (OCIMF). The court held that the supplier's agreement to abide by that standard was an "express warranty" with which the supplier had to comply.

Suppliers should ensure that they are able to comply with any required manufacturing processes or procedures before sinking too many resources into a potential project. A case that illustrates this principle is *Packagen v. BP Exploration & Production, Inc.*[48] *Packagen* involved an alleged arrangement between BP and a Maine supplier of oil containment "boom," which is used to contain oil spills in water. After the 2010 Deepwater spill, BP was desperate for cleanup and containment materials. Although Packagen, the supplier, had never made oil boom before, it had long manufactured packaging materials, and determined that its processes would produce boom at a faster rate than BP's other suppliers.

When Packagen initially contacted BP with a proposal, the BP representative indicated that BP would likely buy all of the product Packagen could make, if Packagen could demonstrate that its manufacturing processes met with the approval of a third-party inspector. Although BP never clarified what approvals were necessary, BP conducted an initial site visit to Packagen's facility and indicated that a supplier relationship was likely. Therefore, Packagen obtained a third-party certification that its boom met ASTM standards, and undertook costly rework of its manufacturing equipment.

BP then asked to see the material specifications for Packagen's product, and discovered that Packagen's boom was compositionally different from the boom that BP bought from other suppliers, which caused BP concern. Accordingly, BP told Packagen that Packagen's boom did not meet BP's quality requirements. However, because BP was still in desperate need for boom, BP conducted a second site visit of Packagen's facility. BP then implemented a new approval process and hired a specialized boom inspector who also indicated to Packagen that a supplier relationship was likely. Unfortunately, BP

---

47   2010 U.S. Dist. LEXIS 133551, 73 U.C.C. Rep. Serv. 2d (Callaghan) 240 (W.D. Mo. Dec. 17, 2010).
48   957 F.Supp.2d 58 (D. Me. 2013).

later determined that its inspector was not sufficiently experienced, and implemented specifications for boom that Packagen's product could not meet. Even so, Packagen's product performed well in a BP boom field test. Therefore, BP identified a number of modifications to Packagen's product that, if Packagen could make them, would qualify Packagen as a supplier. However, by this time, BP had successfully capped the Deepwater Horizon well, and had no further need for boom. Packagen sued.

The court held that Packagen could not prevail on any legal theory against BP. The parties had not entered into a written contract, and Packagen failed to show that BP engaged fraud in its dealings with Packagen. Although the court held that BP made "conflicting representations" about its need for Packagen's product, the court determined that this confusion "may be expected in an emergency" and that "BP's standards and requirements developed over time." The lesson for suppliers is that manufacturing procedures are often important, and it is a good practice to ensure that buyers' manufacturing requirements are defined and achievable before investing in a new project.

### Regulatory Manufacturing Requirements

In the United States and other countries, government agencies responsible for ensuring that products meet safety, health, environmental, and other standards often promulgate manufacturing rules that companies must observe. For instance, the US Food and Drug Administration (FDA) regulates pharmaceutical quality through "Current Good Manufacturing Practices" (cGMPs). cGMPs are standards designed to ensure that drug companies use proper design and manufacturing processes in clean and safe facilities. cGMPs require robust manufacturing processes, raw material monitoring, quality assurance, and testing procedures. In 2010, the FDA initiated its first cGMP regulatory action against GlaxoSmithKline to enforce its cGMPs. Since then, other regulatory actions have followed, and the US Department of Justice has initiated parallel prosecutions against some cGMP violators.

Similarly, the US Federal Aviation Administration (FAA) has developed a set of manufacturing best practices that suggest good manufacturing processes for companies in the aerospace industry. Although not legally binding, the FAA encourages manufacturers to adhere to these manufacturing best practices. Likewise, to minimize pollution, the US Environmental Protection Agency

(EPA) imposes comprehensive manufacturing standards on companies with operations in the United States. To date, the EPA has adopted over nine hundred standards that govern manufacturing, 122 of which are characterized as "major regulations."

———

### Lessons Learned

To ensure effective, robust, and efficient manufacturing practices, supply chain partners should:

- Ensure compliance with emerging manufacturing philosophies, such as the Toyota Way and lean manufacturing, that seek to increase manufacturing efficiency and reduce cost
- Monitor CMs diligently and provide them with clear and precise instructions
- Use automation tools like 3D printing, five-axis milling, and robotics to optimize quality and reduce error and waste
- Use supply chain agreements to ensure that suppliers are using robust and effective manufacturing practices

# CHAPTER 9

# Warehousing and Logistics

## Overview

Warehousing and logistics are critical links in the supply chain that have been steadily evolving over the past 25 years. Warehouses are no longer dusty, stagnant places where finished goods are stored until sold. Today's warehouses are active locations with inventory in motion and are more likely to be called "distribution centers." Although these two terms ("warehouse" and "distribution center") are frequently used interchangeably, distribution centers, or "DCs," have the connotation of goods on the move in the distribution channel.

Another more recent category of warehousing service provider is the third-party logistics provider, or "3PL." 3PLs are outsourced service providers that, in addition to warehousing, typically offer light assembly, kitting, and pick-pack-and-ship services to customers.

### Warehouses and DCs

Finished goods warehouses and DCs are typically owned by manufacturers and are often located on the same property as the company's manufacturing facilities. Finished goods warehouses are usually temporary storage locations. They are used to store goods until there are enough for full truckloads that can be sent to for-hire general merchandise or public warehouses operated by companies specializing in warehousing.

Public warehouses and DCs charge fees for storage based on the amount of storage used and the number of transactions processed. Public warehouse and

DCs can be enormous buildings with fully automated roller lines, packing stations, and automated weighing, sorting, and labeling processes. Public DCs for small goods (e.g., drugstore items or books) may have "pick-to-light systems" in which bins containing items light up when the goods that they contain are needed, making it easier for warehouse workers to find them and greatly enhancing productivity. Smaller warehouses may be completely manual.

The newest type of DC is the eCommerce warehouse, where thousands of items of different shapes and sizes are stored, picked, packed, and shipped to customers who order goods online. These eCommerce centers may be dedicated to one type of product, such as shoes, or they may serve multiple product lines, such as with Amazon.com and Alibaba.com. In some parts of the world, like Russia, eCommerce DCs offer end-to-end services, including website ordering, inventory management, pick-pack-and-ship, delivery via fleet, returns, and restocking. It is common in the fashion industry for manufacturers to use eCommerce warehouses, and to outsource the order and fulfillment processes completely so that they can concentrate on their core business of fashion.

### US Customs General Order Warehouses and Bonded Warehouses

Goods that arrive at US ports of entry, but are not cleared within a specified time (generally, a few days), are removed to general order (GO) storage. These goods are placed under US government supervision until they are cleared to enter the country. There are many reasons why goods may be held in GO storage, including if a company has insufficient funds to pay customs duties, or if required paperwork, such as lead test certificates, is not available. GO storage can be expensive and most importers avoid it. Goods that are in GO storage for more than six months are sold at US Customs auctions.

Bonded warehouses also store goods that have not yet cleared US Customs. Goods arriving at a US seaport may be bound for an inland US city to be cleared by Customs, which is where duties will be paid on the shipment. These goods are moved "in bond," with special customs approval and customs seals on trucks and railcars. When they arrive at their destination, the goods are placed in a US Customs bonded warehouse until formal entry is made. This allows importers to delay paying duties until the goods arrive at their final destination. Bonded warehouses fall under US "CFR19" regulations and require strict adherence to handling and security requirements. (See Chapter 11: Importing and Exporting.)

### Third-Party Logistics Providers (3PLs)

A 3PL is a for-hire company that works with shippers to store, process, and ship goods. 3PLs may provide light manufacturing, such as kitting, relabeling, assembling, and other tasks that add value prior to shipping. 3PLs may also provide warehousing to store goods until the goods are needed to fill customer orders. 3PLs often provide shipping and transportation services as well.

The term "logistics" can include elements of warehousing, transportation management, order processing and optimization, freight rate negotiations, business metrics, freight bill auditing, and much more. There are thousands of 3PLs all over the world that have different models and perform different tasks depending on what their customers want and need. Some 3PLs specialize in specific industries, such as medical products, frozen food, or eCommerce fulfillment. Others provide more generalized services across industries.

The distribution functions performed by 3PLs do not transform 3PLs into "distributors" in the commonly understood or legal sense of that term. True, "distributors" (in the commonly understood sense of that term) take title to the goods in question and resell them for their own profit. For 3PLs, however, title always remains with the manufacturer of the goods, with the 3PL providing only the physical and logistical functions of distribution.

### Systems Integration

In addition to providing services beyond warehousing, most 3PLs also provide IT support for order processing and inventory control. It is not unusual for 3PL IT systems to be at least partially integrated with their customers' IT systems. IT integration allows 3PLs to access order information electronically and update inventory positions and shipping information directly, without needing assistance from customers. 3PL IT systems directly interact with customers' IT systems through an electronic interface or through a more extensive systems architecture.

The details of systems integrations between 3PLs and their supply chain customers should be carefully documented as part of the logistics contract. Access to each other's systems should be limited as much as possible to ensure the integrity of each system and to reduce vulnerability to errors and cyber-attack.

## *Warehouse Layout and Design*

Warehouse layout and design is both art and science. The algorithms that optimize picking and sorting sequences in a distribution environment are the product of complicated engineering calculations. The demand for each product stored in a warehouse has to be taken into consideration, so that fast-moving products are most accessible, and so high-value items are carefully monitored. Location and access to products is driven by the best and fastest way to find and select them for orders. Complementary products are stored in proximity to each other if they are often sold and shipped together (such as sunglasses and cases, or shirts and ties). High-volume items or items that go on sale are constantly moved to the front of the warehouse so that travel time for selection and packing is minimized. The organization required for a large-scale warehouse with thousands, or even millions, of locations, racks, roller lines, and work stations is breathtaking.

Typically, the more optimized, planned, and automated a warehouse is, the lower the cost will be to process orders. Software systems designed to manage warehouses and DCs are expensive and time-consuming to implement, but absolutely essential for running warehousing operations.

Photo Credit: David Cardinal: Warehouse Robots Come of Age. Extreme Tech.

## Controlling Inventories

Control over inventory in public warehouses, DCs, and 3PLs is also complicated and difficult. It is easy to misplace parts in the wrong bin, or to pick and ship too many items or too few. Theft is also a significant problem in many warehouses, as is damage to goods during the pick-pack-and-ship process.

To keep track of inventory, most public warehouses, DCs, and 3PLs execute cycle counting on a daily basis. In cycle counting, a portion of the total inventory is counted and verified each day, with the fast movers and high-value items counted most often. Products are typically designated "A, B, or C" parts, with A's being the most valuable or highest movers. B's and C's are counted less frequently. The entire inventory of goods is counted at least once per year based on computer-generated daily plans. Daily adjustments are made to inventory accounting so that assets are accounted for accurately for financial reporting and the available inventory for shipping is correct. Most public warehouses, DCs, and 3PLs conduct annual wall-to-wall inventory over a short period of time, and suspend all activity in the warehouse until the count is completed, usually over a weekend. Wall-to-wall inventories are also conducted at customer request for a variety of reasons, including addressing accuracy problems, sell-offs, end-of-life products, new product reviews, etc.

## FIFO versus LIFO

Determining how to stock items is an accounting issue that affects processes within public warehouses, DCs, and 3PLs. Some companies follow the "first-in-first-out" (FIFO) method, in which new products are stocked behind older products or in different bins, and the oldest products are picked and shipped first. The other method is the "last-in-first-out" (LIFO) method, in which newer products are selected and shipped first. These inventory accounting methods are based on the preference and accounting policies of sellers and can have a significant impact on the value of inventory being warehoused. In either system, FIFO or LIFO, warehouse workers need to know to select products for orders based on date of manufacture. Some manufacturers require that products with different dates be stored in separate bins or areas, with the computer system directing the picking order. This is particularly important with perishables, such as food and drugs. These date-ordered procedures add complexity to warehouses and to the inventory selection process.

The goal of public warehouses, DCs, and 3PLs is to turn inventory as quickly as possible to fill customer orders and keep inventory refreshed, while minimizing service costs. Consumers in today's environment also expect fast order delivery. Amazon, Zappos, Alibaba, and others have set a very high standard for fast delivery, to the point where consumers now expect delivery in a day or two from all retailers. Customers of public warehouses, DCs, and 3PLs are demanding more and faster services for less cost.

### Using Temporary Workers

Most warehouse businesses have peak shipping times and seasons. Sometimes, fluctuations in labor requirements can be managed through worker overtime. But other times, such as holidays, labor requirements in a warehouse can vary significantly, and the only effective way to manage the variation is by using temporary workers to meet peak demand. However, temporary workers can be problematic.

Temporary workers are given little training and are often assigned the simplest tasks. At peak holiday seasons, for example, temporary workers in retail warehouses box shipments or attach labels to boxes. Unfortunately, temporary workers are notorious for making errors, and their work may not always meet minimum expectations.

For warehouse operators, the use of temporary labor is attractive. Temporary workers do not receive benefits such as health care or retirement, and they often can be assigned the worst or most dangerous warehouse tasks. They are not eligible for job advancement or raises. Instead of converting temporary workers to permanent workers when needed, it is often advantageous for warehouse operators to use "permanent" temporary labor to avoid paying benefits. In recent years, some temporary workers have sued warehouse operators for unsafe working conditions and overtime pay.

### Failure Alert: The Consequences of Poor Inventory Management

A now-defunct Silicon Valley high-tech company was operating in the competitive high-performance graphics market. As required by law, the company reported inventory in its quarterly financial reports, but because it was growing so fast and was profitable, the company overlooked some of its inventory in the reporting process. Its stock price continued to climb.

In reviewing the company's inventory position on certain parts, we noticed off-site inventory at a public warehouse and took a trip across Silicon Valley to see it. We were astonished to find aging electronic junk piled in dozens of racks that obviously had not been touched in years. When we questioned management about why the company was paying for this warehouse full of junk, we were told that the company did not want to write off or write down the inventory value because this would affect stock prices.

Writing off old or obsolete inventory is often a sign of poor supply chain management that companies do not want to admit to. So the aging inventory remained on the books at full value until eventually the company's financial analysts and auditors started asking probing questions. The investigation into the company's inventory manipulation did not end well for several executives.

## Legal Overview

Just as supplier agreements typically set forth the legal rights and duties between supply chain partners, formal agreements are used to set forth the legal rights and duties of companies that deal with public warehouses, DCs, and 3PLs. For routine warehousing and 3PL services, these contracts will typically be on the DC's standard form, which customers may negotiate and amend. For high-value or unusual 3PL arrangements, contract documents may need to be more customized.

Warehouses, DCs, and 3PLs typically operate under service level agreements (SLAs) with their customers. SLAs are contractual agreements in which services such as order fulfilment time or order accuracy are defined. The parties negotiate specific terms regarding picking, packing, and shipping, and the timeframes that need to be met. Sometimes, restocking or reverse logistics are also addressed in SLAs. Failure to meet SLA requirements typically results in penalties to the warehouse. For example, a 3PL may have a 48-hour order-to-ship SLA. If orders are not shipped within this timeframe, the warehouse incurs a penalty. Since most warehouses have integrated systems with their customers, performance to an SLA is relatively easy to track.

In the United States, public warehouse, DC, and 3PL contracts are generally governed by Article 7 of the UCC, which is entitled "Documents of Title." Article 7 has gone the longest of all the UCC articles without significant amendment and had never been modified until 2003, when amendments were introduced to accommodate the increased use of electronic warehousing documents. Originally promulgated in 1952, UCC Article 7 combined several warehousing laws already in existence and codified aspects of "bailment law" (the law that governs when personal property is held by another), set by state law. UCC Article 7 is adopted in some form by all 50 states. Most states have also accepted and adopted the 2003 Article 7 amendments.

For international public warehouse, DC, and 3PL relationships, there is no unified body of law that governs the same way that UCC Article 7 applies in the United States. Therefore, when dealing with international warehousing partners, and particularly if utilizing their services abroad, foreign law will likely apply unless the parties negotiate otherwise. Foreign law in this field can be unpredictable, and for this reason, we recommend being particularly attentive to the choice of law and dispute resolution provisions in international logistics contracts.

### Ownership of Goods

Warehousing, DC, and 3PL agreements should be clear that the warehouse, DC, or 3PL will be providing logistical services only, and that the warehouse is not gaining title or ownership to the goods entrusted to it. This is uncomplicated in US warehousing agreements, and is usually accomplished through a paragraph in the SLA that describes the services the warehouse, DC, or 3PL will perform. Warehouse contracts and warehouse receipts in the US also often include a "statement of ownership," indicating that the customer retains title to the goods in question, and that the warehouse holds only the right to store or distribute goods. If a warehouse, DC, or 3PL contract is ambiguous as to who owns the goods in question and the warehouse, DC, or 3PL enters bankruptcy, there is a danger that the customer's goods could be seized by creditors and liquidated as part of the estate.

For international warehouse agreements, it is particularly important to make sure that the contract provides that the customer retains ownership to the goods. Ownership and title provisions in international warehouse contracts should be vetted and reviewed with counsel in the foreign location, as foreign law may be idiosyncratic as to when and how title to goods transfers between commercial entities, particularly if creditor rights are implicated.

Warehouses, DCs, and 3PLs typically retain a warehouse lien over goods that they handle or store. A warehouse lien entitles the warehouse to collect any amounts owed to it by the customer against any goods the customer leaves in the warehouse's possession. Under UCC 7-209(a), there are two kinds of warehouse liens. "Specific" or "special" warehouse liens entitle a warehouse to proceed against a customer's goods for amounts due and owing on those particular goods. "General" or "spreading" warehouse liens entitle a warehouse or 3PL to proceed against a customer's goods for amounts due by the customer relating to any transaction between the parties. UCC 7-210 requires notice to a customer before goods may be sold to satisfy a warehouse lien.

Customers should ensure that their warehouse agreements give them the right, at least upon reasonable notice, to access, inspect, inventory, and audit goods entrusted to the warehouse or 3PL.

## Maintenance of Goods

Another important aspect covered by warehouse, DC, and 3PL agreements is whether there will be any specific maintenance requirements for the goods entrusted. If goods require special storage conditions (e.g., specific temperature maintenance, anti-humidity storage, etc.), or if particular access is needed (e.g., by industrial vehicle), this needs to be spelled out in the SLA.

Increasingly, storage of some types of goods is being regulated by law. In 2013, for instance, the United States passed the Drug Quality and Security Act (DQSA)[49] in response to a meningitis outbreak caused by poor handling of prescription drugs. The DQSA imposes greater handling, tracking, reporting, registration, and other requirements on companies in the prescription medication supply chain, including warehouses, DCs, and 3PLs. As the provisions of the DQSA go into effect over the next several years, warehouses, DCs, and 3PLs will have to ensure that they are in compliance. Among other things, the DQSA will require warehouses, DCs, and 3PLs to register their facilities with the US Secretary of Health and Human Services.

Similarly, in 2011, the United States enacted the FDA Food Safety Modernization Act (FSMA),[50] requiring all food transporters in the supply

---

49   21 U.S.C. § 301 note.

50   21 U.S.C. § 2201 note.

chain, including warehouses, DCs, and 3PLs, to implement greater measures to ensure the safety of food. A proposed rule under the new legislation, which is close to achieving final approval, is the Sanitary Transport of Human and Animal Food rule, which will require greater standards and controls for food transportation. In 2015, China also enacted an unprecedented food safety law in response to a contaminated milk scandal that caused the death of several infants. This new law requires greater safety controls by all players in the food supply chain in China. Again, warehouses, DCs, and 3PLs will have to ensure that they are in compliance.

Sometimes, goods entrusted to a warehouse or 3PL can be commingled with similar goods belonging to other customers. Other times, there are reasons not to allow commingling. In some instances, it may make sense to require in the warehouse, DC, or 3PL agreement that a customer's goods have dedicated space in the warehouse that will not be used by any other customer. On the other hand, some warehouses, DCs, and 3PLs (particularly overseas) reserve the right to move goods to other warehouses, as needed. If customers prefer or need their goods to stay in their original location, this should be addressed in warehouse SLAs.

Of course, additional services and more specific or highly regulated services come at a price, and "scope creep" is something warehouses, DCs, and 3PLs are generally on the lookout for. Expect an increase in contract price as you increase your service requests.


### Liability and Indemnity for Loss, Damage, Theft, or Mishandling

A legal issue that comes up frequently in warehouse, DC, and 3PL relationships is liability and indemnity for loss, damage, theft, or mishandling of goods entrusted to these entities.

Warehouse theft is a massive drain on US companies, so much so that in April 2010, the US FDA issued a letter to US companies expressing concern about the increase in cargo and warehouse thefts of FDA-regulated products. Recent news stories concerning more bizarre warehouse thefts include a September 2013 theft of $90 million in prescription drugs from a warehouse in Connecticut, a December 2012 theft of 10 million pounds of maple syrup from a Quebec storage facility, and a theft of $65,000 in chicken wings from storage warehouses in Georgia shortly before Superbowl 2013.

Warehouse thieves are sophisticated, and often have inside help from warehouse employees.

For warehouse, DC, and 3PL relationships in the US, Article 7 of the UCC provides strict rules governing warehouse liability for loss or damage to customer goods. UCC 7-204(a) states that a warehouse is liable for damage or loss to customer goods "caused by its failure to exercise care with regard to the goods that a reasonably careful person would exercise under similar circumstances." In other words, warehouses, DCs, and 3PLs will be held liable for any damage or loss caused by their own negligence.

This is a hard and fast rule that cannot be modified by agreement. Indeed, UCC 7-202(c) provides that warehouse contracts may not include any terms that "impair" a warehouse's "duty of care under Section 7-204." Moreover, UCC 1-102(c) states that "the obligations of good faith, diligence, reasonableness, and care prescribed by this act may not be disclaimed by agreement."

An illustrative case that enforces UCC 7-204(a) is *Butler Manufacturing Co. v. Americold Corporation*,[51] which involved a warehouse fire that destroyed a customer's business records. The warehouse contract limited the warehouse's liability to damage caused by its gross negligence or willful injury. The court held that this limit of liability clause was unenforceable since it violated the duty of care set forth in UCC 7-204, which cannot be amended by contract.

However, UCC Article 7 does allow warehouses, DCs, and 3PLs to limit the damages that customers may collect in the event of loss or damage to their property while in storage. UCC 7-204(b) states, "Damages may be limited by a term in the warehouse receipt or storage agreement limiting the amount of liability in case of loss or damage beyond which the warehouse is not liable." Therefore, damages limitations in warehouse contracts are common. Warehouse, DC, and 3PL agreements often limit the amount of recoverable liability per occurrence, per pallet, per unit of goods, or per pound. It is also common for warehouse agreements to disclaim consequential damages.

In addition, warehouses, DCs, and 3PLs often limit the time in which a customer can assert claims for loss or damage. Usually, warehouse, DC, and 3PL contracts require a customer to assert claims within a specified period of time (often 60 days), and set time limits for when a customer may file any

---

51  835 F.Supp. 1274, 22 U.C.C. Rep. Serv. 2d (Callaghan) 318 (D. Kan. 1993).

legal action stemming from loss or damages claims (often nine months or one year).

Non-US warehouse, DC, and 3PL relationships (not governed by the UCC) are not uniform as to how they approach liability or indemnification for loss, damage, theft, or mishandling, or as to whether and they enforce contractual limitations on damages. Therefore, it is important to have robust contact provisions that set forth the parties' rights and duties and that choose a law to govern the agreement that will duly enforce those rights and obligations.

### Warehouse-Related Insurance

To guard against damage for loss, damage, theft, or mishandling of goods, it is common for one or both parties to a warehouse SLA to obtain insurance to cover the goods entrusted to the warehouse, DC, or 3PL. Typically, a warehouse, DC, or 3PL's ordinary commercial policy will not cover damage to customer goods, so if insurance for customer goods is needed, it is usually procured independently.

There are a lot of high-quality insurance products on the market for warehoused goods. Procuring insurance often requires due diligence on the warehouse, DC, or 3PL to ensure its reputability and integrity.

### Choice of Law and Dispute Resolution Provisions in Warehouse Contracts

Although the law in the United States is fairly uniform as it relates to warehousing, DC, and 3PL contracts, because international law is unpredictable, it is important to insert clear choice of law and dispute resolution provisions in warehouse, DC, and 3PL contracts with non-US vendors. A sample provision that chooses New York law and arbitration before the London Court of International Arbitration is below.

#### 3PL Contract Choice of Law and Forum Selection Clause

This Contract and the legal relationship between 3PL and Customer shall be governed by a construed in accordance with the substantive laws of New York State, including the version of Article 7 of the Uniform Commercial Code then in force, notwithstanding any conflicts of laws rules. Any lawsuit or other action involving any dispute, claim, or controversy relating in any way to this Contract or to Customer's Goods shall be brought as an arbitration before the London Court of International Arbitration as the exclusive forum for such disputes.

(See also Chapter 20: Dispute Resolution Clauses in Non-US Supply Chain Contracts.)

### *Avoiding Inadvertent Liability*

One final legal topic that bears mention in warehouse, DC, and 3PL contracts is avoiding inadvertent liability—either the inadvertent liability of the warehouse for acts of the customer or the inadvertent liability of a customer for acts of the warehouse.

From the warehouse, DC, or 3PL's perspective, the biggest risk of inadvertent liability is for product liability claims arising from goods entrusted to the warehouse. The rule in most states in the United States is that a company that is merely a "passive conduit" for getting goods to market will not be liable for product liability claims in connection with those goods. If a company has "control" over the manufacturing or distribution process or "substantial ability" to control the manufacturing or distribution process, however, the company does bear risk for liability for product liability claims. Warehouses, DCs, and 3PLs should be vigilant, therefore, in defining their relationships with their customers' products.

Likewise, customers can inadvertently become liable for employment claims asserted by the warehouse, DC, or 3PL's employees. To avoid this, customers should always deal at arms-length with warehouses, DCs, and 3PLs. Excessive entwinement with the warehouse, DC, or 3PL's employees can risk liability. If this is a concern, the warehouse, DC, or 3PL's independent contractor status should be expressly stated in the SLA, and the warehouse, DC, or 3PL should be made to indemnify the customer against any employment claims brought against the customer by the warehouse, DC, or 3PL's employees.

———

## Lessons Learned

When working with warehouses, DCs, and 3PLs, companies should:

- Understand the many services that modern warehouses, DCs, and 3PLs offer
- Integrate IT with warehouses, DCs, and 3PLs, but only to the extent necessary for the warehouse, DC, or 3PL to do its job
- Carefully track, monitor, and report all inventory being stored
- Understand that in the US, warehouses, DCs, and 3PLs cannot disclaim liability for their own negligence, but they can limit damages and shorten claims periods
- Be clear about who has title to any goods being entrusted to a warehouse, DC, or 3PL
- Be aware of increasing regulation of warehouse, DC, and 3PL functions, and take whatever steps are necessary to ensure compliance
- Take steps to prevent warehouse theft
- Purchase insurance for warehouse-related losses

# CHAPTER 10

# LOGISTICS AND TRANSPORTATION PARTNERS

## Overview

Logistics can be loosely thought of as the process of getting products to the right place at the right time. Logistics providers can include combinations of warehousing operations, transportation for-hire services, private fleet operators, airlines, steamship lines, freight forwarders, and delivery agents. Logistics can also mean 3PLs (third-party logistics providers), which are outsourced services that perform a variety of logistics-related tasks. (See Chapter 9: Warehousing and Logistics.) There is clearly some crossover in the services provided between logistics, warehousing, and distribution vendors.

Logistics and transportation carriers are regulated by federal laws governing for-hire services, such as driver hours and safety. But since the 1980s, the rates that logistics partners charge have not been governed by federal law. Today's shipping customers sign private contracts for rates and services with the carriers serving them.

Freight forwarders do not own transportation assets such as cargo ships or aircraft themselves. They simply buy space from transportation companies and resell it at a mark-up. This situation provides an opportunity for mutually beneficial contracts between shipping customers and logistics providers. For example, a freight forwarder may purchase 20 container positions for passage from Shenzhen, China, to Oakland, California, then resell the container space to its own shipping customers. By buying the container space in bulk and selling portions of the space at a premium, the forwarder makes a profit.

These profit margins allow freight forwarders to negotiate prices with shipping customers, provide services, and prepare the documents required for international cargo shipments.

## SLAs (Service Level Agreements)

SLAs between customers and transportation providers commonly include percentage-on-time arrival clauses. For example, logistics providers or transportation carriers may promise to deliver a particular customer's shipments 98 percent on time to an agreed schedule. This means that the shipping customer's freight will get priority in consolidated shipments and the earliest possible dispatch. If a logistics provider is also hired to provide pick-pack-and-ship services, it will schedule these processes to meet the SLA requirements. These agreements are common in supply chains between transportation and logistics partners. SLAs often include a penalty if the SLA is not met as promised. Penalties are typically rate reductions or credits applied to invoices for failure to perform.

## Transportation Management Systems (TMS)

Transportation providers do more than just transport goods. In most cases, logistics and transportation companies also provide "freight routing" services (i.e., choosing which carrier to use for a specific route) based on cost and expediency of service. For example, a transportation company may choose more economical two-day service via truck rather than overnight shipment by air, if there is not an imminent due date for the cargo. Transportation providers commonly use transportation management systems (TMS) software to develop load-builder plans, route optimization, and freight rate audits. TMS can be integrated across carrier systems and shipping customer systems to electronically communicate the status of shipments in transit and track hand-offs between carriers, such as from an airline to a delivery driver. For shipping customers that are more sophisticated and use more software to run their operations, the information that flows to transportation partners will be more automated. From a legal perspective, transactions between transportation partners create evidence records that can be examined if a dispute arises.

### Reverse Logistics

Reverse logistics is the process of bringing goods back to the supplier for repair or disposal. For example, let's say your cell phone is under warranty and it breaks. Your carrier replaces it, and your old phone is shipped to a repair hub for refurbishment. This reverse transportation routing is a logistics service that is generally provided economically to shipping customers. Transportation providers will generally collect products that are planned for a reverse logistics route over a period of time, say a week or a month, and will return them in bulk to take advantage of bulk freight rates. Reverse logistics services may include shipment back to the buyer or customer, as well as further processing once the goods arrive at a repair facility.

Recycled goods also go through a reverse logistics process. If a shipping customer recycles cardboard, the cardboard's journey may go all the way to China, where the cardboard is processed and turned into other products. For electronics, recycled goods may go to special facilities where valuable minerals are stripped out before housings and other parts are destroyed or recycled. Europe is particularly keen on recycling things like TV sets and may require that manufacturers take used products back once they have reached end-of-life. Planning for any company's reverse-logistics needs years in advance can be complicated and uncertain at best. A TV, for example, can last as long as 15-20 years, and the future of reverse logistics processes are uncertain that far out. Therefore, it is best to anticipate reverse logistics issues, but be flexible in planning.

### 3PLs (Third-Party Logistics Providers)

In our chapter on warehousing (Chapter 9), we discuss the role 3PLs play in warehousing and distribution. But 3PLs often provide transportation management services as well, including transportation carrier selection and negotiating on behalf of shipping customers. 3PLs sometimes also provide warehousing, pick-pack-ship services, light assembly, and other processes specific to a particular shipper.

The growth in the 3PL industry has been remarkable in the past 20 years, primarily because shipping customers want to outsource logistics services so they can focus on their core businesses. 3PLs can scale and offer software solutions and a variety of services to shipping customers that do not wish to perform these functions on their own.

### Field Service Hubs

Companies that repair goods in the field typically require storage for parts in many locations around the world. For example, if an aircraft has a mechanical failure, repair or replacement parts need to be located quickly and installed on the aircraft, wherever it is in the world, to get the aircraft back in service. If spare parts are not available locally, they have to be brought in from other locations.

As a result of their worldwide repair needs, airlines and other equipment companies keep spare parts at field service hubs. It is common to outsource spare-parts storage services to logistics providers that can ship parts immediately when needed. In addition, many field service hubs offer inventory management and restocking services when repair parts get low. Field service hubs also work under SLAs that are typically strictly enforced.

## Legal Overview

There are many legal considerations involved in the physical process of moving products along the supply chain. When disputes arise during this process, it is generally because products have been damaged, lost, or delayed. These disputes can occur between supply chain partners, and they can occur between shipping customers and logistics providers such as 3PLs.

Between supply chain partners, allocation of transportation risk is accomplished through the supply chain agreement. An arcane vocabulary of shipping and delivery terms has developed to allocate transportation risks and responsibilities between supply chain partners in their contracts. Between shipping customers and transportation partners, on the other hand, there is a vast web of laws and international treaties that determine transportation carrier liability.

### Transportation Rights and Duties between Supply Chain Partners

Most supply chain agreements expressly state which party bears the responsibility for delivering goods to the buyer and allocate the risk of loss, damage, or delay to goods during transport. This is good practice.

In US supply chain relationships, if the parties do not allocate responsibility for delivery and risk of loss in their contract, the UCC supplies default rules. Under the UCC, if a supply chain contract does not specify a place for delivery, the buyer is responsible for transporting the goods from the supplier, and bears the risk of loss during delivery.[52] If a supply chain contract requires or authorizes a supplier to ship goods by carrier but does not specify the destination, the risk of loss passes to the buyer when the supplier delivers the goods to the carrier.[53] If a supply chain contract requires the supplier to deliver goods to a particular destination, the risk of loss passes to the buyer when the goods are delivered.[54] Unless the supply chain contract specifies otherwise, neither party is obliged to purchase insurance.

For supply chain relationships with international partners, the default rules governing logistics and transportation are typically supplied by the CISG (the Convention on the International Sale of Goods). (For a more extensive discussion about the CISG, see Chapter 7: International Procurement.) Under the CISG, if a supply chain contract is silent as to which party is responsible for delivery, the supplier must place the goods at the buyer's disposal at the location where the goods were manufactured or, if no such place exists, at the supplier's place of business.[55] If a supply chain contract requires the supplier to deliver goods to a carrier but does not require delivery to a particular location, the supplier must deliver the goods to the carrier and is not responsible for their transport to their ultimate destination.[56] If the contract requires the supplier to deliver goods to a particular location, the risk of loss passes to the buyer when the goods are delivered at that destination.[57] As with the UCC, unless an international supply chain contract specifies otherwise, neither party is obliged to purchase insurance.

However, supply chain parties can change these default rules by contract. In fact, contract provisions specifying delivery instructions are so common that standard abbreviated delivery terms have become customary in supply chain contracts. The most common sources of delivery terms come from the

---

52  UCC § 2-308.
53  UCC § 2-509.
54  UCC § 2-509.
55  CISG Art. 31.
56  CISG Arts. 31(a), 67(1).
57  CISG Arts. 67(1), 68.

UCC for US supply chain contracts, and from the International Commercial Terms (Incoterms) for international supply chain contracts. Some industry and trade groups (such as the Revised American Foreign Trade Definitions) have also devised delivery terms that complement (and sometimes contradict) the terms used by the UCC and Incoterms. Moreover, in some instances, the UCC and Incoterms use same terms, but give them different meanings. Therefore, if you use abbreviated delivery terms in an agreement, it is important to specify which terms you are using.

The UCC uses the following delivery terms:

### UCC Delivery Terms and Their Meanings

**FOB** **"Free on Board" (place of shipment).** Supplier bears the cost and risk of transporting goods to the carrier at the place specified. Risk then passes to buyer, and buyer pays all further delivery costs.[58]

**FOB** **"Free on Board" (destination).** Supplier bears the cost and risk of transporting the goods to the destination and tendering delivery to buyer. Risk passes to buyer when buyer accepts the goods or after a reasonable amount of time to accept the goods.[59]

**FOB** **"Free on Board" (vessel or vehicle).** Supplier bears the cost and risk of transporting the goods to the vessel or vehicle identified and loading goods on board. Risk then passes to buyer, and buyer pays all further delivery costs.[60]

**FAS** **"Free Along Side" (port or vessel).** Supplier bears the cost and risk of transporting the goods to the vessel identified in the manner usual in that port, or on a dock designated by buyer. Supplier must also obtain and tender a receipt for the goods in exchange for a bill of lading.[61]

**CIF** **"Cost, Insurance, and Freight."** The price of goods includes the cost of insurance and freight to the named destination. Supplier's responsibilities include securing carriage and loading, and supplier must tender all documents necessary to perfect buyer's rights to the goods being transported.[62]

---

58  UCC § 2-319(1).
59  Ibid.
60  UCC § 2-319(1).
61  UCC § 2-319(2).
62  UCC § 2-320.

**C&F** **"Cost and Freight."** The price of goods includes the cost of freight to the named destination. Supplier's responsibilities include securing carriage and loading, and supplier must tender all documents necessary to perfect buyer's rights in the goods being transported.[63]

**Ex-Ship** **"From the carrying vessel."** Requires delivery once a ship has reached the named destination. Supplier must discharge all liens and furnish buyer with direction that puts the carrier under a duty to deliver the goods. Risk of loss passes to buyer when the goods are unloaded from the ship.[64]

**No Arrival No Sale.** Supplier must promptly ship goods but assumes no obligation that the goods will arrive unless supplier causes the non-arrival. If goods are lost or materially damaged, buyer may proceed as if there has been casualty, allowing avoidance of the contract.[65]

International Incoterms, by contrast, use the following terms and definitions:

**Incoterms 2010**

**EXW** **"Ex Works" (place of delivery).** Supplier must make goods available at supplier's place of business. Risk then passes to buyer, and buyer pays all delivery costs. Applies to any mode of transport.

**FCA** **"Free Carrier" (place of delivery).** Supplier bears the cost and risk of delivering goods to the carrier nominated by buyer at the location identified. If delivery occurs at supplier's place of business, supplier is responsible for loading onto the carrier. If delivery occurs elsewhere, buyer is responsible for loading. Applies to any mode of transport.

**CPT** **"Carriage Paid To" (destination).** Supplier bears the cost of delivering goods to the carrier and pays cost of carriage. Buyer pays all further delivery costs. Supplier has no obligation to purchase insurance. Applies to any mode of transport.

**CIP** **"Carriage and Insurance Paid" (place of destination).** Supplier bears the cost of delivering goods to the carrier and pays cost of carriage, and must buy insurance to that point. Buyer then

---

63    Ibid.
64    UCC § 2-322.
65    UCC § 2-324.

bears responsibility for insurance and delivery to the final destination. Applies to any mode of transport.

**DAT** **"Delivered at Terminal" (destination terminal).** Supplier bears the cost and risk of delivery to destination port, including insurance and unloading from the carrier. At destination port, the cost and risk passes to buyer. Applies to any mode of transport.

**DAP** **"Delivered at Place" (destination).** Supplier bears the cost and risk of delivery until goods are unloaded at destination. Buyer pays all duties. Applies to any mode of transport.

**DPP** **"Delivered Duty Paid" (destination).** Supplier bears the cost and risk of delivery to final destination. Buyer is responsible only for unloading. Applies to any mode of transportation.

**FAS** **"Free Alongside Ship" (port of shipment).** Supplier bears the cost and risk of delivery alongside vessel designated by buyer at port of shipment, and for ensuring that goods can be exported. Buyer bears the cost and risk for the remainder of the journey. Applies only to transport by water.

**FOB** **"Free on Board" (port of loading).** Supplier bears the cost and risk of delivering goods to the port of shipment and loading them on board vessel designated by the buyer. Responsibility for costs and risks then passes to buyer. Applies only to transport by water.

**CFR** **"Cost and Freight" (port of destination).** Supplier bears the cost and risk of delivering goods to port of destination, but risk of loss transfers to buyer once goods are loaded onto the vessel. Supplier is not required to purchase insurance. Applies only to transport by water.

**CIF** **"Cost, Insurance, and Freight" (to port of destination).** Supplier bears the cost and risk of delivering goods to port of destination, but risk of loss transfers to buyer once goods are loaded onto the vessel. Supplier must purchase insurance until goods reach port of destination. Applies only to transport by water.

Note that the UCC and Incoterms have three terms in common—CIF, FAS, and FOB—but define them differently. For example, "FOB" under the UCC dictates that risk of loss passes to the buyer at the named location, whereas under the Incoterms, "FOB" dictates that risk of loss passes to the buyer at the port of shipment.

If the source of delivery terms is not specified in the contract, a court will have to decide which definitions apply. In *St. Paul Guardian Ins. Co. v. Neuromed Medical System & Support*,[66] for instance, the parties disputed the meaning of a "CIF" term in the underlying contract. The court held that because the contract specified that the CISG was the governing law, and the CISG incorporates the Incoterms, the Incoterms' definition of "CIF" controlled.

### Rights and Duties between Transportation Providers and Shipping Customers

Transportation providers are highly regulated, and the law generally dictates exactly when they can be held liable for lost, damaged, or delayed cargo. Most transportation providers know exactly how to limit their liability to the extent the law allows, and do so as a matter of course. Transportation providers' standard contract terms are normally not negotiable, and courts routinely enforce those terms. Therefore, our discussion on the liability of transportation providers will talk less about minimizing or avoiding disputes, and instead will discuss what rights companies have when working with them. Be aware that the regulations described in this section apply only to "public" or "common" carriers. Privately chartered transportation providers' liability is governed by contract.

### Air Carrier Liability

The 1978 US Airline Deregulation Act (ADA) limits the legal claims that shipping customers may bring against public air carriers, such as American Airlines Cargo, United Cargo, FedEx, UPS, and DHL. Congress enacted the ADA to end government regulation of commercial air services and to lower air-freight prices by exposing the industry to free market forces.

The ADA has been held to preempt—and prohibit—nearly all state law claims against public air carriers, including common law and tort actions. Contract claims, however, are the exception, and public air carriers may be

---

66   2002 U.S. Dist. LEXIS 5096 (S.D.N.Y. Mar. 26, 2002).

held liable to shipping customers for breach of contract. In *American Airlines v. Wolens*,[67] for example, the US Supreme Court held that breach of contract claims are not preempted by the ADA because contract claims are obligations that air carriers voluntarily assume.

Contract disputes between shipping customers and public air carriers are governed by federal common law, rather than the law of any particular state. Under federal common law, air carriers cannot disclaim liability entirely, but they can limit their liability to the value of the cargo being shipped. To be protected by these limits, air carriers must give shipping customers reasonable notice of the liability limits and an opportunity to pay a higher rate if a customer wants additional coverage. The way most air carriers comply with these rules is by assigning shipments a low presumed value and corresponding liability limit (often $100). Shipping customers can increase their liability coverage to the declared value of the cargo, but will be required to pay more to ship the goods.

Most air carriers impose a maximum value on the items they agree to ship, and disclaim liability above that amount. Courts enforce these limitations. *Trieber & Straub, Inc. v. United Parcel Service, Inc.*,[68] for instance, involved UPS's policy not to ship merchandise valued over $50,000. In *Trieber & Straub*, the plaintiff, a jewelry store, shipped a $105,000 diamond ring, even though the merchandise was valued over UPS's $50,000 limit. The jewelry store declared the ring's value at $50,000 and purchased the maximum $50,000 liability coverage. When UPS lost the ring, the jewelry store made a claim against UPS for the $50,000 coverage amount. UPS refused to pay the claim on the grounds that its service rules prohibited shipments valued over $50,000. The Seventh Circuit Court of Appeals enforced the UPS rule, and denied the jewelry store's claim, even though the jewelry store only sought to recover the amount of coverage it had purchased.

Internationally, public air carriers are governed by an international treaty regime that began with the 1929 Convention for the Unification of Certain Rules Relating to International Carriage by Air, also known as the "Warsaw Convention." The Warsaw Convention sought to create uniform rules for the international air transport of people and cargo. In 1999, the Montreal

---

67  513 U.S. 219 (1995).

68  474 F.3d 379 (7th Cir. 2007).

Convention replaced the Warsaw Convention and modernized its rules. The Montreal Convention has over one hundred signatories and governs most international air shipments.

Under the Montreal Convention, public air carriers are presumed to be liable for lost, damaged, or delayed cargo. Public air carriers can avoid liability if they prove that the loss, damage, or delay was due to certain specifically enumerated reasons beyond the carrier's control, such as a defect in the cargo itself, a packaging defect caused by someone other than the carrier, war, or government action. Unless the parties agree to a greater liability amount, an international air carrier's liability is limited under the Montreal Convention to an artificial currency limit of 19 "special drawing rights" (SDRs) per kilogram of cargo. The International Monetary Fund publishes conversion rates between SDRs and real currencies on a daily basis. (Presently, SDRs are valued at 0.657 cents per US dollar. Thus, liability for the loss of a 10-kilogram package today would be approximately $125.)

As with air shipments in the United States, international air shipping customers and carriers can agree by contract to increase an air carrier's liability, generally in exchange for increased pricing. These agreements are documented through "air-way bills," which the Montreal Convention requires. The Montreal Convention also provides that, to be entitled to recovery, an aggrieved shipping customer must notify an air carrier of its claim in writing within 14 days after discovering the damage or non-delivery. Failure to make a timely complaint will bar recovery. The Montreal Convention also includes a two-year statute of limitations to initiate litigation.

### Water Carrier Liability

The liability scheme for water carriers is less uniform than the scheme that governs air carriers. Internationally, shipments by water are governed by a complex web of international treaties. The first such treaty is the International Convention for the Unification of Certain Rules Relating to Bills of Lading of 1924, known as the "Hague Rules."

The Hague Rules prevent water carriers from disclaiming all liability for lost, damaged, or delayed cargo, but limit liability to $500 per package, unless the parties agree to a higher amount by contract. The Hague Rules provide defenses for damages that are not the fault of the carrier, much like the air carrier rules do. A water carrier also has a defense if it conducted adequate "due diligence" to ensure the seaworthiness of a vessel. Approximately 50 countries today are signatories of the Hague Rules, including the United States, which implemented the Hague Rules into its domestic law through the Carriage of Goods by Sea Act (COGSA).[69]

After approximately 40 years of the Hague Rules, many states became interested in correcting provisions of that treaty that they felt were problematic. In 1968, the Brussels Protocol to the Hague Rules was signed by several countries, which became known as the "Hague-Visby Rules." The Hague-Visby Rules made minor changes to the Hague Rules, the most notable of which allowed carriers to hire independent contractors to discharge their due diligence obligations. The United States is not a signatory to the Hague-Visby Rules, but there are few conflicts between the Hague Rules and the Hague-Visby Rules.

After the Hague-Visby Rules were negotiated, many countries, particularly developing countries that feared exploitation by first-world water carriers, demanded more widespread changes to the international water shipping rules. This demand resulted in the 1978 United Nations Convention on the Carriage of Goods by Sea, called the "Hamburg Rules." The Hamburg Rules deviate significantly from the Hague and Hague-Visby Rules, including that the Hamburg Rules do not require shipping customers to show bills of lading or similar documents to prove liability against water carriers. The Hamburg Rules also abolished water carriers' due diligence defense. However, the 30 or so countries who have signed onto the Hamburg Rules do not include any of the major shipping nations, so the implementation of this treaty has not significantly affected international cargo delivery by water. The US is not a signatory to the Hamburg Rules.

The final treaty relating to international water shipments is the United Nations Convention on Contracts for the International Carriage of Goods Wholly or Partly by Sea, called the "Rotterdam Rules." The Rotterdam Rules were adopted in 2009, but are not yet in force since they have not been ratified by most of their signatories, including the United States. The Rotterdam Rules modernize the Hague/Hague-Visby Rules by extending the period when carriers are responsible for cargo to include the entire period in which

---

69  46 U.S.C. § 1300, *et seq.*

the carrier has possession of the cargo, rather than merely the time the cargo is on the carrier's vessel ("tackle-to-tackle"). The Rotterdam Rules also increased water carrier liability via a formula that is based on cargo weight, and extended the statute of limitations for claims against international water carriers to two years. If the Rotterdam Rules come into force, signatory countries will be required to renounce all previous treaties concerning international water carriers.

Water shipments that occur via common carrier within the United States between two or more states are governed by the Carmack Amendment,[70] which was enacted in 1936 to govern railroads and motor carriers and was expanded in 1978 to cover interstate water carriers. The Carmack Amendment preempts all state and common law claims against interstate water carriers, forbids interstate water carriers from totally disclaiming liability for damage caused by lost, damaged, or delayed shipment, but allows interstate water carriers to limit their liability to the declared value of cargo. Like the Hague and Hague-Visby Rules, the Carmack Amendment permits defenses for damage or loss that is not the carrier's fault. The Carmack Amendment has a nine-month notice period, in which a shipper must notify its carrier of claims, and a two-year statute of limitations.

Water shipments that occur strictly within the borders of one US state are governed by state law, and normal common law actions are available.

### Motor and Rail Carrier Liability
In the United States, interstate and international motor and rail cargo transportation is also governed by the Carmack Amendment. If cargo is lost, damaged, or delayed, the Carmack Amendment presumes liability on the part of motor and rail carriers. It allows carriers to limit their liability to the declared value of the cargo, so long as they maintain tariffs within guidelines promulgated by the Interstate Commerce Commission (ICC), give shipping customers a reasonable opportunity to choose between two or more levels of liability, and issue bills of lading.

———

70   49 U.S.C. § 14706.

## Lessons Learned

When determining responsibility for transportation and logistics, and while working with transportation and logistics partners, supply chain partners should:

- Be aware that there are many different ways to structure logistics and transportation services and investigate all possible options
- Understand that transportation providers' liability is often limited by statute or international treaty
- Allocate the risk of loss, damages, and delay of goods with supply chain partners
- Be aware that there are standard abbreviations that commercial parties use to establish their contractual delivery and insurance obligations
- Be aware that there are several different sets of delivery term abbreviations, and specify which one you intend to use

# CHAPTER 11

# IMPORTING AND EXPORTING

## Overview

Most companies today have at least some international supply chain relationships that require the import and export of goods across borders. Companies and nations have always traded with one another. The Silk Road in China began in approximately 200 BC and is considered the first global supply chain, trading goods across Asia and Europe. In the last 50 years, the movement of products around the world has become more commonplace, despite arcane regulations that govern importing and exporting in nearly every country.

The processes and regulations regarding importing and exporting, or "trade compliance" as they are also called, are constantly changing. For example, companies may not currently export to US-embargoed countries such as North Korea or Syria or Cuba. As political conditions change and sanctions are lifted on Cuba, however, export regulations from the United States to Cuba will also change. Import and export regulations are constantly changing around the world and reflect current economic and political values.

### *The Politics of Importing*

Most countries of the world apply restrictions, quotas, and import duties to protect domestic industries from competing foreign goods. The purpose of duties and import restrictions is to make imports more expensive and the import process more difficult. But import restrictions are not always popular domestically.

If you recall, the Boston Tea Party was a result of high tariffs on imported tea and other products, for which the colonists had no say. These taxes were intended to promote Britain's political agenda and increase revenues extracted from the colonies. Few products were made in the colonies at that time, so the colonies had no choice but to import goods from overseas and pay the high tariff duties.

Once America won its independence, tariffs collected on imports were the major source of funds for the nation's coffers. In fact, prior to ratification of the 16th Amendment in February 1913 (which authorized a federal income tax), the federal government relied entirely on import tariffs for revenue. Today, however, import duties represent a very small percentage of US tax revenue and do little to protect domestic industry.

Over time, global trade has increased significantly. The World Customs Organization (WCO), established in 1952, was formed to encourage and facilitate trade among nations. But even with the World Trade Organization (WTO) and the WCO and other international pro-trade bodies, importing remains a difficult and complicated process.

### *Importing Into the United States*
To import products into the United States, an importer needs to (1) classify the goods being imported using the Harmonized Tariff Schedule of the United States (HTSUS), (2) determine the value of the goods being imported, and (3) identify the country where the goods were made or produced, known as the "Country of Origin." These three pieces of information and associated documentation will allow an importer to file a customs entry document (USA CF 7501) to import goods into the United States.

If goods are regulated by an additional US government agency, such as the FDA or the FAA, there may be additional import requirements. For example, if a company imports medical devices, the import process may require FDA certificates. If a company imports wine or spirits, shipments may require certificates from the Bureau of Alcohol, Tobacco, and Firearms (ATF).

Filing a US Customs entry form is very much like filing a tax return with supporting documents and receipts. An entry summary document (CF 7501), together with commercial invoices, shipment packing lists, any required certificates, lead test results, and other documents, must be submitted to the CBP (US Customs and Border Protection), along with the payment of duties, taxes, and fees. In addition, commercial importers must file entry information electronically via the US Customs Automated Commercial Environment (ACE) system. Commercial importers must now electronically submit shipment and transaction information before their shipments leave the foreign port of embarkation (known as "10+2 Importer Security"). This is a new requirement since September 11, 2001.

### Anti-dumping and Countervailing Duties

When a US domestic industry believes it is being harmed by imports that are sold below fair market value, an industry association may file an anti-dumping and countervailing duty petition with the United States International Trade Commission (USITC). These lawsuits are complicated and often require teams of accountants, lawyers, and experts to prove that the goods have been undervalued.

If successful, countervailing duties are applied to the imports in question and can make the imported product prohibitively expensive. For global companies that import and export, this complicates supply chain operations, and it may be years before the harmed industries see any countervailing duty relief payments.

### Licensed US Customs Brokers

Most companies use licensed US Customs brokers to prepare entry documents, clear customs on their behalf, and arrange to have goods delivered. Licensed US Customs brokers must pass a rigorous test about the laws and practices that govern imports, as well as a background investigation. Brokers are then licensed by CPB to perform importing functions on behalf of customers. Generally, brokers help with document preparation and provide regulatory guidance to importers. Licensed US Customs brokers can also assist importers to electronically file documents and physically examine goods.

### Import and Export Documents

There are many documents associated with international shipments including:

- Truck, rail, sea, and air freight bills
- Commercial invoices

- Packing lists
- Insurance certificates
- Tests and quality certificates
- Regulatory certificates, such as from the FDA and ATF
- Export declarations
- Import entry summaries (USA CF 7501)
- Others

For companies involved in legal disputes regarding exporting or importing, there will likely be many documents associated with each shipment at issue that are discoverable and relevant. Importers are required by law to keep import records for five years after the goods' date of entry. However, many importers retain import records for much longer, usually in accounts payable files. Import records show transaction values, quantities, part numbers, inspection certificates, insurance values, and other items that may be helpful to an import/export case.

### Foreign-Trade Zones (FTZs) and Temporary Imports

Once a shipment has physically cleared customs, it can be delivered to the end user, or to an interim party such as a Foreign-Trade Zone (FTZ), or a repair facility for "temporary imports." FTZs are special-purpose zones where goods stay temporarily, usually for further assembly or manufacture. No tariffs are imposed on products in the FTZ until the goods are imported to their final destination.

Temporary imports are often used for items coming back to the United States for repair or refurbishment, which can be re-exported within one year, without tariffs. Temporary imports and FTZs require additional filings, documents, and control over the goods while they are in the United States.

The United States operates a number of FTZs within its territory. US FTZs are considered to be "outside" the commerce of the United States, even though they physically operate in the United States. The United States is not alone in creating FTZs. Many other countries also allow FTZs in their territories, which internationally are usually called "special economic zones." For example, *maquiladoras* in Mexico are Mexican factories that import raw materials at zero or reduced tariffs and assemble finished products for export. These are Mexican special economic zones.

In the United States, FTZs are usually in or adjacent to US ports of entry on public land. US law also allows foreign trade "subzones," which operate on private property within 60 miles of US ports of entry, and which also allows tariff-free treatment of goods. Today, there are over 230 FTZ sites and almost four hundred subzones in the United States.

FTZs and subzones present special benefits in supply chains because they provide inverted tariff benefits to trading partners. Inverted tariff benefits arise when the tariffs imposed on a product's imported components are higher than the tariff on the fully assembled product. By manufacturing or assembling components into finished products in FTZs or subzones, companies avoid component tariff rates and instead pay finished-product tariff rates, which may be lower.

Setting up operations in FTZs and subzones is complex and cumbersome, but many companies reap substantial tariff benefits by doing it. The most famous example occurred in the 1960s when Volkswagen imported all of the parts required to build VW Beetles into an FTZ. Inside the FTZ, Volkswagen assembled the cars and then imported fully assembled cars into the United States, thus benefitting from a lower tariff rate.

FTZs are also sometimes used when US companies want to delay importing. For example, US companies import liquor to FTZs year-round to be bottled, but only import the bottles into the United States, as needed or just before peak selling seasons, such as the holidays. Tanks of liquor can be brought in months before they are needed, and tariff payments are postponed until the liquor is bottled and physically shipped out of the FTZ.

### Counterfeit Goods

In November 2011, the US Senate Armed Services Committee held hearings on counterfeit parts in US military supply chains, including electronic parts used to manufacture weapons and other Department of Defense equipment. Investigators found that counterfeit or suspect electronic parts had been installed or delivered to the military for several weapons systems and military aircraft, such as the Air Force's C-17, the Marine Corps' CH-46 helicopter, and the Army's Theatre High-Altitude Area Defense (THAAD) missile system.

Counterfeiting is not limited to electronics or goods sold to the government. Automotive parts, industrial goods, purses and accessories, watches, consumer products, and even aircraft parts, can also be counterfeited. Counterfeiters are getting better and better at their craft, to the point that counterfeits may now be indistinguishable from the real thing. Indeed, it can be so difficult to tell counterfeit from legitimate parts that professional industrial buyers are often fooled. Even the price of counterfeits may be equivalent or close to the price of legitimate parts, thus avoiding buyer suspicion.

The only way to control counterfeiting is for companies to maintain control over their supply chains. This means verifying and monitoring all parts suppliers, distributors, subcontractors, and manufacturers. Even with careful monitoring, however, importers can be fooled by counterfeit parts. As a result, importers may be fined and penalized by US Customs, which ensures that counterfeit goods are not imported into the United States. Penalties range from small fines to hundreds of thousands of dollars in fines, depending on the importer's lack of control over its imports, or level of negligence or intent in importing counterfeit goods.

### Failure Alert: Penalties and Fines from Supplier Counterfeiting

A Silicon Valley buyer of imported optical memory parts from China conducted what the buyer thought was a thorough evaluation of its Chinese suppliers. For every new supplier in China, the US buyer's technical staff validated sample parts, did visual and electronic inspections, and checked references. The buyer stated on every purchase order that the buyer would only accept legitimate and genuine parts—no counterfeits.

When US Customs inspectors found counterfeit products in a $50,000 shipment of optical memory products from the company's supplier in China, they confiscated the shipment. The company and buyer, totally unaware of the counterfeits, were fined $240,000, although assistance from a trade compliance attorney, the fine was reduced. Ultimately, the goods were not allowed to leave US Customs' custody, and instead were destroyed. The money the buyer spent to purchase the goods from the Chinese supplier had to be written off as a loss.

To avoid this from happening in the future, the Silicon Valley company now tightly controls its global supply chain every step of the way by making regular trips to its suppliers in China, auditing them thoroughly, and reducing its number of suppliers to a manageable few.

### Exporting from the United States

According to studies cited by the US Department of Commerce and the US Trade Representative,[71] companies that export products outside of the United States are more economically stable and grow at a faster rate than those that do not export. Although there are many business benefits to exporting, the process can be complicated, especially for technology or defense-related products.

The two US agencies that regulate exports from the United States are the Department of Defense and the Department of Commerce. The Department of Defense regulates the export of products related to the military or that have military uses, including products that could have a dual commercial and military use. To ship these types of goods out of the United States, an exporter must comply with the International Traffic in Arms (ITAR) regulations and apply for Department of Defense export licenses.

The Department of Commerce regulates exports of non-military commercial products. For commercial products, exporters must first classify the products to determine whether a special export license is needed, and then must conduct "restricted parties screening." For the first step—classification and licensing—goods are assigned a classification number from a list the Department of Commerce maintains called the "Commerce Control List." The Commerce Control List includes 10 product categories that the Department of Commerce pays special attention to, including nuclear materials, chemicals and toxins, sensors and lasers, telecommunication equipment, navigation and avionics, marine equipment, and others.

Certain classification/destination combinations require special licenses prior to shipment. High-tech hardware and software, in particular, may require special export licenses related to encrypted software and communications frequencies. Many exported goods are classified under the designation "EAR99 – No License Required."

The second step—restricted parties screening—requires exporters to check the recipient of the goods against the Department of Commerce's "Restricted Parties Screening Lists." The US government uses software to perform restricted parties screening automatically. If a recipient of exported goods is identified as a restricted party, the exporter must stop the shipment, and may be required to report the attempted transaction to the Department of Commerce. After

---

71   *See, e.g.,* Institute for International Economics, Working Paper 05-10, "Importers, Exporters, and Multinationals: A Portrait of Firms in the US that Trade Goods," September 2005.

September 11, 2001, the Department of Commerce's list of restricted parties ballooned to over a million names.

The Department of Commerce recommends that restricted parties screening be executed during a number of stages during the export process, including:

- When a customer record is created in a company's business software system
- Before technical discussions with potential customers
- At the time an order is accepted
- Before software downloads to customers
- For all visitors to company locations
- Annually for all employees of the company
- For employment candidates

In addition, the US government regards some technical discussions, brochures, and white papers that may implicate national security interests, to be "deemed exports," particularly if discussions occur with foreign nationals, foreign universities, or foreign governments. Deemed exports may require special licenses from the Department of Commerce before the discussions take place. Software shipments and downloads, especially if the software is encrypted, are also subject to the classification and restricted parties screening processes.

### *The Role of Trade Compliance*

Many companies treat trade compliance as an administrative task and assign it to first-line supervisors, rather than providing higher-level oversight or responsibility. Treating trade compliance as a low-level function may, however, be unwise, since there are significant financial and legal consequences for companies that do not follow proper trade compliance and reporting procedures. We know of one company, a bicycle seller, who lost millions of dollars in holiday sales, when a large shipment of Chinese-made bicycles was held up at Customs at a California port. The main issue was incorrect paperwork, which could have been avoided with better corporate oversight. In other cases, where Export Administration Regulations are violated, criminal penalties can reach 20 years imprisonment and $1 million per violation. Administrative monetary penalties can reach $250,000 per violation, or twice the value of the transaction, whichever is greater.

Now, it is more common for larger companies to place trade compliance together with their internal audit, SOX, risk, and tax departments, increasing the visibility and stature of trade compliance. New titles for this grouping include the "Office of Compliance" or "Regulatory Compliance Office."

## Legal Overview

Import and export law is a creature of international trade law and policy. Originally called *lex mercatoria*, or the "law of merchants," the notion that trade between nations should generally be free and unrestricted has been a prominent economic philosophy in western countries since Adam Smith's *Wealth of Nations* in 1776. Although there have been historical aberrations, such as the United States' trade policy during the Great Depression, the trend in the United States, and increasingly worldwide, has been toward imposing fewer burdens on free trade.

Import/export law between countries is fragmented and idiosyncratic. Since import/export law has been the result of an evolutionary process between nations over time, it would be impossible to cover all aspects of international import/export law in this chapter. Here, we provide an overview of the origin and principles of international trade law and the import/export rules that govern international trade in supply chain relationships.

### The General Agreement on Tariffs and Trade (GATT)

The grandfather of import/export treaties is the General Agreement on Tariffs and Trade (GATT), which was originally signed in 1947 in Geneva by the 23 world nations that were then most involved in global trade, including the United States. China was an original GATT member in 1947, but renounced the treaty after the Communist Party took over China in 1949. In 1986, China announced its desire to rejoin the GATT community, and was readmitted in 2002.

GATT's primary purpose was to avert further war after World War II ended. But its next main purpose was to remove barriers to trade between countries by reducing tariffs on foreign goods. Since 1947, GATT has gone through multiple rounds of negotiations, amendments, and further interpretations, most of which have lowered import/export tariffs. GATT provides the framework for the import/export rules that nearly all companies operating in the world follow today. These rules apply to supply chain purchases and govern the international trade aspects of supply chain relationships.

The most recently completed round of GATT negotiations, referred to as the "Uruguay Round," involved 123 countries. The Uruguay Round began in 1986 and ultimately resulted in the formation of the WTO in 1995, pursuant to an international treaty referred to as the "Marrakesh Agreement." The sometimes-maligned WTO now has 160 member countries, and its goals include promoting free trade, providing a mechanism for dispute resolution between countries, and facilitating future trade negotiations. The Uruguay Round did not necessarily advance the cause of uniformity in international import/export law, however. Due to the sheer number of participating nations, Uruguay Round negotiations became fragmented, resulting in "plurilateral" agreements between some but not all GATT/WTO countries, which is one reason why import/export law remains so complex today.

Another factor that contributes to the complexity of import/export law is that international trade treaties do not treat all industries uniformly. Under the pre-Uruguay GATT negotiations, agriculture was almost entirely excluded from tariff negotiations, and protectionism in agriculture was widespread. During the Uruguay negotiations, agricultural exporting countries (such as Australia, Brazil, and Canada) objected to protectionism in agriculture (because they wanted to export more), which resulted in the 1995 Agreement on Agriculture. The Agreement on Agriculture lessened some of the market-distorting tariffs on agricultural products, though tariffs continue to this day, albeit at reduced levels.

GATT continues to allow pockets of significant protectionism by permitting heightened tariffs on imports that "cause or threaten serious injury to domestic producers." This exception has been invoked by different GATT members at various points in time, including by the United States to protect its domestic steel industry. GATT also allows member nations to limit exports if doing so is in their national interest. For example, in the 1980s, Japan restricted its exports of cars.

### *Harmonized Laws Governing Imports and Exports*

In connection with the emerging GATT framework, in 1948, several of the original GATT countries adopted the Convention establishing the Customs Cooperation Council, which was later renamed the WCO (World Customs Organization). The WCO governs the customs aspects of nearly all international import/export trade. The WCO's mission is to harmonize international customs and facilitate international trade. To that end, since 1983, the WCO has maintained the Harmonized System (HS) of goods, which classifies all goods that are traded between nations, for the purpose of creating a more uniform customs system. The HS classifies goods based on their composition and/or use, and assigns each product a 10-digit classification code number. Each country uses the same system for classifying goods, but sets their own tariff rate for each classification category.

To date, the HS has over 17,000 classification codes that are organized in 99 chapters. Because of this complexity, it can be very difficult for new or even established importers and exporters to determine how products should be classified. The HS has been criticized for being arcane, difficult to use, and counterintuitive, and therefore likely to generate needless disputes. As an example, the same food product may be classified under different HS categories, depending on if it is fresh, frozen, or cooked. The United States has adopted the HS as the HTSUS (Harmonized Tariff Schedule of the United States). More than two hundred countries that also use the HS have adopted it into their domestic laws as well.

Improper classification of goods that are imported and exported within supply chains is a common occurrence. Errors in HS classification can cause products to be confiscated at international borders, and can subject importing companies to fines and penalties. Seemingly minor variations in classification can result in large differences in the tariffs that apply to imported goods. New products are particularly susceptible to being misclassified, especially if they resemble more than one already-classified product, which is almost always the case. In addition, classification categories sometimes change, multiplying the potential for confusion.

In the United States, disputes about HS classifications are adjudicated by the United States Court of International Trade (formerly known as the US Customs Court). Appeals from the Court of International Trade are heard by the US Court of Appeals for the Federal Circuit. Courts adjudicating HS disputes are called upon to make excruciatingly fine distinctions to classify products, and their decisions affect supply chain operations.

For instance, in the appellate decision of *Value Vinyls, Inc. v. United States*,[72] the lower court originally held, in favor of an importer, that a man-made textile component was "a product with textile components in which man-made fibers predominate by weight over any other single textile fiber." The US government appealed to the Federal Circuit, arguing that this "predominate by weight" HS category was inappropriate because the product was made entirely of man-made fiber, and therefore should have been classified as "textile-other." Under the importer's classification, the tariff was 4.2 percent. Under the government's classification, the tariff would have been 5.3 percent.

In support of its position, the government cited a previous Court of International Trade case that interpreted the word "predominate" to require that a product have two or more components. The Federal Circuit disagreed, however, reasoning that the previous decision was limited to the facts of that case, and upheld the lower court's ruling in favor of the importer. While the difference between a 4.2 percent tariff and a 5.3 percent tariff may seem small, aggregated all of the products the importer purchased, the impact was millions of dollars.

The lesson from this case is that customs classifications rest on fine distinctions that often require special expertise to perform correctly. Most companies use experienced advisors for their import and export operations to avoid the serious consequences that are imposed if customs classifications are wrong. In the event of an incorrect customs classification, the government will require the prompt payment of unpaid tariffs. US law also provides for additional penalties if an incorrect classification was negligent, grossly negligent, or fraudulent.[73] Knowingly misclassifying a customs shipment is a crime under US law, punishable by fines and prison sentences.

### NAFTA and Supply Chain Relationships

A relatively recent import/export legal innovation in the United States has been the adoption of the North American Free Trade Agreement (NAFTA)

---

72   568 F.3d 1374 (Fed. Cir. 2009).

73   19 U.S.C. 592.

between the United States, Mexico, and Canada. The product of extensive negotiations, NAFTA was formally signed into law in 1993 by all three signatory nations. Among other effects, NAFTA eliminated almost all tariffs between the member countries, with some exceptions for agricultural goods.

Under NAFTA, Mexican *maquiladoras* (a type of special economic zone) have become wildly popular supply chain options for assembling component parts into finished products. Labor costs are often cheaper in Mexico than in the United States and other countries, and since most *maquiladoras* are near the United States-Mexico border, they are logistically convenient and accessible. As with FTZs in the United States, Mexican *maquiladoras* can import raw materials and sub-components tariff-free, and pay tariffs only when finished products are exported. This often saves money in supply chain operations.

NAFTA is not the only common customs market in the world. The European Economic Community (EEC) is a common customs market among European states that was created in 1957. Since its creation, the EEC has been renamed the European Union (EU), and it now has 28 member states. There are no tariffs on trade between EU members, and they have a common tariff system for trading with the outside world. Other common customs markets include the 10-member Association of Southeast Asian Nations (ASEAN), the Southern African Customs Union (SACU) between five countries in southern Africa, and the Southern Common Market (MERCOSUR), which includes a number of countries in South America. The United States is currently negotiating possible terms of a Trans-Pacific Partnership with a number of Pacific Rim countries.

———

## Lessons Learned

Supply chain partners that import or export goods across international borders should:

- Understand that import/export law is often influenced by politics
- Consider using licensed customs brokers to assist with importing and exporting

- Use care when selecting customs classifications, as the HS classification system is cumbersome and complex, and errors can result in penalties
- Consider using FTZs for final assembly of goods to avoid paying high component-part tariffs
- Comply with Export Administration Regulations for classification, licensing, and restricted parties screening before exporting from the United States
- Be aware of the import and export benefits provided by NAFTA and other common market treaties

# CHAPTER 12

# WARRANTIES

## Overview

Warranties are legally binding promises that manufacturers make about their products—sometimes to supply chain partners, and sometimes to end users. Warranties take many forms. In most cases, warranties guarantee a product's functions, features, operation, material composition, and/or perhaps its ability to successfully integrate with other components. Broader warranties may also guarantee the quality and speed of repair service provided by field service personnel. Warranties protect buyers and can be expensive for suppliers. Therefore, warranties are at the heart of many supply chain legal disputes.

As a business matter, warranties are interrelated with field service. Field service organizations perform repairs and service, whether or not warranty coverage exists.

Most companies now recognize that there are substantial margins to be made in field service. Even for companies that experience price pressure on their products, field service is still an area for major profitability and customer loyalty. Cisco Systems, a very large Silicon Valley networking hardware company, reports that up to 15 percent of its revenues are generated through field service consulting and repairs. Field service and sales of repaired, refurbished, and aftermarket parts are among the highest margin segments of industrial business.

In addition, generous warranty service may be what is required to stay competitive or ahead of the competition. A great warranty may be the deciding factor in a customer's decision to buy a product or to choose one supplier over another. Warranties may also contribute to company branding. Companies with the best warranties may be seen as better companies with superior products. For example, automobiles with the best warranties are often perceived as having the highest quality cars.

Therefore, the importance of warranties and field service should not be overlooked. To maintain long-term customer loyalty through the product life cycle, particular attention should be given to product warranties and executing field service during the warranty period. As soon as the warranty period is over, the profitable field service and repair cycle begins.

### *Warranties in the Sales Cycle*

The quality and extent of product warranties are often major considerations for customers when they buy new products and equipment. Customers (whether B2B buyers or end-product consumers) are likely to consider warranties as part of the product-pricing package and will weigh and consider the scope of warranties that are extended during the sales process. A supplier's sales staff may be reluctant to bring along field service personnel to a negotiation session with a buyer for fear of causing delay in finalizing a deal. But field service personnel can provide valuable perspective as to what can and cannot realistically be included in warranty coverage. To avoid litigation, it is important to clarify warranty terms and to have these terms reviewed by legal counsel and the company's service organization, before including them in a contract.

Performance warranties, which guarantee the way a product will perform, can be problematic and should be drafted carefully, particularly if a product is engineered to order or is newly developed. Engineers may be overly optimistic about the performance of their creations, and may inadvertently make promises that cannot be supported (at least not economically). It is important that reasonableness govern all warranty discussions and promises to customers.

As a general rule, warranties for expensive industrial products are usually customized and individually negotiated. Manufacturers typically have some standard terms and conditions that provide a starting point for specific customer warranties. The parties will then negotiate the particulars, such as repair response times and product integration responsibilities.

Warranties for consumer products are different. Consumer product companies typically provide "thin" warranties, such as 90-day and return-to-factory replacement or repair warranties. Minimal, thin warranties make it possible for sellers to sell enhanced or extended warranties, as well as service contracts to consumers. These premium extended warranties minimize customer down-time and can be extremely lucrative for manufacturers and retailers.

### *Warranting Repair Services*

Supply chain contracts sometimes include repair warranties. Repair warranties may require field repairs to be performed within a certain amount of time, such as within 24 hours. Repair warranties may also include different response levels, such as two-hour or four-hour response times for mission-critical equipment and 24-hour response times for less critical parts, etc. Short-repair-time warranties require service organizations to make repair parts available for immediate use, often in multiple locations. For example, spares for mission-critical aircraft repairs must be readily available on a worldwide basis to avoid "aircraft-on-ground" (AOG) situations. Skilled mechanics must also be immediately available to perform mission-critical repairs. However, less critical aircraft components, such as passenger seat lightbulbs, may wait for overnight or weekly maintenance repairs. Buyers and customers often demand carefully tailored multi-level warranties to ensure that service response times meet their needs and expectations. For big global operations such as airlines, this means having inventories of spare parts and field service personnel always available to respond in any worldwide location.

In addition, supply chain contracts may also be used to guarantee repair quality and repair success rates. Buyers and customers may demand that first-time repair success rates, known as "first-time fix" (FTF), be as high as 75-80 percent, and may carefully track performance to FTF standards. If an FTF rate is included in a supply chain contract, the supplier must employ experienced field service personnel for that customer because inexperienced repair people may not be able to perform repairs as promised. Other key performance indicators (KPIs) often required by customers with respect to repair warranty coverage include:

- **Equipment uptime:** The most important overall KPI; very high uptime requirements, such as for phone companies, will require equipment redundancy or on-site parts and technicians to assure no downtime. Definitions vary by customer.
- **MTTR:** Mean time to repair.

- **MTBF:** Mean time between failures.
- **SOFR:** Service order fill rate. Percent availability and delivery of all parts needed for repair.
- **Customer satisfaction after repair:** Percent satisfaction in pre-defined and agreed categories.

### Repair Feedback

Gathering field service data from warranty and non-warranty repairs is important. Statistics regarding failures or difficult repairs should drive product improvements, developments, and new features and functions. If safety issues are found, feedback from field service personnel should drive swift response actions.

Field service personnel need to be brutally honest when they provide feedback on product performance in the field. Field repair information, in and out of warranty, gives companies critical information on customer experience. No matter how great a company's product is, there will be instances where it does not perform adequately or as expected in the field. How a company reacts will determine, in large part, whether the company's customers become or remain loyal.

Finding counterfeit parts during service happens frequently in the industrial machinery and electronics industries, particularly if cheap repairs have been made. (See Chapter 7: International Procurement and Chapter 11: Importing and Exporting.) Today, counterfeits are difficult to detect and nearly impossible to detect with the naked eye. Even if a customer does not know that counterfeit parts were used during a repair, counterfeit parts will generally invalidate warranty coverage. Counterfeits are typically discovered when field service personnel try to validate serial numbers of parts used in previous repairs.

### Purchasing Warranties from Suppliers

On the procurement side of supply chains, buyer purchasing staffs evaluate product warranties as part of any deal being offered. Trained to look for valuable items to add to negotiations, buyers pay close attention to warranties because warranties often represent significant additional value in the deal. Buyers are also trained to ask for extended warranties at no charge. While granting an extended warranty may seem like a good idea to a supplier's sales person trying to close a deal, extended warranties may pose significant risk to suppliers if complying with extended warranties becomes prohibitively expensive. To help mitigate this risk, it is prudent to carefully define what is and is not covered in any extended warranty before the contract is signed.

We caution clients to make sure that their legal and engineering staff carefully review all warranties and that they conduct complete risk assessments before executing supply chain contracts containing warranties.

### *Using Refurbished Parts for Warranty Repairs*

Refurbished parts are components that have been used and then repaired, or remanufactured to be used, for warranty and non-warranty repairs. In electronics, refurbished parts are commonly used to repair computers, routers, printers, keyboards, etc. Take Dell Computers, for example. If a part such as a keyboard on your Dell laptop fails, Dell will exchange your keyboard for a refurbished one via two-day delivery. You are expected to disassemble and reassemble your laptop to install the new keyboard, following the written instructions that come inside the box. In the computer world, refurbished equipment is usually not defective, but because it is used, it is far less expensive. Using refurbished parts for warranty repairs can create significant profit margins for companies.

Remanufactured parts are another category of parts frequently used in warranty repairs, often in the automotive and industrial machinery industries. Remanufacturing involves removing non-functioning components and adding in new parts at the part-module level and possibly at the component level, and the repair or replacement of worn-out or obsolete components. Remanufactured auto parts and industrial machines are expected to meet the same customer expectations as new machines, and are usually warrantied that way.

For repaired, refurbished, and remanufactured products, companies must work closely with legal counsel to ensure that warranty contract language is clear, and that parts sold "same as new" carefully follow legal definitions.

## Legal Overview

Warranties that are included in supply chain contracts and POs are legally binding, and set forth the quality, performance, and reliability standards to which a supplier's product must conform, as well as the consequences of performance failures. Since warranties usually come into play when a buyer believes that something has gone wrong, warranties are often at the frontier of supply chain disputes. Under US law and in much of the world, warranties can be either "express" or "implied." In addition, suppliers may "disclaim" or otherwise "limit" warranty coverage. In the supply chain context, technical specifications often set forth detailed product warranties.

Warranties that are unclear, not definitively agreed to, ambiguous, or oppressively one-sided often become the subject of supply chain disputes. The key to avoiding warranty disputes is to ensure that product warranties are clear and precise. When dealing with warranties between supply chain partners, we recommend three best practices. First, warranties and technical specifications should be drafted in clear and simple language. Second, all implied warranties should be disclaimed. And third, supply chain partners should consider whether they should limit the available damages for breach of warranty to an easy-to-ascertain amount. Each of these best practices will be discussed in turn.

### *Drafting Clear Express Warranties and Specifications*

For supply chain contracts in the United States, express warranties are created in three ways: by making an "affirmation of fact or promise," by furnishing a "description of the goods," or by providing a "sample or model."[74] An "affirmation of fact or promise" is an oral or written statement, in a supply chain contract or otherwise, representing that the products being supplied will have certain characteristics. A "description of the goods" is not much different from an "affirmation of fact or promise" and is an oral or written statement about the product. "Samples and models" are representative examples of the product with which all products that are delivered under the contract must conform.

An oddity of US warranty law (and a vestige of its origin in tort law) is that express warranties are not required to be in writing or included in a

---

74   UCC § 2-313(1).

contract to be binding. Rather, under the UCC, an express warranty arises if a representation about a product forms "part of the basis of the bargain" between the parties. This somewhat loose standard means that an express warranty can be created not just during contract negotiations, but also before or after a contract is executed. The UCC reinforces this by stating, "It is not necessary to the creation of an express warranty that the seller use formal words such as 'warrant' or 'guarantee' or that he have a specific intention to make a warranty."[75] Thus, suppliers are sometimes surprised to find that they are held to warranties created outside the four corners of supply chain agreements. For this reason, controlling the warranty-creation process is important.

It is possible to limit warranties to those that are expressly included in a supply chain contract, and we recommend this as a best practice. To prevent pre-contract representations from being interpreted as warranties, it is important to include an "integration clause" in the contract. An integration clause makes the written contract the full and final statement of the parties' rights and duties, such that any representations made outside of the contract are without legal effect. A sample integration clause states something like, "This Agreement constitutes the entire, full, and final agreement between the Parties and supersedes all prior agreements, statements, representations, and negotiations, whether or not relied upon."

Without an integration clause, pre-contract statements can be construed to be express warranties. With complex products, this can be especially problematic. The case of *Scientific Components Corp. v. Sirenza Microdevices, Inc.*[76] illustrates the care that suppliers must take to limit express warranties to those stated in the contract. Sirenza, the supplier, contracted to supply Scientific Components with audio amplifiers. The amplifier data sheet stated that the amplifiers were "unconditionally stable," but the parties did not incorporate the data sheet into their contract. Instead, the buyer provided Sirenza with comprehensive specifications for the amplifiers that did not promise stability, and that contained an integration clause. After receiving consumer complaints about the amplifiers' lack of stability, however, Scientific Components sued Sirenza.

Notwithstanding the contract specifications that did not guarantee stability and the contract's integration clause disclaiming pre-contract representations,

---

75    UCC § 2-313(2).

76    399 Fed. Appx. 637, 73 U.C.C. Rep. Serv. 2d (Callaghan) 1 (2d Cir. 2010).

the court held that the supplier's data sheet created a binding warranty. In part, the court's decision was a product of the supplier's litigation mistake, since the supplier failed to raise the contract's integration clause properly as a defense. But this result most likely could have been avoided if the supplier had included a provision expressly disclaiming all warranties not contained in the specifications in its contract.

An integration clause will prevent pre-contract statements from becoming warranties, but an integration clause will not protect suppliers from post-contract statements becoming warranties. To prevent post-contract statements from being construed as warranties, supply chain contracts should state that contract modifications may be made only by a signed writing. Certain post-contract engineering documents that are routine parts of product development, such as Preliminary Design Reviews (PDR), Critical Design Reviews (CDR), Failure Mode and Effects Analysis (FMEA), and Production Parts Approval Process (PPAP) documents, sometimes contain statements that seem like warranties. Generally, however, documents such as these are intended simply to be part of the iterative design process. However, without an anti-modification clause, they can be construed as just that. (See Chapter 18: Changing the Supply Chain Agreement.)

For complex products, warranties are most often set forth in contract specifications that are either issued by a buyer, or that a buyer and supplier agree on collaboratively. When it comes to drafting product specifications that contain warranties, it is important to be clear about what is being warranted. As most product engineers know, not all specifications are created equally. Design specifications dictate how a component should be made, and often include material choices, dimensions, and tolerances. Performance specifications, on the other hand, describe what a product must be able to do. Some specifications require suppliers to conduct product testing. Other specifications require proof that products can perform under specified environmental conditions. Many specifications include combinations of these different types of requirements. Whatever the case, specification language should be clear to avoid disputes.

If product specifications are set forth in a separate document from the PO or supply chain agreement, the specifications should be expressly incorporated into the contract documents. Specifications should also be subject to a provision-by-provision review process, the same as other contract terms, in which both parties can evaluate their willingness to live with each provision. Sample language that adopts an appropriate procedure is as follows:

### Specification Warranty and Review

Supplier warrants that the Components shall conform to the specifications and drawings ("Specifications") furnished by Buyer, and that Supplier has had a full opportunity to review the Specifications and determine Supplier's ability to comply with Specifications. Buyer's Specifications are fully incorporated into this Agreement. In the event of any conflict between Specifications and any other document incorporated into or constituting this Agreement, the Specifications should take precedence.

For international supply chain contracts, the law governing product warranties under the CISG is similar to the UCC in the United States. Article 35 of that CISG provides that binding quantity, quality, and description obligations (the CISG does not use the term "warranty") can be created through verbal or written statements, or by furnishing samples or models. Unlike the UCC, the CISG limits warranties to terms that are "required by the contract." However, since the CISG does not require supply chain contracts to be in writing to be enforceable, in reality, the practical effect of pre- and post-contract representations on warranties is not meaningfully different under the CISG than it is in the United States.

### *Disclaiming Implied Warranties: The Implied Warranty of Merchantability*

Under US law, contracts for the sale of goods include certain "implied warranties," unless the contracting parties affirmatively disclaim them. There are two principle implied warranties under the UCC. The first is the "implied warranty of merchantability," which provides that, unless excluded or modified, all goods sold by "merchants" (experienced sellers) will be "merchantable," meaning that they will "pass without objection in the trade" and "are fit for the ordinary purposes for which such goods are used."[77]

---

77  UCC § 2-314.

The implied warranty of merchantability is set forth in UCC § 2-315. The implied warranty of merchantability is not a promise that goods will be of the "highest quality." Rather, it is a promise that goods will simply be fit for their "common and ordinary purpose." For example, cars that are fit to drive pass this standard, even if they do not carry all the performance features a customer may have wanted. The implied warranty of merchantability also requires consistency; products must be "of even kind, quality, and quantity within each unit and among all units involved."[78]

Litigation involving the implied warranty of merchantability most often arises in the context of consumer sales. In contracts between sophisticated commercial parties, such as with supply chain contracts, the implied warranty of merchantability is seldom invoked and seldom appropriate. According to the leading UCC commentators, "Sophisticated business buyers should rarely prevail under 2-315. A right under 2-315 is but a substitute for the express warranties that ought to arise out of the buyer's specifications stated in the contract. A suit under 2-315 is a tacit admission of fault by the buyer's purchasing managers."[79]

The majority view among US courts is that "specially manufactured products," which would include those that are made to comply with a buyer's specifications or that are made for a specific buyer, have no "ordinary purpose" and thus carry no implied warranty of merchantability. Thus, a buyer's specifications will generally displace the implied warranty of merchantability. Consequently, courts frequently hold that there is no implied warranty of merchantability in supply chain contracts.

There are outliers, however. In *Scientific Components Corp. v. Sirenza Microdevices, Inc.*,[80] which we discussed previously in this chapter, the court also addressed whether the buyer's specifications displaced the implied warranty of merchantability. Although the court recognized the many cases in which "specifications void the implied warranty of merchantability," the court nevertheless held that because the buyer's specifications were "not inconsistent with the implied warranty of merchantability," the buyer's claim for breach of the implied warranty of merchantability should not be dismissed on summary

---

78   Ibid.

79   J. White & R. Summers, *Uniform Commercial Code* 684 (5th ed. 2002).

80   399 Fed. Appx. 637, 73 U.C.C. Rep. Serv. 2d (Callaghan) 1 (2d Cir. 2010).

judgment. Therefore, even for custom-designed products, disclaiming the implied warranty of merchantability is the best practice.

The implied warranty of merchantability can be disclaimed by contract (except in Mississippi, where the warranty of merchantability cannot be disclaimed). However, the disclaimer must be "conspicuous," and in writing, and must specifically mention the word "merchantability." Alternatively, a supplier can disclaim all warranties at once, including the implied warranty of merchantability, by stating that goods are being sold "as is," "with all faults," or by using other language that "calls the buyer's attention to the exclusion of warranties and makes plain that there is no implied warranty."[81]

For supply chain contracts between international parties, the CISG also includes an implied promise that goods "[a]re fit for the purposes for which goods of the same description would ordinarily be used."[82] But, unlike the UCC, the CISG allows this implied warranty to be disclaimed without requiring "conspicuous language" or any other formal requirement.

### *Disclaiming Implied Warranties: The Implied Warranty of Fitness for a Particular Purpose*

The implied warranty of fitness for a particular purpose is the second implied warranty that can arise in the supply chain context. An implied warranty of fitness for a particular purpose has been extended when a supplier "has reason to know any particular purpose for which the goods are required," and "the buyer is relying on the seller's skill or judgment to select or furnish suitable goods."[83] Thus, there are two elements to this implied warranty: (1) the supplier's knowledge of the buyer's purpose, and (2) the buyer's reliance on the supplier's skill or judgment.

The implied warranty of fitness for a particular purpose is in some ways the opposite of the implied warranty of merchantability. The implied warranty of merchantability promises that products are fit for their "ordinary purpose." The implied warranty of fitness for a particular purpose, on the other hand, promises that products are fit for a special purpose of the buyer. But, like the implied warranty of merchantability, the implied warranty of fitness for a

---

81    UCC § 2-316(3)(a).

82    CISG, Art. 35.

83    UCC § 2-315.

particular purpose can be disclaimed using "conspicuous language" in writing. The disclaimer for a warranty of fitness for a particular purpose does not have to use any specific wording.[84] An "as is" or "with all faults" disclaimer is also sufficient to disclaim the implied warranty of fitness for a particular purpose, as well as any other warranties that might otherwise apply.[85]

For international supply chain contracts, the CISG has a similar implied warranty. Under the CISG, products must be "fit for any particular purpose expressly or impliedly made known to the seller at the time of the conclusion of the contract."[86] A disclaimer of the warranty of fitness for a particular purpose under the CISG does not have to be conspicuous and need not contain any particular wording to be effective.

Most cases support the notion that a buyer's specifications will displace the implied warranty of fitness for a particular purpose. Indeed, the leading UCC commentators have observed, "[S]ophisticated buyers rarely rely upon sellers' skill in selecting the proper product. That, too, should be taken care of by the purchasing agents of the buyer, who in most circumstances can be expected to develop their own specifications and to write those specifications into the agreement."[87]

But, again, not all specifications are created equally. For design specifications, in which a buyer dictates how a supplier's product should be made, it is easy to see why the implied warranty of fitness for particular purpose should be displaced. In those cases, the buyer is clearly not relying on the supplier's skill and judgment. But for performance specifications, in which a buyer simply specifies what it wants the product to do and leaves it to the supplier to accomplish these objectives, it is less clear that the implied warranty of fitness for a particular purpose should be displaced. In those situations, the buyer is not dictating how to satisfy its requirements, it is simply stating what its requirements are, and may indeed be relying on the supplier's skill and judgment to ensure that the product functions as needed.

Several court decisions bear out this distinction. In *HWH Corp. v. Deltrol Corp.*,[88] for instance, an Iowa district court held that there was a question of

---

84   UCC § 2-316(2).

85   UCC § 2-316(3)(a).

86   CISG, Art. 35.

87   J. White & R. Summers, *Uniform Commercial Code* 684 (5th ed. 2002).

88   2009 U.S. Dist. LEXIS 26380, 68 U.C.C. Rep. Serv. 2d 393 (N.D. Iowa Mar. 19, 2009) (applying Iowa law).

fact for a jury to decide as to whether a valve supplier breached its implied warranty of fitness for a particular purpose. During pre-contract negotiations, the supplier assured the buyer that its valves would perform better than valves made by the buyer's other supplier. The buyer issued performance specifications that set forth strength requirements, but did not dictate how the valve had to be made. Rejecting the supplier's motion for summary judgment, the court held that the buyer's performance specifications did not displace the implied warranty of fitness for a particular purpose because they "were requirement drawings, and were not complete design drawings."

A buyer's testing regiment can also displace the implied warranty of fitness for a particular purpose. In *Dow Corning Corp. v. Weather Peachtree Doors and Windows, Inc.*,[89] a federal district court granted summary judgment against a buyer of silicone sealant on its claim for breach of the implied warranty of fitness for a particular purpose. Because the buyer conducted its own testing and investigation of the sealant, and several times requested changes to its formulation, the court determined that the buyer did not rely on the supplier's expertise.

Because courts are not always consistent, however, we believe the best practice for avoiding supply chain disputes is to disclaim the implied warranty of fitness for a particular purpose, whether or not the buyer has issued detailed specifications, and whether or not the buyer conducts its own testing of the supplier's product. If a buyer has a particular purpose that it needs the supplier to meet, this should be set forth clearly in the parties' supply chain contract.

### Limiting Breach of Warranty Damages

Another way that supply chain partners can control warranty coverage is to limit the damages that a buyer can recover in the event of a warranty breach. Indeed, this is a common practice in supply chain contracts, and courts almost universally enforce contractually-agreed limitations on breach of warranty damages.

Under the UCC, the damages normally available to a buyer for breach of warranty are calculated as the difference "between the value of the goods as accepted and the value they would have had if they had been as

---

89   790 F.Supp.2d 604, 74 U.C.C. Rep. Serv. 2d (E.D. Mich. 2011) (applying Michigan law).

warranted[.]"[90] In practice, for supply chain products, this calculation usual-ly amounts to the full cost of replacing defective products. The UCC also al-lows buyers to recover "incidental and consequential damages" for breach of warranty.[91] "Incidental damages" are costs incurred in dealing with a breach of warranty, such as the cost of storing defective parts.[92] "Consequential damages" are any other damages that flow from the warranty breach that "could not reasonably be prevented by cover and otherwise,"[93] and include buyers' lost profits.

It is common for supply chain contracts to limit breach of warranty dam-ages to a refund of the purchase price and/or to repair or replacement of the non-conforming products. It is also common to expressly bar recover of con-sequential damages. Obviously, these limitations favor suppliers. But, adopt-ing these limitations can be helpful to both buyers and suppliers because they minimize disputes. Calculating difficult-to-quantify damages can be conten-tious. It may be sensible for both parties, therefore, to limit warranty damages to those that can be easily calculated.

The UCC imposes rules on how breach of warranty damages may be lim-ited. If a supply chain contract limits breach of warranty damages, the contract should expressly state that any damages that are available are the "sole" or "exclusive" damages that the buyer may recover.[94] If language like this is not included in the contract, courts may treat the available remedies as allowable, but not exclusive. An example of a well-worded warranty damages limitation clause is as follows:

**Limitation on Damages**
Buyer's damages for breach of any warranty provided in, or in connec-tion with, this Agreement shall be strictly limited to repair or replace-ment of non-conforming goods, which shall be the exclusive remedy available to Buyer in the event of a breach of any warranty. In no event and for no reason shall Supplier be liable to Buyer for consequential, incidental, special, or indirect damages.

---

90  UCC § 2-714(2).
91  UCC § 2-714(3).
92  UCC § 2-715(1).
93  UCC § 2-715(2).
94  UCC § 2-719(1)(b).

The UCC also states that there are circumstances in which warranty damages limitations are unenforceable. Namely, a court can strike down a damages limitation that "fails of its essential purpose."[95] Similarly, a consequential damages exclusion may be invalidated if excluding consequential damages is "unconscionable."[96] It is extremely unusual for courts to strike down damages limitations clauses in contracts involving sophisticated commercial parties, however. When courts strike down damages limitations in the supply chain context, it is generally because the contract limits damages to repair or replacement of defective parts, and the supplier is recalcitrant in making repairs, or the defect at issue is unrepairable. Including a refund of the purchase price as an allowable item of damages generally avoids any possibility that a damages limitation will be invalidated.

*BAE Systems Information and Electronics Systems Integration, Inc. v. SpaceKey Components, Inc.*[97] illustrates this point. The supplier of space equipment warranted that its product would be "radiation resistant" to a certain standard, but later determined it could not meet the standard. The contract limited the buyer's damages to repair/replacement, or a refund of the purchase price. The court found that although repair and replacement were impossible, the damages limitation did not fail of its essential purpose because the supplier could refund the purchase price.

There are occasional outliers, however. For example, in *Marvin Lumber and Cedar Co. v. Sapa Extrusions, Inc.*,[98] a federal district court held that a contract for the sale of wood that limited breach of warranty damages to a refund of the buyer's purchase price failed of its essential purpose. The court's reasoning was that "the purchase price amounted to only a small fraction of the overall repair cost when the product failed, which cost was foreseeable to the seller." We feel that this analysis is highly questionable, and that most courts would have decided the case the other way.

Supply chain parties may also agree to limit the time in which a buyer may claim breach of warranty. Under the UCC, the statute of limitations

---

95   UCC § 2-719(2).

96   UCC § 2-719(3).

97   752 F.3d 72, 83 U.C.C. Rep. Serv. 2d 623 (1ˢᵗ Cir. 2014) (applying New Hampshire law).

98   964 F.Supp.2d 992, 81 U.C.C. Rep. Serv. 2d 279 (D. Minn. 2013) (applying Minnesota and/or Pennsylvania law).

for breach of warranty is four years.[99] However, the UCC allows parties to limit this period to "not less than one year,"[100] and limitations of this type are common.

For international supply chain contracts, the CISG also allows parties to limit the damages available for breach of warranty. Likewise, the CISG allows parties to limit the time in which warranty claims may be asserted.

―――――

## Lessons Learned

To create valid and enforceable warranties and to avoid warranty disputes, supply chain partners should:

- Ensure that their warranty programs meet necessary cost and profitability targets
- Be prepared to negotiate warranty coverage with supply chain partners
- Use warranty and non-warranty repair information to learn valuable information about product quality and performance
- Consider offering or purchasing extended warranties
- Ensure that warranties, including those contained in technical specifications, are drafted in clear and precise language
- Use integration clauses to prevent pre-contract representations from being construed as warranties
- Use no-oral-modification language to prevent post-contract representations from being construed as warranties
- Disclaim implied warranties
- Consider limiting breach of warranty damages to an easy-to-calculate figure

---

99  UCC § 2-725(1).

100  Ibid.

# CHAPTER 13

# RECALLS

## Overview

Product design and the manufacturing process are not always perfect, and sometimes, companies must conduct product recalls and field service actions to repair products or to remove defective products from the market. In a recall, a manufacturing company removes products from use. In a field service action, the manufacturing company arranges to repair or modify products in the field. Both recalls and field service actions are costly and inconvenient.

In some situations, product recalls and field service actions are precipitated by safety issues or serious product defects that require immediate attention. These field service actions are generally treated as emergencies, and the supply chain must react with haste and efficiency to repair or replace defective products and restore customer trust. In other cases, recalls and field service actions involve less significant customer convenience or experience issues. Either way, recalls or field service actions are usually costly and bad for brand image.

Take Apple's "Antennagate" scandal a few years ago. When consumers reported that the iPhone 4 lost its signal when held in a certain way, Apple offered to provide a free phone case to every iPhone-4 owner. Steve Jobs, then Apple CEO, held a press conference to announce the case offering, apologized for the product failure, and explained the steps the company was taking to correct the problem. In the meantime, the iPhone-4 defect caused a blogging frenzy dubbed "Antennagate." Shares of Apple fell $1.61 to $260.09 in response to the announcement.[101] Not only was the iPhone-4 service action expensive, but Apple suffered a blow to its reputation and lost significant market value. The Apple employees responsible for the failure left the company.

When a company determines that a recall is appropriate, it typically must reverse its logistics process so that merchandise can be returned to the manufacturer (unless it is appropriate to discard the recalled product). It is also common for a company conducting a recall to notify its consumers and a supervising government agency, such as the Consumer Products Safety Commission or the FDA, that a recall is in process. The notification process may involve emailing customers, posting notices in stores, and advertising campaigns. If a recall involves safety issues, such as E. coli in food or a potentially harmful toy, word needs to get out fast.

It has been estimated that the average cost of a recall involving food or consumer products is $10 million in supply chain, legal, and consultant fees, which does not include other, indirect financial impacts like damage to reputation and lost sales.[102] This figure also does not include the human costs associated with recalls and harmful products, such as customer injuries.

According to a recent survey of supply chain and operations executives, only 48.4 percent of companies that responded said they would be able to execute a recall within hours.[103] The remaining 51.6 percent answered that it would take them days or even weeks to act. Delay and inaction often exacerbate the negative consequences that are associated with recalls and field service actions. For this reason, best-practice companies have recall execution plans in place before a crisis erupts.

### *Retail Recalls*

Retail industry recalls and field service actions are often the most challenging to execute because they involve reaching a large population of customers, whose identities generally are unknown, very quickly. In retail supply chains, field service actions involve first identifying and removing defective products

---

101    Bloomberg: *Apple's IPhone Executive Mark Papermaster Leaves After Antenna Complaints*, by Arik Hesseldahl. August 8, 2010, 7:27 AM PT.

102    "Recall Execution Effectiveness: Collaborative Approaches to Improving Consumer Safety and Confidence," Deloitte/GMA, May 2010.

103    "On the Trail to Traceability," RedPrairie, June 2012.

from shelves and storage areas, and then quarantining the products from further access by consumers. Retailers conducting recalls must next locate and direct consumers who have already purchased defective items to return to the store and obtain an authorized refund. Sometimes, the refund process can be administered via the Internet or mail. Savvy companies use social media to advertise retail recall actions. All returned products must be quarantined until dispositioned for destruction or until they are returned to a collection center.

Many companies use traceability software solutions and data mining tools to locate recalled products in retail stores, ecommerce pipelines, warehouses, in transit, and at other locations in the supply chain. The effectiveness of these software tools varies because not all of them allow companies to see their inventory positions in real time. Lot and serial-number tracing software, however, does allow this visibility, and in general, we recommend using it. Finding defective inventory is often partially a software task and partially a manual task, especially when expediency is required.

Large retailers with multi-store locations typically have recall protocols in place that direct how stores are notified to remove products from shelves, and quarantine defective products in designated staging areas. Once recalled items are segregated and quarantined, they must be dispositioned for the next step, which is usually destruction under supervision or a return to the vendor. Destruction under supervision is often the preferred solution; it ensures that defective items do not return to commerce on the grey market or are sold as used goods at swap meets and online sites, such as eBay and Craigslist. In international commerce, this is particularly problematic where back-channel sales of this sort are highly profitable. Unless defective goods are destroyed under supervision and the destruction is confirmed with photos and signed documents, defective products are often sold again and again.

The most famous defective product recall in the United States was the 1982 recall of Tylenol, after a series of deaths caused by potassium-cyanide-laced Tylenol capsules were sold by retailers. The adulterated bottles were traceable to secure factory production lines, which led Johnson & Johnson to conclude that the cyanide was introduced post-production. Johnson & Johnson first distributed warnings to hospitals and distributors and halted Tylenol production and advertising. Even though investigators and the company knew the capsules were tampered with in the retail channel, on October 5, 1982, Johnson & Johnson initiated a nationwide recall of Tylenol products.

An estimated 31 million bottles of Tylenol products were in circulation, with a retail value of over $100 million. All recalled products were subsequently destroyed.

The Tylenol case is often used as a case study in college business ethics classes because of Johnson & Johnson's swift and decisive action. Although Johnson & Johnson understandably feared the enormous revenue loss that would result from the recall, its executives took bold action to remove all products from retail shelves and offer refunds to consumers who had already purchased the product. However, the result for Johnson & Johnson was surprisingly good. Consumer confidence in the company and the product was affirmed. Sales and profits soared after the recall, and Tylenol became the most popular over-the-counter drug in the United States. The incident inspired the pharmaceutical, food, and consumer-products industries to develop tamper-resistant packaging and improve quality controls. Pharmaceutical capsules were replaced with tablets to reduce the opportunity for tampering. Tampering with consumer products was made a federal crime.

### Destroy or Return

Whether to destroy or return recalled items to the supplier is often a financial decision. It may be less expensive to destroy goods than to pay to return defective products to the seller. If products have come from a foreign location, China for example, returning items may not be possible, since the Chinese government prohibits the import of defective goods.

Sometimes, companies performing recalls or field service actions may want to preserve samples of defective products for testing and failure analysis. When this is the case, supply chain professionals must work closely with quality assurance personnel to select products for testing and arrange appropriate reverse logistics to ensure that products are not further damaged during the return process. We have seen retailers rough-handle goods once they know the goods have been recalled. Mishandling, however, may cause companies to lose valuable information about the defective product, which may be crucial to making important changes and improvements, or if a buyer pursues legal action. All parties involved in the reverse logistics process should be instructed to carefully handle items being returned.

If a product is being retrofitted or repaired in the field, field service processes and personnel must be engaged. In a retrofit or repair situation, repair kits are typically shipped to field service personnel or to the product or customer site to await installation. Again, it is important for defective parts to be carefully handled and returned to a designated facility for analysis and reverse engineering.

### Planning Ahead for Recalls and Field Service Actions

Sometimes supply chain managers, particularly in industrial goods companies, will delay designing recall and field service action protocols. Having an established recall process, however, reduces the supply chain's exposure to the negative impacts of recalls and field service actions, and prepares the company for action when a recall occurs. Written policies and procedures governing recalls and field service actions are best, with step-by-step instructions that can be followed if a recall or field service action is required.

These are some of the typical steps in a corporate recall or field service action process:

- Notifying appropriate government agencies and following communications protocols with those agencies
- Notifying and engaging personnel as needed to initiate and administer the recall or field service action, such as executive management, supply chain/logistics, legal, quality assurance, marketing and communications, field service, and outside experts; if needed, many companies designate an internal recall team
- Setting up the accounting information needed to document recall and field service costs and pay for recall services as needed
- Identifying all defective or unsafe products at point of sale, on shelves, in storerooms, and in distribution centers using inventory location or traceability software
- Instructing retailers to remove defective products from shelves and quarantine defective goods in a storage area
- Identifying all products in transit, in warehouses, at other storage locations, and at supplier locations using inventory location or traceability software, and providing quarantine instructions

- Stopping production and procurement of product, and quarantining all work-in-process
- Instructing retailers and distributors as to the protocol for paying refunds and collecting returned products
- Aggregating defective products into central collection areas
- Determining if recalled products should be destroyed or returned
- Selecting sample products for testing and analysis, and shipping the samples to designated locations
- Destroying or returning recalled products

## Legal Overview

From a legal perspective, the subject of recalls raises the specter of government regulation—in the United States and sometimes abroad. In the United States, most product recalls involve a federal regulatory agency, and possibly state regulators as well. Internationally, recall authority becomes more complex. This section will discuss how recalls and field service actions work from a legal point of view, and will offer best practices for allocating responsibility for recalls and field service actions within supply chains in a way that best avoids legal disputes.

Longer supply chains and increased complexity may negatively impact product quality and reliability. As a result, product recalls and field service actions are on the rise. 2014 was a record recall year for the US National Highway Traffic Safety Administration (NHTSA), having overseen the recall of almost 64 million affected vehicles). Recalls and field service actions have become common in many industries, including food, toys, automotive, aerospace, and pharmaceuticals. Even clothing companies experience recalls, as the 2013 see-through yoga pants scandal at Lululemon demonstrated.

Recalls should never be handled without the help of experts. Due to the sheer number of potential government agencies involved, different standards, and different potential bases for liability, companies should always involve, at minimum, competent and experienced legal counsel who can interface with the regulator and manage litigation risk. Logistics assistance is often also important for companies that do not have experience with the reverse supply chain procedures that recalls often entail. Public relations assistance can be invaluable in handling recall and field service action publicity—which, for publicly traded companies especially, can be a minefield of potential liability.

### Regulatory Authority Over Recalls

In the United States, the federal government has many agencies that oversee the manufacture and sale of products. In aviation and aerospace, the governing agency is the FAA (Federal Aviation Administration). For food, cosmetics, pharmaceuticals, and medical devices, it is the FDA (Food and Drug Administration). For automotive products, it is NHTSA (National Highway Traffic Safety Administration). For consumer products, it is the Consumer Product Safety Commission (CPSC). Each of these agencies oversees products and product recalls, but their practices and procedures vary.

**The Federal Aviation Authority (FAA):** The FAA regulates aviation and aerospace products. Because of the safety-critical nature of these products, the FAA involves itself in nearly every aspect of aircraft-parts manufacturing. All safety issues must be reported to the FAA immediately upon discovery. Post-sale "service bulletins" are commonplace in the aviation industry, and the FAA has the authority to mandate these. Aviation recalls and field service actions are relatively easy to administer, since aircraft owners are a smaller population, aircraft ownership is registered with the FAA, and aircraft location is easily tracked. The FAA must approve and monitor all upgrade, recall, and retrofit programs.

If an aerospace or aviation defect causes an "unsafe condition," the FAA may order an "airworthiness directive," in which the FAA mandates that the manufacturer perform certain actions to address the safety issue until it has been resolved. Emergency airworthiness directives require remedial measures to cure the unsafe condition before affected aircraft may be flown. Non-emergency defects are classified as "urgent," which means that remedial measures must be taken within a short but not immediate period of time. Airworthiness directives are coordinated internationally, and foreign regulators, such as the European Aviation Safety Agency in Europe, the Civil Aviation Safety Authority in Australia, the Directorate General of Civil Aviation in India, and the Civil Aviation Administration of China, work together to address aviation safety issues.

**The Food and Drug Administration (FDA):** The FDA is involved in all recalls relating to food, pharmaceuticals, and medical devices, though its authority is not the same across these areas. The FDA has plenary power to order recalls of food and medical devices. For pharmaceuticals, the FDA can mandate a recall only if contamination is discovered during production. If a pharmaceutical defect is discovered after production, the FDA can require going-forward preventative measures and can encourage the manufacturer to recall the product, but the FDA cannot mandate a post-production recall. For public relations purposes, however, food and drug manufacturers often conduct recalls voluntarily.

FDA recalls can be difficult to administer because food and over-the-counter pharmaceuticals are sold in large quantities, are usually not tracked to the end user, and are often consumed before a recall can be effectively publicized. Automated traceability technologies help track products as far as grocery store or drug store shelves, but generally not to ultimate consumers.

Recalls are relatively common (unfortunately) in the food industry. According to the Center for Disease Control and Prevention, one out of every six Americans becomes sick from contaminated food each year. By way of the Food and Drug Administration Amendments Act of 2000, the FDA established a Reportable Food Registry to track contamination reports and speed up the detection of food contamination. The US Department of Agriculture Food Safety and Inspection Service is a separate agency that oversees meat and poultry in the United States. This agency coordinates meat and poultry recalls, and monitors the effectiveness of recall actions.

**The National Highway Traffic Safety Administration (NHTSA):** NHTSA is the US federal agency responsible for motor vehicles, tires, and child safety seats and restraints. NHTSA maintains a database of all consumer safety complaints concerning automotive products, and investigates defective product reports that involve possible safety issues. Automotive manufacturers must report all safety issues to NHTSA as soon as they are discovered. NHTSA has the power to mandate product recalls and field service actions. NHTSA actively monitors and manages all automotive recalls.

Since motor vehicle users are registered with local government agencies, and most automotive companies have dealer networks, NHTSA recalls are relatively easy to administer. In addition, NHTSA maintains a page on their website listing all active recalls that consumers can access. The week this chapter was written, automotive manufacturers announced 10 new recalls, all of which were recorded on NHTSA's website. NHTSA cannot mandate recalls for vehicles that are over 10 years old when a defect is found.

**The Consumer Product Safety Commission (CPSC):** The CPSC provides oversight for the 15,000+ "consumer products" under its jurisdiction. Consumer product manufacturers must report to the CPSC if they become aware of potential safety issues. By virtue of the Consumer Product Safety Improvement Act of 2008, the CPSC has the power to mandate recalls, although the vast majority of consumer product recalls are voluntary. The CPSC maintains a searchable database of product-related injuries.

The CPSC was created in 1972 by virtue of the Consumer Product Safety Act, and is charged with administering and enforcing six additional consumer-related laws: the Flammable Fabrics Act of 1953, the Federal Hazardous Substances Act of 1960, the Poison Prevention Packaging Act of 1970, the Children's Gasoline Burn Prevention Act of 2008, and the Virginia Graeme Baker Pool and Spa Safety Act of 2008. Consumer product recalls are often difficult to administer, since manufacturers typically do not track sales to ultimate customers. Therefore, to be effective, consumer product recalls often involve extensive publicity.

### Other Agencies

The agencies described above are those that are most commonly involved in product recalls and field service actions, but they are not the only federal agencies that could be involved. The ATF (Bureau of Alcohol, Tobacco, Firearms, and Explosives) oversees recalls and field service actions involving alcohol, tobacco products, and guns. The EPA (Environmental Protection Agency) oversees recalls and field service actions involving pesticides and vehicle emission control systems. The US Department of Housing and Urban Development (HUD) oversees recalls pertaining to manufactured housing products. And the Coast Guard oversees recalls for watercraft equipment.

### State Laws

State agencies generally do not have extensive involvement in product recalls and field service actions, precisely because the federal government is so involved. Federal law governing product safety is often so extensive that it is said to "occupy the field," which means that states are not allowed to legislate in these areas. That said, all 50 states have attorney general investigatory powers, consumer protection laws, and health and safety regulations that can be asserted against companies that fail to follow federal law recall or field service mandates, or if their products endanger consumers.

## International Laws and Standards

To date, the United States has the most highly developed regulatory product recall and field service laws of any country. But other countries' laws are beginning to catch up. In 2004, the European Union enacted the General Product Safety Directive, which requires manufacturers to conduct safety analyses before bringing products to market, among other measures. The EU, however, has not yet enacted laws that would require recalls of unsafe products.

Japan, on the other hand, has implemented laws governing recalls, but its regulations are not as extensive as in the United States. China does not have specific laws governing product recalls, but it does enforce its criminal laws against makers of unsafe products. Famously, two corporate executives were executed and several others were sentenced to life imprisonment in connection with a 2008 infant milk formula contamination incident that resulted in several deaths and several hundred thousand instances of sickness. (Indeed, the Chinese milk scandal also resulted in China's very first personal injury legal claims and the enactment in 2015 of China's first-ever Food Safety Law.)

## Recall and Other "Post-Sale" Legal Duties

In the United States, under some circumstances, injured consumers may sue manufacturers that fail to conduct recalls when they should, that do not administer recalls diligently, or that fail to warn consumers about product defects that are discovered after the products at issue have been sold. These lawsuits are usually styled as product liability and negligence actions and are governed by state law. The states are divided as to whether manufacturers owe what are called "post-sale duties" to warn consumers about product defects and to recall defective products.

The rule historically has been that companies have no post-sale duty to warn consumers about defective products, or to recall defective goods. This rule is changing, however. The first state to hold that manufacturers may have a post-sale duty to warn was Michigan in the 1959 case, *Comstock v. General Motors*.[104] In this landmark decision, the Michigan Supreme Court held that GM had a duty to warn customers about brake failures that GM learned about after the vehicles at issue had been sold. Today, approximately half the states have held that manufacturers have post-sale duties to warn consumers about product defects in at least some circumstances.[105] Some states impose a duty to warn for all defects. Other states limit the duty to warn to defects that are "latent," meaning those that would not be apparent to the consumer at the time of sale.

Only a few courts have held that manufacturers have a post-sale duty to recall defective products. Cases in California, Connecticut, and New York have imposed recall duties on manufacturers, though even in those states, the case law is mixed. Cases in a handful of other states recognize a duty to recall when ordered by a government agency, or a duty to exercise due care when conducting a recall if a manufacturer voluntarily assumes the duty to do so (including California, Connecticut, and Georgia).

The recently promulgated Third Restatement of Torts recognizes a post-sale duty to warn and a limited duty to recall when a government agency has mandated a recall. The Third Restatement also imposes a duty to use due care when conducting recalls if a company has voluntarily undertaken a recall or field service action.[106] These Restatement provisions have not yet been adopted in a majority of states, however.

A manufacturer's decision to conduct a recall or other field service action may have other implications in personal injury litigation. For example,

---

104   358 Mich. 163 (1959).

105   Alaska, Arizona, Colorado, Connecticut, Georgia, Hawaii, Iowa, Kansas, Louisiana, Maryland, Massachusetts, Michigan, Minnesota, New Jersey, New Mexico, New York, North Carolina, North Dakota, Ohio, Pennsylvania, South Dakota, Washington, and Wisconsin impose post-sale duties to warn on product manufacturers. Alabama, Arkansas, California, Delaware, Florida, Idaho, Illinois, Indiana, Mississippi, Missouri, Montana, Nebraska, Oklahoma, Oregon, Rhode Island, South Carolina, Tennessee, Utah, Vermont, West Virginia, and Wyoming do not impose post-sale duties to warn. The remaining states, Kentucky, Nevada, New Hampshire, Texas, Utah, and Virginia, are either split, inconsistent, or uncertain.

106   Restatement (Third) of Torts §§ 10-11.

a voluntary recall or field service action may help a company to avoid punitive damages because undertaking a recall shows care and diligence. A recall may also be used negatively against a company, however, since personal injury plaintiffs may cite the recall or field action as evidence the manufacturer knew its product was dangerous. A recall or field service action that implies that the same defect exists in a large number of products may also make class action litigation more likely.

### Contracts Governing Recalls in the Supply Chain

How product recall costs are allocated between supply chain partners is usually a matter of contract. In some industries, particularly the automotive industry, it is common to allocate responsibility for recall costs in advance. Often, automotive supply chain contracts apportion recall costs by formula, with a percentage to be paid by the supplier and the remainder to be paid by the buyer, without regard for the parties' actual level of fault. In industries where recalls are common—and the automotive industry certainly is one of them—this can work.

In other industries, supply chain partners more commonly allocate responsibility for recall costs according to the degree of the parties' fault that contributed to the underlying product defect. In most cases, the supply chain partner that will bear the majority of the recall costs should be the one to decide whether to conduct a recall and to design and administer the recall. Often, supply chain partners will form joint recall committees to coordinate the field action.

Depending on your industry, the best practice might also be to specify in the contract which supply chain partner will be responsible for administering recalls or field actions, interfacing with regulators, and informing the public. In automotive recalls, for example, the vehicle manufacturer often has better access to customer contact information and superior relationships with regulators, such that it often makes sense for the vehicle maker, rather than a component supplier, to coordinate and lead a recall or field service action.

Supply chain disputes periodically arise concerning whether recall costs were "reasonably incurred." Typically, the party claiming that recall costs were excessive will claim inefficient labor, poor recall management, and/or excessive scope to try to reduce its liability. To avoid supply chain disputes about the appropriate scope of a recall or field service action, we recommend consulting with recall administration experts before implementing a recall.

### Case Study: Meatballs and the Supply Chain

We'd like to discuss now a topic near and dear to our hearts: meatballs. In *General Mills Operations, LLC v. Five Star Custom Foods, Ltd.*,[107] a food manufacturer sued its meatball supplier for breach of contract after the supplier's meatballs became the subject of a USDA-recommended recall. The trial court allowed the buyer to recoup its recall costs from the supplier on the basis of language in the parties' agreement that the supplier "shall promptly pay or reimburse [buyer] for all costs and damages (including lost profits) incurred by [buyer], including, without limitation, costs for ... recall."

Because the contract provision was clear and straightforward and specifically mentioned recall costs, the case was able to be decided on summary judgment and did not require a trial. We recommend clear language like this that allocates responsibility for recall costs between supply chain partners.

------

### Lessons Learned

When conducting product recalls or other field service actions, supply chain partners should:

- Plan ahead for recalls and field service actions so they can be executed quickly and efficiently, including written instructions and a budget
- Determine what government agencies should be notified in case of a recall; establish written procedures for notification; be prepared to work with regulators
- Enlist the help of recall experts in designing and administering product recalls and field service actions
- Allocate responsibility for recall costs between supply chain partners in supply chain contracts

------

107   703 F.3d 1104 (8th Cir. 2013).

# CHAPTER 14

# INFORMATION TECHNOLOGY

## Overview

Just 20 years ago, supply chain operations focused on moving goods from suppliers to manufacturing to customers. Today, those same supply chain processes also move information. Information about inventories, supplies, raw materials, and finished goods drives the day-to-day decisions made in global supply chains. Information also drives the location and amount of inventory required, delivery and manufacturing schedules, the location of field service parts, and much more. Customers now demand electronic information showing where their shipments are and when they will be delivered. Information technology (IT) has gradually evolved from being a "nice-to-have" service to being an absolute necessity demanded by customers. Information technology is also often a strategic advantage in a competitive business environment.

There are two principal functions that supply chain information technology supports:

- **Planning:** Helping companies determine what to do in the future
- **Execution:** Helping companies implement plans, decide what should happen next, and look in the rearview mirror to analyze and interpret what has already happened

These two halves of supply chain operations are critically supported by information and software systems. Both halves are essential in running a manufacturing business and are often the front-line in avoiding supply chain disputes. Having more information leads to a greater ability to cooperate.

## *Forecasting and Planning Software*

Forecasting and planning IT programs may be a part of bigger business IT systems, such as ERP (enterprise resource planning) systems, or they may be individual software packages called "point solutions." For either alternative, or some combination of both, the approach to planning is essentially the same and consists of forecasting demand, production planning, and inventory planning.

Forecasting software executes a complex set of algorithms and calculations that attempt to predict the future. In a production environment, the variables might include things like buying trends and preferences, seasonality, and complementary product purchases such as a printer and a cable. The variables are weighted and prioritized and fed into the predictive algorithm.

Generally, manufacturers prepare twelve-month rolling forecasts that are updated regularly with current information, and adjusted as unknown contingencies become clearer. For example, if an apparel company is trying to predict sales of red dresses for the holiday season, they will look at past years' sales of dresses, seasonal purchases of red garments, fashion trends, sales of red handbags and other accessories, and will then feed these predictors into the computer software to prepare a forecast. The red-dress forecast may be developed in the spring for the following holiday season, and will be adjusted each month to enable the manufacturer to plan for and make quantities that can be sold—not too many and not too few. If the manufacturer makes too many red dresses, stores will have to take markdowns to sell off excess inventory. If the manufacturer makes too few red dresses based on a faulty forecast, the manufacturer and the retailers will miss revenue opportunities. To make just the right amount of products, forecasts must be accurate.

Now multiply the red-dress prediction over hundreds or thousands of products across various garment assortments, and geographic and demographic preferences, and you can start to understand the magnitude of the computer-modeling challenges in a production environment. These same principles apply to all industries when it comes to forecasting.

The variables will be different in industrial product forecasting versus consumer products, but the same principles generally hold true. Forecasts are adjusted on a periodic basis as products are sold and trends are identified. Companies may model alternate versions of a forecast to plan for what might happen if a product is wildly popular or a dismal failure. This information helps business executives make informed decisions. Forecasts may also provide valuable information for suppliers that need to plan their own production. But suppliers must understand that forecasts are just that—predictions that cannot be fully relied upon. Just like the weatherman's prediction of rain, forecasts are not 100 percent reliable. Overreliance on forecasts can cause supply chain disputes. Appropriate reliance, on the other hand, leads to harmony.

Once a forecast is complete and acceptable to management, production planning begins. Planners use end product forecasts to plan each stage of production and to schedule delivery of the components needed to build the end products. Production planning uses software to coordinate production schedules and to determine where the products can be fit into the overall factory schedule. Much like a giant, dynamic 3D puzzle, planners shift and rearrange schedules through the use of software to optimize the production shop floor. In addition, planning software keeps track of priority customers and suggests new schedules that may not be optimal from an overall perspective, but will allow the best customers to be served first. Planning software takes into account inventory on hand, inventory/work-in-process (WIP) and long-lead-time items. The software automatically generates requisitions for parts needed to support the plan. These requisitions are then sent to purchasing so that parts can be procured in time to meet production schedules.

The use of accurate IT to make all of this happen is essential in a complex manufacturing environment. With thousands of parts and many suppliers and priorities, it would be mostly impossible to forecast and plan without software tools.

### Execution Software

Execution software is the second category of IT used in supply chains. Again, execution software may be a part of a bigger business system like an ERP system, or may be an individual "point solution" software package. Execution software records and tracks business transactions that occur in the normal course of business. Day-to-day activities, such as order management, accounting, purchasing, production, and logistics, each involve one or more supporting business transactions that are recorded by execution software and that can be traced and audited.

The key to execution software is the relationship between functions. For example, if raw material is needed for production, the production-planning function of the software will generate purchase requisitions and will forward them to purchasing, which will then place POs with the appropriate suppliers. Requisition numbers can be cross-referenced with the corresponding POs, so there is an audit trail of what was requested and subsequently ordered. The requisitions and POs will also typically include general ledger account numbers so the proper cost accounting can take place when goods are paid for. POs will trigger accounts payable events, so that when raw materials are received, receipts will be recorded in the system and payment will be authorized. Thanks to execution software, almost every supply chain and procurement transaction can be cross-referenced and linked together. This is important for coordinating supply chains, and for documenting transactions in a way that all supply chain partners agree is reliable. This helps avoid disputes.

### ERP Systems

Business management software programs are often referred to as ERP (Enterprise Resource Planning) systems. The most basic ERP systems usually include accounting, purchasing, manufacturing, and warehousing/logistics functionality. A more extended systems architecture may also include engineering, marketing, HR, import/export, budgeting, and other enabling software. In addition, ERP systems have functionality within modules that can be used to address specific needs, such as lot traceability for agri-business or ingredient mixing recipes for chemical compounds.

ERP systems include both supply chain forecasting/planning functionality as well as execution functionality. A company may choose to use some or all of the ERP-system functions by turning on or off specific modules or functions within modules. Some companies may choose to use only the basic implementation, while others will implement most or all of the functionality.

Large ERP-system implementations are often difficult and lengthy due to the complexity of the ERP software and multiple functions within a business that are affected. For a transaction that generates a production plan, purchase requisition, PO, receiving records, and an accounts payable sequence, the ERP software has to work in each functional module AND across all of the modules.

ERP implementations are complicated at best and nearly impossible in the worst scenarios. ERP implementations generate their fair share of legal disputes, which we discuss in the second half of this chapter. During an ERP implementation, the implementation team must understand all of the company's processes in detail and must configure the ERP software to match the current or recommended new processes.

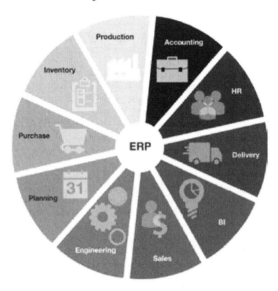

The typical ERP implementation may take six months to several years for larger companies and may require expensive outside consultants to help. Very few companies are able to handle ERP implementations on their own unless they have hired former ERP consultants into their own staffs. Careful implementation planning is critical, since ERP implementations often go wrong, and disputes are common. The most popular ERP systems are SAP and Oracle, with Microsoft Dynamics in third place and gaining rapidly in popularity. There are also dozens of tier-two ERP packages that are less expensive to implement and operate. These tier-two packages may be just what a smaller company needs.

### Point Solutions versus ERP Systems

Some companies have unique business requirements that can only be handled, or are handled best, using specialty software packages. Standard ERP systems may not fully address a company's unique needs and may have to be supplemented. Supplemental software packages are also referred to as "point solutions" and are usually much smaller implementations. For example, a point-of-sale system at a gas pump may require software not offered in a big ERP system. This special software must be implemented and integrated or developed by software engineers separately. International-trade compliance software is another common point solution deployed and integrated with ERP systems.

Instead of using full-blown ERP systems, smaller companies often use accounting packages (QuickBooks is the most popular) and a small tier-two or tier-three business system for their operations. However, even these implementations are complex and may require several months of work before the implementation is complete and the business system can go live.

### The Software Selection Process

IT systems typically require extensive evaluation to ensure that the functional requirements of the business match the software functionality. Once a company chooses software, there is often a lengthy price negotiation process with the software vendor and a complicated contract process. Software is generally priced or licensed by the number of concurrent users, called "license seats." Sometimes software vendors also charge for each transaction in the system. In addition, there are annual software license maintenance fees that are typically 20-25 percent of the software list price. Maintenance fees allow for access to help lines and sometimes access to developers, and rights to upgrades and bug fixes. For the big ERP systems, relationships with software vendors can last 20 years or more, with maintenance fees over time constituting most of the software revenue.

The software selection process can be conducted by an internal team or by outside consultants hired to identify requirements and assist in the software evaluation. The process includes these steps:

- Identifying and documenting the "current state" of the business, including mapping business functions and identifying "must-haves" and "nice-to-haves"

- Identifying and short-listing potential software vendors and reviewing software functionality
- Preparing an RFX (RFI/RFQ/RFP) for vendor responses
- Evaluating RFX responses against business requirements and against other vendors
- Coordinating software demonstrations by short-listed vendors and evaluating demonstrations
- Identifying gaps where software does not meet business needs
- Selecting the software vendor(s)
- Negotiating costs and contract terms
- Implementing the new software

Sounds pretty sequential and straightforward, right? But this selection phase is extremely critical. If IT consultants do not have experience in their client's industry, they may lead a company to the wrong software or make errors in judgment about how the business requirements are best met. During the software selection process, it is important to hire the most experienced consultants you can find to ensure that their recommendations are viable and strong. Companies that try to save money by hiring cheap consultants or do the selection themselves will often get just what they pay for.

It is also critical during the selection process to determine what, exactly, software packages can and cannot do. We always recommend giving vendors several business scenarios to demonstrate, so they can show how their software handles the most important unique requirements of the business. We cannot emphasize enough the need for preparation during this part of the process. Many lawsuits have been filed against software companies that have promised functionality during the demonstration phase and then are accused of not delivering. This always makes us wonder how prepared the customer-selection team was in asking probing questions and validating critical business scenarios, and what the software company promised but did not deliver.

### Cloud versus Behind-the-Firewall Software

Companies also have to decide if they want to operate software from behind their internal firewalls on their servers, or to allow software to operate "in the cloud." Software operates equally well in both circumstances. The cloud is nothing more than software and services that run via the Internet. Cloud software can be less expensive, since monthly rental fees can usually be expensed and not capitalized on companies' balance sheets, whereas purchased software is typically capitalized as an asset. However, the cloud is less secure. Companies often choose to operate business software from behind their firewalls if they are concerned about getting hacked in the cloud, or that operating with cloud-based software will allow competitors to access confidential information.

### *Disputes with IT Implementation Consultants*

Countless lawsuits have been caused by software implementations that do not go as planned. These lawsuits generally involve cost overruns and missed milestones, and often the client is forced to stop the implementation or find another consulting firm to assist. In our experience, IT implementation problems happen most often when consultants have held themselves out as experts in a particular industry, but in fact are not. Sometimes a consulting firm will pitch experienced consultants and then switch to lower-cost subcontractors or remote overseas configuration shops. If the price of implementation has been negotiated too low, consultants may find ways of economizing to improve margins (to the customer's detriment).

To avoid IT implementation disputes, you should be diligent when selecting consultants. We recommend picking a team that is experienced in your industry, checking their references, and being vigilant in project oversight. You certainly can and should ask to review and approve every consultant who is added to the implementation team. Reject team members that are not credentialed, and do not be afraid to ask to replace any consultant who is missing deadlines, cannot get along with others, or appears to lack knowledge about your industry. Never skimp on selecting and managing IT implementation consultants. You often only have one shot to get IT implementation right.

Another critical strategy for avoiding legal disputes with IT consultants is to carefully oversee IT implementation work. All delays and changes in schedule should be fully explained and approved. Implementation consultants' work product should be reviewed on a regular basis—at least every two weeks during implementation—and should be compared against promised milestones and deliverables. Keep the communications lines open to discuss and debate issues. Escalate significant issues to a project-steering committee for resolution.

## Finding Records in IT Systems

Most business software is built on relational databases. For all practical purposes, every transaction record can be related to other transactions, and most can be cross-referenced. If you are looking for cause-and-effect transactions (such as forecasts related to raw materials purchasing or customer orders related to payments), you should be able to find transaction records in several areas of an ERP system. Most ERP systems also have easy report-writing functionality so that just about any user can pull a report and look at data. Reliable evidence of every step in the supply chain can be found and produced, if it is needed, and this in turn helps maintain good supply chain relationships.

## Using Agile Methodology in IT Development and Systems Implementation

Using an alternative to full-scale IT implementation, called "agile," can also help avoid implementation disputes. Agile IT implementation techniques became popular in the early 2000s. The agile approach is to include many incremental milestones in an IT implementation plan. At each milestone, the agile implementation team releases an increment of the code and deploys it for use, versus the old fashioned method of waiting until the entire system is completed and then going live. An agile deployment may mean that each functional area, such as accounting, purchasing, warehousing, etc., is deployed separately, and integration of the parts happens at a later date. Each incremental deployment is expected to elicit feedback, drive iterations, and evolve the software. The agile method has its advantages, but be aware that its iterative process may wreak havoc with supply chain contracts that are written based on defined scope and deliverables.

## IT Systems Trends

In addition to cloud computing and agile deployments, several other trends are guiding IT systems use in most companies. The use of "Big Data," the "Internet of Things," the use of smart phones for business, wearables, imaging, and drone delivery, are all information-driven supply chain technologies that may have an effect on legal disputes.

## Use of Big Data

More and more companies are using Big Data to find trends and guide strategic supply chain direction. "Big Data" is a term that describes data sets so large and complex that they require special software to process and analyze. In terms of supply chains, Big Data may be used to shorten the order-to-delivery cycle and may help with forecasting trends and understanding customer ordering patterns. Once analyzed, the Big Data is then fed back into day-to-day operations to make informed decisions about process improvements and efficiencies. Use of Big Data may also drive new behaviors such as long-lead-time parts ordering and the buildup of certain inventories in anticipation of customer needs. Big Data can provide interesting business insights not previously available, much of which will impact supply chain functioning.

Over-reliance on Big Data, however, can sometimes create supply chain disputes. For example, if a 3PL (third-party logistics provider) builds a new warehouse in anticipation of new storage requirements resulting from Big Data analysis, but these needs do not materialize or the 3PL's customers source their storage needs elsewhere, then friction between supply chain partners is created. Thus, it is important for supply chain partners to understand that Big Data trend analysis is predictive, but may not be fully accurate. Big Data analysis should not become the only point of input regarding what might or might not happen in the future, and should not be treated as a substitute for human analysis or for actual communication with supply chain partners.

## The Internet of Things (IoT)

The Internet of Things (IoT) is an emerging phenomenon that describes how it is now possible to remotely track all sorts of products and materials by embedding them with wireless monitoring devices. Once embedded, the status and location of products and materials can be assessed—and sometimes even controlled—remotely through the Internet.

The IoT opens up the possibility of far more extensive transaction records and traceability of data than are available today through more traditional IT, adding to the ways attorneys and clients can mine information in support of supply chain cases. The IoT is yet another repository of evidence that can be audited and that will also be subject to discovery and disclosure obligations.

### Supply Chain Partner Systems

Companies also may rely on their supply chain partners' IT systems to provide data for their end-to-end business data models. Suppliers' systems may interface with customer procurement portals online, or they may use EDI (electronic data interchange) to communicate information. Suppliers are often given the ability to download buyer forecasts and submit invoices electronically through buyer-IT systems. To the extent that using supply chain interface points and processes is required or desired by buyers, these requirements should be clearly defined in supplier contracts so that all parties understand the expectations and performance measurements.

Other supply chain partners, such as logistics and warehouse service providers, may actually fulfill customer orders through their customers' IT systems. Warehouse providers that control finished-goods inventory must maintain a high level of inventory accuracy, since inventory is recorded as an asset in the owning company's financial statements. Thus, the security and integrity of supply chain partners' IT systems must be considered when allowing partners direct access to your IT systems.

## Legal Overview

Selecting and implementing IT systems can give rise to complex and problematic legal disputes. Problems in this area tend to involve communication and expertise—or the lack thereof. IT clients sometimes need a particular solution, but may not be able to describe their needs with precision to IT vendors. In addition, IT vendors and consultants may rely on sales personnel that do not fully understand the capabilities and features of their products, or who may not have sufficient experience in their clients' industry to know what IT capabilities and features are most important. Compound these issues with the fact that IT solutions and implementations are usually expensive and time-consuming. This is a frequent recipe for litigation.

### The Law Governing IT Disputes

IT disputes are similar to other supply chain disputes, but do have some special features. We have discussed supply chain relationships between suppliers and buyers as being governed by Article 2 of the UCC for contracts between

US entities, and the CISG for contracts between US and non-US entities. The UCC and CISG, however, apply only to contracts for "goods." Courts have struggled with the question of whether software and other IT products constitute "goods" or "services."

In the United States, service contracts are governed by state common law. The common law is the set of legal principles that have been established over time through judge-made case law, and, unlike the UCC, is not codified in state statutes. Alternatively, if an IT contract has a choice-of-law clause, the governing law will be the common law of the chosen state. The common law of contracts between states can sometimes vary significantly on issues that affect IT relationships, which companies with IT partners should be aware of.

US courts have reached inconsistent decisions about whether the UCC applies to software and other IT-related contracts. Some courts draw a distinction between IT products that are "off-the-shelf," meaning not customized for a particular company, on the one hand, and those that are customized, on the other hand. Off-the-shelf IT products are classified as goods, and those contracts are governed by the UCC. Customized IT products, by contrast, are classified as services, and those contracts are governed by state common law.[108] But this view is not uniform. Many courts have applied the UCC to IT contracts with significant customized aspects. For example, in *Micro Data Base Systems, Inc. v. Dharma Systems, Inc.*,[109] the Seventh Circuit held that the UCC governed a contract for custom-designed business management software. Many other cases simply conduct no analysis as to whether the UCC applies to IT contracts.[110]

Under the CISG, which governs international contracts, courts and other tribunals almost uniformly hold that off-the-shelf IT products are goods governed by the CISG, while customized or developmental IT products are not. For international contracts that are determined to be service contracts, it is difficult to predict what the governing law will be, since different countries use different tests to determine choice of law. Contract law can vary dramatically among different countries. For this reason, for international IT contracts, it is

---

108  *See, e.g., Simulados Software, Ltd. v. Photon Infotech Private, Ltd.*, 2014 U.S. Dist. LEXIS 61047, 82 U.C.C. Rep. Serv. 2d (Callaghan) 528 (N.D. Cal. May 1, 2014); *Systems America, Inc. v. Rockwell Software, Inc.*, 2007 U.S. Dist. LEXIS 8483 (N.D. Cal. Jan. 26, 2007).

109  148 F.3d 649, 35 U.C.C. Rep. Serv. 2d (Callaghan) 747 (7th Cir. 1998).

110  *See, e.g., SER Solutions, Inc. v. Masco Corp.*, 103 Fed. Appx. 483 (4th Cir. Jul. 1, 2004).

particularly important to include a choice-of-law clause selecting the law that will govern the contract. (See Chapter 7: International Procurement.)

There is more than just academic interest at stake in whether the UCC or the common law applies to contracts for IT products. State common law generally does not include any of the implied warranties that are included in every contract governed by the UCC. For IT contracts, implied warranties can create important causes of action for software that fails to perform as expected. In addition, statutes of limitations (meaning the amount of time an injured party has to file a lawsuit) are often different between the UCC and the common law. Under the UCC, the statute of limitation for contract actions is four years. Under states' common law, however, statutes of limitations vary and can be up to 15 years for written contract actions. The common law also differs from the UCC in how it treats differences between contract offer and acceptance terms. Under the UCC, depending on several factors, minor differences between offer and acceptance terms are either incorporated into the contract or are rejected, but a contract is nevertheless formed. Under the common law, however, even minor differences between offer and acceptance terms are usually deemed to prevent contract formation.

### Legal Aspects of Failed IT Relationships

IT relationships often fail when IT products or services do not have the functionality that customers expect. Often, poorly trained IT sales representatives make promises about functionality that their product cannot support. Other times, IT vendors are too hasty to affirm that their products will operate compatibly with their clients' existing systems. Failed IT implementations can be costly, frustrating, and time-consuming to resolve. Therefore, it is particularly important in IT vendor relationships to ensure at the outset that customer expectations will be met.

Companies seeking IT products and services should also be aware that IT contracts tend to be one-sided in favor of IT vendors. Standard IT contracts generally disclaim warranties, limit damages to repair or refund of purchase price, limit the timeframe in which customers can assert claims, and avoid making firm commitments about product capabilities or functionality. It is important for customers to understand that IT contracts are usually negotiable, however, particularly for larger implementations. Even "boilerplate" provisions (which often end up being very important) can be negotiated.

Courts are often sympathetic to customers in IT disputes—possibly because the consequences of failed IT implementations are so catastrophic. In *SER Solutions, Inc. v. Masco Corporation*,[111] for instance, a faucet manufacturer entered into a contract with an IT vendor for customized IT business software. The IT vendor verbally represented that its products would meet the customer's needs, but as the project went on, the IT vendor missed implementation dates and could not make its software coordinate with the customer's existing systems. Although the parties' contract included no performance guarantees, the court held that a clause in the contract stating that the IT vendor's software would interface "correctly" with the customer's system was a binding promise that the new software would perform the functions that the customer needed.

Similarly, in *Hodell-Natco Industries, Inc. v. SAP America, Inc.*,[112] an IT vendor stated in its marketing materials that its product would provide "robust and fully integrated" financial and sales software. Although the IT vendor and its customer, a fastener and chain wholesaler, finalized and signed an agreement that superseded all prior representations, the court held that the customer could nevertheless assert claims against the IT vendor for fraud, fraudulent inducement, and negligent misrepresentation based on the IT vendor's failure to live up to the representations it made in its pre-contract marketing materials.

In *BHC Development, L.C. v. Bally Gaming, Inc.*,[113] the court found a way around the general rule that contract damages limitations provisions are enforceable, and allowed additional damages against an IT vendor. In this case, a casino contracted with a software developer for business software. Although the parties' contract limited damages to recovery of the customer's purchase price, the court held that the damages limitation clause in the contract did not apply to the customer's negligent misrepresentation claim because the claim was based on representations made before the parties entered into their contract. These decisions should cause IT vendors to exercise caution in making representations they cannot fulfill.

---

111    103 Fed. Appx. 483 (4ᵗʰ Cir. Jul. 1, 2004).
112    2010 U.S. Dist. LEXIS 143144 (N.D. Ohio Sept. 2, 2010).
113    2014 U.S. Dist. LEXIS 64124 (D. Kan. May 9, 2014).

## *IT Data as Evidence*

Although poorly implemented IT projects can have catastrophic effects and can precipitate legal disputes, effective IT can meaningfully aid companies' supply chain relationships. In the ordinary course of business, supply chain partners routinely rely on data contained in their own and their partners' IT systems to clarify actions that are needed, evaluate success, and coordinate their activities going forward. Data provided by IT systems is generally considered to be objective and fair.

Having accurate data is also important if a supply chain dispute results in litigation. Under most countries' contract law, damages must be proven with sufficient certainty to be recoverable. The way commercial damages are often proven is through data maintained in one or both parties' IT systems. Having an accurate understanding of damages is also essential for negotiating settlements in supply chain disputes.

IT data is often used to negotiate pricing with supply chain partners. Generally, most supply chain contracts set product price at the outset of the supply chain relationship, but many long-term contracts provide for periodic price readjustment during the contract as well. Price readjustments are common in natural resource contracts, such as for natural gas, coal, and metals, which often incorporate "price reopener" provisions. Whether pricing is set at the outset of the supply chain relationship, at readjustment periods, or both, supply chain partners must have an accurate understanding of their costs and profit expectations to effectively negotiate pricing. This is where IT data comes into play. With accurate IT data, supply chain partners can most accurately assess their historical costs, and can best project how these costs will develop in the future.

Understanding production costs and anticipated profit can be particularly challenging for supply chain contracts that involve highly engineered products. Highly engineered products involve many components and sub-components whose pricing may vary over time, uncertain labor hours for product assembly (which may include rework), and up-front product development costs. Ensuring that highly engineered products generate appropriate profits often requires complex cost calculations and comparisons with products made for other customers, both of which require reliable IT data. In our experience, highly engineered products are where pricing most often goes wrong, but are the most difficult to renegotiate. Indeed, for highly engineered products, buyers usually expect that production costs will decrease over time as suppliers achieve greater efficiencies in their manufacturing processes, or as technology improves. Therefore, buyers are likely to resist requests for price increases.

———

## Lessons Learned

To ensure accurate, robust, and functional IT systems, companies should:

- Employ competent outside IT consultants with relevant industry experience
- Follow a robust selection and implementation process for IT products
- Ensure that any new IT products coordinate with existing systems
- Insist on demonstrations to ensure that new IT can successfully perform the company's most unique business functions
- Understand that emerging trends, such as Big Data and the Internet of Things, can provide valuable information, but resist the urge to over-rely on these new trends at the expense of human expertise and communications with supply chain partners
- Negotiate all IT contract terms, including "boilerplate" terms like damages limitations
- Include a choice-of-law clause in all IT contracts, and particularly in international IT contracts

# CHAPTER 15

# Executive Oversight of the Supply Chain

## Overview

Over the past 25 years, the supply chain has earned a place in the C-suite. Today, companies understand that supply chain issues impact financial performance, stock value, and corporate reputation. Several significant trends, changes, and evolutions in the business ecosystem have made executive management's oversight of the supply chain much more important. Companies must now ensure that their supply chains around the globe operate ethically, or risk bad press and damage to their brands. In addition, corporate executives today are under 24/7 scrutiny. Executives are expected to know what is going on in their corporate operations at all levels all the time. Executive oversight of the supply chain has become a corporate reality.

Supply chain failures impact executive management more than ever before. A cautionary example comes from the alleged Toyota unintended-acceleration cases. Although thousands of consumers reported instances of unintended vehicle acceleration between 2000 and 2010, Toyota was charged with being slow to address the problem and slow to make changes to its products. A widely suspected cause was Toyota's rapid expansion of its supply chain operations in the years leading up to the problem and its executives' failure to properly monitor supplier quality. The press reported that Toyota's executives blamed one possible cause after the next, without completing a thorough root-cause analysis. The appearance of Toyota's CEO on the *Today* show, where he appeared defensive and confused, further hurt Toyota's brand image. Toyota's response to the unintended-acceleration cases is now used in business school classrooms as a case study of how not to handle a supplier-related media crisis.

### ERP Systems

Significant changes in business over the past two decades require companies to rethink their approach to managing supply chain issues at the executive and board level. Probably the most significant change in supply chain management has been the introduction of ERP (enterprise resource planning) software. (See Chapter 14: Information Technology.) As companies began deploying ERP systems in the 1990s, they created corporate-wide visibility, including visibility into cause-and-effect relationships within supply chains. This visibility has allowed companies to identify and solve problems more easily in a cost-effective manner. Corporate officers and board members are expected to ensure that their companies use state-of-the-art ERP technology, and that the information that ERP systems provide is understood and acted upon appropriately. ERP records can also become evidence if a company becomes involved in a supply chain dispute.

Because business functions in ERP systems are linked in a relational way, ERP systems can eliminate the corporate problem of the left hand not knowing what the right hand is doing. Gone are the silos and barriers between departments that plagued organizations in the past. Company functions form an interrelated ecosystem, and executive management is expected to have visibility into and control over the ecosystem.

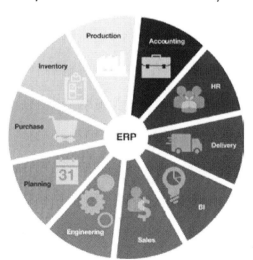

ERP systems are linked in a relational way to business processes. Cause-and-effect relationships become visible and more manageable.

Using the ERP technology available today, supply chain monitoring is not only possible, it is readily achievable. For example, if company executives want to identify where conflict minerals are used in the company's products, most ERP systems will allow executives to research all of the component parts on the company's bills of material and the suppliers associated with each part. This information should enable the company to identify the components that may contain conflict minerals, which the company can then further investigate. While C-suite executives will most likely have someone else do the research, executives' job is to ensure that the information exists and is obtainable through system queries and reports.

### Globalization Trends Impacting Executive Oversight

Globalization and the trend toward more open markets have made executive oversight of supply chains more difficult. In the 1980s and 1990s, importing and exporting became strategies as worldwide competition began to grow and as low-cost country manufacturing became a reality. Companies started to establish manufacturing sites in foreign countries, particularly China, to take advantage of low labor costs and fewer operating regulations. On the export side, as the WTO (World Trade Organization) accepted new member countries and as these new members opened their markets, manufacturers pushed to sell products globally. Consequently, executive managers today are expected to stay abreast of and be aware of potential global opportunities, especially those that can reduce production costs.

Improved communication technologies like email, Skype, and SMS text messaging have made it possible to cope with globalization, as has the explosion of information available on the Internet. Business processes have also adapted to globalization, as shown by the emergence of electronic banking, supplier-buyer portals, and electronically submitted customs clearance.

It is not just the global mega-companies of the Fortune 500 that are international today; many smaller and medium-sized businesses consider themselves to be global businesses. With globalization comes much more responsibility to control worldwide operations, however. Managers and executives must oversee their companies' global operations. Trade compliance, which was previously thought to be an administrative task, must also be properly managed at the executive level.

### *Corporate Social Responsibility (CSR)*

Corporate social responsibility (CSR) issues now require companies to monitor all aspects of their operations to ensure that they support global business norms and do no harm to local communities, consumers, or the environment. The vanguard of any CSR program is necessarily the board of directors and executive management.

CSR includes things like paying a living wage in every country, guarding against inhumane treatment of workers, and ensuring no forced labor or unpaid overtime, no child labor, no conflict minerals, and no uncontrolled pollution.

Some companies have CSR programs that extend to suppliers, subcontractors, and their sub-suppliers and sub-subcontractors. How far an organization takes CSR is a matter of company policy and strategy. Investors and consumers of big global brands can be demanding in this area and sometimes pressure companies to invest in broad, global CSR programs that include regular audits of global facilities and suppliers. Other companies may hire outside firms to manage their CSR initiatives.

Environmental programs are rapidly gaining visibility as we learn more about global warming. Investors and socially conscious customers now demand reporting on carbon footprint data and environmental protection measures, particularly as increased government regulation becomes likely. Even though some countries may not regulate as strictly as the United States, if a company has manufacturing sites in those countries, the company will still be subject to CSR demands. Executive management must plan for and manage CSR programs whether they are executed by internal staff or outsourced. More focus will be placed on these programs in the future, and customers and investors will be watching every move.

For instance, 2015 saw a rash of putative consumer class action lawsuits in California, alleging that manufacturers and retailers such as Costco and Nestlé obtained seafood products from the waters off the coasts of Thailand and Indonesia from fishing boats that used forced labor. Compliance officers around the world took note, and many companies increased their supply chain monitoring efforts as a result. This is a trend we expect to continue.

### Security Trends Impacting Executive Management

In the aftermath of 9/11, the US government turned its attention to global supply chain security to ensure that terrorists were not shipping "terror" in ocean containers, trucks, or aircraft. Supply chain security prior to 9/11 was minimal compared with afterward. Before 9/11, the US government maintained a "Denied Parties List" of several thousand people and companies that were not permitted to receive shipments, domestic or international. After 9/11 however, the list, now called the "Restricted Parties List" by the Department of Commerce and the "Blocked, Denied, Entity, and Debarred Persons List" by the Office of Foreign Assets Control (and other national security lists maintained by the US government) ballooned to more than a million entries. To ensure that they do not inadvertently deliver items to people or entities on these lists, most companies have implemented software to screen shipments and payments. Executives can be held accountable by the US government for violations.

In addition, executives now need to worry about cyber security breaches. No longer are just the computer "geeks and nerds" held accountable, but executives are also charged with budgeting enough money and hiring the right talent to keep company and customer information safe. We used to say that supply chain was all about moving goods around the world. Today, it is also about moving information, but that information is vulnerable to attack and must be protected.

### Megatrends

Executives are always watching for new trends that may change the corporate strategy or impact operations. Supply chain "megatrends" cause disruption and often change the way companies do business. Megatrends that are likely to affect operations must be understood by executive management, and a strategy must be put in place to address them. Failure to understand megatrends at the executive level can jeopardize companies' success.

**Lean Manufacturing:** One such megatrend is lean manufacturing. (See Chapter 8: Manufacturing.) "Lean" is the most recently popularized approach in a long history of optimization and quality-assurance manufacturing initiatives. Some predecessors to the lean movement include quality circles, total quality management (TQM), the Toyota Way, Deming's Quality Management, and Six Sigma. Generally, these methodologies break down processes to their fundamentals to remove cost, streamline manufacturing and business-related processes, and improve quality.

While some of these approaches have been with us for 50 years or more, they do not exist at all in some countries or are deployed in a very limited way. In addition, lean initiatives often fail due to improper controls, inadequate metrics to measure success, and lack of commitment. If you find yourself in the middle of a legal dispute because of a faulty or defective product, executive management may be asked to justify why they failed to monitor lean or other methodology implementations around the world. Many companies that outsourced manufacturing to China have been forced by investors and the public to "reshore" back to the United States and Europe amidst discoveries of failed or totally inefficient manufacturing operations.

**Reshoring:** The reshoring movement in America has incentivized companies to bring manufacturing back to the United States. Evaluating what can be built effectively in America has received enormous attention since the 2012 presidential elections, when both Democrat and Republican candidates blamed China for stealing American jobs. Recent surveys of consumers and research by the Reshoring Institute (www.ReshoringInstitute.org) indicate that consumers are willing to pay 10-15 percent more for goods made in America.

Reshoring is complicated, and requires the guiding hand of executive management, often with the help of experienced outside consultants. To maintain cost-competitiveness with offshore manufacturing, American manufacturing operations need innovation and automation, which executive management must underwrite. Extracting labor costs out of manufacturing, granting tax and other incentives for manufacturers in the United States, and building products that Americans actually want are some of the keys to reshoring successfully. Reshoring projects require careful monitoring by executives to align with corporate strategy and maintain reasonable cost control.

**Shifting Markets to Asia:** Today, most of our products and advertisements target North American and Western European consumers. But with the rise of the middle class across Asia—China in particular—the location of middle-class consumers is shifting. Making products that appeal to Asian consumers is key to tapping the largest markets in the world. This shift in consumer location should cause companies to reevaluate their supply chain footprints because, in many instances, it may be more efficient to source components from the same location that new consumer markets are found in. For example, instead of the minty-fresh toothpaste sold in America, a company may be more successful developing a green-tea-flavored brand for the Asian market. Neglecting major markets will leave a company behind its competition. Shareholders and others will hold executive management responsible for these failures.

### *The Importance of Metrics to Executive Management*

Most organizations have developed KPIs (key performance indicators) that allow executive management to track and understand their companies' performance. KPIs also track the performance of global supply chains, which have dozens of day-to-day KPIs. Lower-level monitoring of a broad spectrum of supply chain KPIs, which are typically grouped into activity, quality, and productivity metrics, can help executive management oversee the bigger picture. Companies should establish measurement bands (upper limits and lower limits) to compare their performance against. Anytime activity is outside of the acceptable bands, it is cause for investigative action. Executive management should always have access to high-level supply chain metrics.

Activity KPIs compare actual supply chain performance against expected or planned targets. The principal activity KPIs measure production, but beyond production, companies should also measure on-time order fulfillment and production turnaround time (e.g., the order date to the ship date). The faster a company can turn inventory, the faster it frees up working capital, and in turn, the higher its customer satisfaction ratings will be. Executive management ultimately is charged with ensuring that supply chain personnel investigate changes in activity KPIs as soon as they occur to interpret any higher-level issues that exist, especially those that may affect customer shipments or product quality.

Quality KPIs are the second group of supply chain metrics that executive management must monitor at a high level. Quality deterioration is almost invariably a forerunner for customer issues, excessive scrap and waste, and brand image issues. Underneath the high-level quality metrics that executive management monitors should be a host of individual metrics for each product and process that supply chain personnel oversee closely. Cascading metrics can be important when defending product liability lawsuits because they show that the company proactively managed product quality and reliability at every step in the design and manufacturing process.

Productivity KPIs form the third group of supply chain metrics that executive management must watch. Productivity metrics show how well a company uses its assets, which includes people and machines. Labor productivity is an important metric to watch after making operational changes, such as introducing new and more efficient machines. Labor productivity is also easy to compare with competitors and to other industries because information on company revenues and number of employees is typically publicly available. If a business is unproductive as compared to its peers, you can be sure analysts and investors will notice, and so may their lawyers.

Of course, executive management should also monitor costs across their supply chains. However, it is important to recognize that there is always a trade-off in focusing on costs alone. If a company is focused exclusively on driving out costs, quality and on-time deliveries may suffer. We include costs as an important productivity measure because when costs are analyzed alongside output and on-time performance figures, executive management gets a more complete picture of supply chain performance.

### Don't Overdo It

While it is important for executive management to monitor and be attuned to company performance metrics, it is also easy to get sidetracked and measure the wrong things, or have too many key metrics. The best-in-class and world-class companies generally have five to ten key daily metrics that their senior executives focus on. We recommend that the five to ten metrics that are most important to your company be reviewed daily, and revisited and recalibrated once or twice per year with the executive team. When business conditions and corporate goals change, so should the metrics.

The most critical metrics and KPIs will vary by industry. The key is to consistently measure what is important to your business.

You get what you measure.

### *How Executive Management Should Address Disruptions*

In our chapter on supply chain risk (Chapter 17), we discuss the many different types of business disruptions that can occur. Some disruptions such as tornadoes, earthquakes, fires, and snowstorms are not predictable and must be planned for as emergency responses. Other disruptions such as supplier bankruptcy and systems failures can be predicted, and alternative plans can be developed. It is the responsibility of corporate executives to assure that emergency plans are in place for unpredictable risks and that business alternatives are developed for risks that are predictable.

## Legal Overview

The legal consequence of executive management's failure to monitor the supply chain adequately is often shareholder litigation. Shareholder litigation alleging improper or inadequate management can be time-consuming and distracting, and a drain on company resources. This section will discuss what shareholder lawsuits entail and how to manage them.

### *Shareholder Derivative Lawsuits*

The first type of lawsuit that shareholders assert in response to perceived executive failures is shareholder derivative lawsuits. Shareholder derivative lawsuits are brought by one or more shareholders who purport to be acting on behalf of the corporation and are asserted against the corporation's officers and directors in their individual capacities. Shareholder derivative lawsuits generally allege that corporate officers and directors breached their fiduciary duties to the corporation by not adequately managing the corporation, or by managing it for their own gain. Shareholder derivative lawsuits seek to compel the defending officers and directors to reimburse the corporation for the corporation's damages. Any damages that are awarded in shareholder derivative lawsuits go to the corporation. They do not go to the shareholders who initiated the litigation. Shareholder attorneys may, however, recover attorneys' fees.

Officers and directors used to be given wide berth in managing companies, and were held to a lenient standard known as the "business judgment rule," which was often asserted as a defense in shareholder derivative lawsuits. But in 1985, this changed when the Delaware Supreme Court decided the landmark case of *Smith v. Van Gorkom*.[114] *Smith v. Van Gorkom* held for the first time that officers and directors could be liable for failing to adequately inform themselves about corporate affairs. As a result of *Smith v. Van Gorkom*, shareholder derivative lawsuits became much more common and have been used as a way to hold officers and directors responsible for supply chain failures.

### Shareholder Securities Class Actions
In response to the proliferation of shareholder derivative lawsuits following *Smith v. Van Gorkom*, Delaware amended its state law to allow corporations to more broadly indemnify officers and directors named as defendants in shareholder derivative lawsuits. Every other state soon followed Delaware's lead. (Delaware is the state of incorporation for the largest number of US companies. Consequently, Delaware is often a national leader in corporate governance issues.) The effect was that derivative lawsuits against a company's officers or directors were ultimately paid by the corporation. As a consequence, a second type of shareholder litigation against officers and directors emerged—securities class actions.

In securities class actions, shareholders allege that a corporation's officers and directors violated federal securities law by making false or misleading statements about the corporation to the investing public, or that the company's officers and directors failed to disclose material information about the corporation to the investing public when they had a duty to do so. To prevail, plaintiffs must prove "scienter," meaning that the officers and directors acted with intent to deceive or with reckless disregard that they were defrauding the market.

Called "10b-5" suits, securities class actions are generally asserted pursuant to Section 10b-5 of the US Securities Exchange Act of 1934. These

---

114    488 A.2d 858 (Del. 1985).

lawsuits are brought as class actions on behalf of all of the company's shareholders because fraud on the market affects the value of all shares. In contrast to derivative litigation, any recovery by shareholders in securities class actions is the plaintiffs' to keep. To curb the growth of securities class actions, Congress enacted the Private Securities Litigation Reform Act of 1995, which implemented additional pleading requirements, limited discovery, and imposed rules on who could serve as class representatives. But securities class actions are still popular—and lucrative.

Supply chain problems and supplier disputes can lead to securities class actions just as they can to shareholder derivative lawsuits. Securities fraud allegations can also lead to criminal and civil investigation by the Securities Exchange Commission and the Department of Justice.

### Simultaneous Shareholder Lawsuits

When shareholder lawsuits come, they often come in waves, which is why they can be so disruptive and expensive. Often, shareholder derivative lawsuits and securities class actions are brought simultaneously, forcing companies to defend on multiple fronts using multiple law firms and experts, often in multiple courts. As an example, shareholders filed almost one hundred separate securities class actions and 50 derivative lawsuits in the wake of the alleged Enron fraud.

Typically, if a securities class action has any promise of substantial recovery, not one but several lawsuits will be filed as plaintiffs' attorneys compete with each other to lead the class and recover the biggest fees. The more well-known and respected shareholder attorneys will generally represent the largest shareholders, which are often institutional investors. Other shareholder attorneys will file copycat actions on behalf of smaller shareholders, sometimes in the same court but sometimes elsewhere.

In addition, securities class actions have not completely replaced derivative lawsuits. Plaintiffs' attorneys who lose the race to lead a securities class action sometimes will file a derivative lawsuit based on the same facts, as in Enron. Derivative cases typically generate lower legal fees, but for many shareholder lawyers, it is still worth it. Often, corporations will insist on settling all shareholder actions at once, so the derivative cases will share in the recovery with the securities class actions.

### *Supply Chain Shareholder Litigation against the Hershey Company*

In November 2012, the Louisiana Municipal Police Employees' Retirement System, an institutional shareholder, initiated a books and records lawsuit in Delaware Chancery Court against the Hershey Company. The lawsuit sought access to Hershey corporate records that allegedly would prove that Hershey's executive management knew that Hershey's cocoa suppliers in West Africa used illegal child labor to harvest cacao. (Books and records lawsuits do not directly allege corporate mismanagement, but shareholders file them to get access to corporate records that later become the basis for mismanagement lawsuits against executive management.)

In August 2013, the special master assigned to the Hershey case recommended that the plaintiff's complaint be dismissed, stating that it was not based on credible evidence of wrongdoing. In March 2014, however, the Delaware Chancery Court overruled the special master's recommendation, holding that the plaintiff stated a claim sufficient to allow the books and records lawsuit to go forward, bringing the case one step closer to becoming full-scale shareholder litigation.

### *Supply Chain Shareholder Litigation against Apple*

Before the iPhone, iPad, and iPod, Apple's main products were personal computers. During the Christmas season of 1995, Apple planned to launch a new line of PowerMacs, prompted by record-breaking consumer demand. Unfortunately, however, Apple's forecasts were catastrophically low, and its supply chain was not able to react in time, resulting in lost sales and profits to the company.

Shareholder actions quickly followed and were litigated for years. The company fired its then-CEO Michael Spindler and after another failed CEO, recalled Steve Jobs to the top job. But the damage was done. Apple's PC market position never fully recovered, and Apple floundered until it introduced the iPod in 2001.

### *Avoiding Shareholder Lawsuits Based on Supply Chain Issues*

Making supply chain management and oversight a priority at the executive management level goes a long way toward avoiding costly and distracting shareholder litigation. In providing appropriate supply chain oversight, companies should take a number of steps.

First, it is helpful if at least one member of the board or executive management team has supply chain experience. Indeed, companies with complex supply chains are increasingly seeking out operational experts to provide experienced and qualified board-level oversight. Second, companies should ensure that officers and board members receive regular supply chain reports that discuss in detail any major supply chain issues the company is facing. Third, it is also important to ensure a high level of coordination and communication between the corporate supply chain and finance functions. What shareholders need to see is that executive management is providing appropriate and competent oversight of the supply chain area, including the trends and megatrends that we discussed in the first part of this chapter.

———

## Lessons Learned

To ensure that executive management approximately discharges its fiduciary duties, and to safeguard companies from costly and time-consuming shareholder lawsuits relating to supply chain issues, companies should:

- Facilitate the hiring of competent and highly trained supply chain professionals
- Ensure executive management oversight of supply chain megatrends, such as ERP systems, globalization, CSR issues, data security, lean manufacturing, and reshoring initiatives
- Provide executive management with access to meaningful and appropriate supply chain performance metrics
- Avoid excessive focus on cost-cutting
- Look for board members with supply chain expertise

# CHAPTER 16

# CORPORATE SOCIAL RESPONSIBILITY AND THE SUPPLY CHAIN

## Overview

In Chapter 15 on executive oversight of the supply chain, we discussed the role of executive management in monitoring supply chain performance. One supply chain area that requires particular executive and corporate attention is corporate social responsibility (CSR) issues. CSR issues can, and often do, result in supply chain disputes. And probably more than any other supply chain topic, failing to manage CSR issues can expose companies to negative publicity. Furthermore, some CSR measures are mandated by law.

### *What Is Corporate Social Responsibility?*

Corporate social responsibility is the term used to describe the practices a corporation adopts to be a good global, community, and environmental citizen. CSR practices can be financial, like giving money to charitable organizations, or they can be operational, like adopting corporate practices that reduce the size of a company's carbon footprint. From a media perspective, CSR most often becomes an issue when something goes wrong, like when a company uses child labor, contributes to human rights abuses, or harms the environment.

Moreover, CSR monitoring is now literally everywhere. Due to the rise of social media, anyone can break a CSR story. In July 2014, Target stores' policy of allowing open gun carry went viral via Facebook, with social media users pledging not to shop at Target until it banned weapons in its stores.

After a few weeks of this, Target changed its ways. On the other hand, some companies, like Ben & Jerry's, The Body Shop, and Tom's Shoes, use CSR to their advantage, and have generated positive media attention through their CSR initiatives.

CSR pressures come from consumers, shareholders, and the public at large. Shareholder pressure happens both when shareholders engage in activism to encourage the companies in which they invest to take up socially responsible corporate practices, and when they choose which companies to invest in based on their corporate CSR records. While some shareholders push for CSR measures, however, other shareholders sometimes oppose CSR spending, arguing that corporate profits should be used solely to increase shareholder value. So CSR is an issue with both supporters and detractors.

Although CSR has its roots in the early Industrial Age, CSR became more prominent in the late twentieth century. Influenced by principles that first took root in the more idealistic EU as well as corporate disasters such as the Exxon Valdez oil spill, CSR has taken off in the US since the 1990s. Over the last five years, CSR has become recognized as a priority by nearly every US public company, and many privately held companies too. Younger consumers and voters have indicated that CSR principles are a priority for them, which has also influenced the rise of CSR in corporate culture.

### CSR and Global Supply Chains

CSR issues have begun to factor prominently in supply chains. Today, companies are not only held responsible for only their own CSR practices, but for ensuring that their suppliers are socially responsible as well. The American Bar Association has recently taken up this issue, and has disclosed that it plans to send letters to the chief executives at all Fortune 500 companies, demanding that they end human rights abuse in their supply chains.

A recent CSR issue that has received a lot of publicity is child labor in the chocolate industry. Cocoa, chocolate's main ingredient, comes principally from suppliers in West Africa. In the early 2000s, it was widely publicized that much of West Africa's cocoa was harvested by child laborers in dangerous and exploitative conditions. Many of the child laborers were believed to have been kidnapped and illegally trafficked as well. Indeed, Cargill and other American companies are currently involved in litigation brought by African workers who claim that they were kidnapped as children and forced to work at West African cocoa plantations that were suppliers to American companies.

Under public pressure, the chocolate industry has engaged in efforts in West Africa to end child labor. Many non-profit and human rights groups are spreading awareness about the companies that may buy cocoa harvested using child labor, and the media has reported on these efforts. As we discussed in the last chapter, these pressures have led to a shareholder suit for books and records against The Hershey Company, seeking evidence of child labor in Hershey's supply chain.

Another prominent CSR issue is supply chain "sustainability," or ensuring that a company's practices do not cause unnecessary pollution or deplete natural resources. Recent studies have found that supply chain sustainability is increasingly a concern among consumers and investors, and the push for sustainability has led to more environmentally friendly supply chain practices.[115] In addition, more companies than ever are conducting sustainability audits of their suppliers, particularly in the food and beverage industry. Corporate sustainability reports to investors have been another product of the sustainability drive. Larger companies have started hiring managers specifically to oversee supply chain sustainability practices.

IKEA has famously been out-front on its supply chain sustainability efforts, with its wooden pallet phase-out project (in favor of paper pallets) and its focus on creating transportation efficiencies. IKEA has learned how to market sustainability, touting the reduction of its carbon footprint in connection with its sustainability initiatives. Similarly, Best Buy has received positive media attention for its involvement with the Electronics Industry Citizenship Coalition and the Conflict Free Sourcing Initiative.

## Legal Overview

As a legal matter, CSR issues have advanced the most as a result of shareholder advocacy. In the United States, this has occurred through Security Exchange Commission (SEC) Rule 14a-8, which allows shareholders to submit proposals to be voted on at annual shareholder meetings. To be eligible for a shareholder

---

115    *See, e.g.,* "Key Sustainability Issues in the Electronics Industry: Sustainability Industry Report," The Supply Chain Resource Cooperative, June 18, 2012; "Improving Sustainable Supply Chain Efforts Among Retail Leaders," Retail Industry Leaders Association, 2011.

vote, shareholder proposals must affect all of a corporation's shares, and cannot relate merely to an individual grievance of the proposing shareholder. In addition, corporations may refuse a shareholder proposal if it relates to the corporation's "ordinary business operations," meaning tasks that "are so fundamental to management's ability to run a company on a day-to-day basis that they could not, as a practical matter, be subject to direct shareholder oversight."[116] However, the SEC has indicated that shareholder proposals that relate to ordinary business matters may not be excluded from a company's annual meeting materials if they also relate to significant social policy issues. If a company intends not to submit a shareholder proposal to a vote at the annual meeting, it will petition the SEC for a "no-action letter."

During the 1960s, corporations and the SEC granted broad discretion to corporate management, and interpreted the "ordinary business operations" exception to the SEC shareholder proposal rule expansively. This view began to change with the 1970 D.C. Circuit Court of Appeals decision, *Medical Committee for Human Rights v. SEC*.[117] In that case, a Dow Chemical Company shareholder submitted a proposal to stop Dow's sale of napalm, a chemical agent used in the Vietnam War. Arguing that the decision to sell a particular chemical was an issue of managerial discretion, Dow refused to include the proposal in its annual meeting materials. The SEC initially sided with Dow and issued Dow a no-action letter, but the shareholder appealed to the D.C. Circuit. The D.C. Circuit Court held that management's interest in running the day-to-day operations of the company did not trump the shareholder's right to petition other shareholders to change the corporation's actions.

Also in 1970, an activist group called the Project for Corporate Responsibility approached GM with nine CSR proposals for inclusion in GM's annual meeting materials. GM was initially resistant, and many of the proposals were voted down, but the movement attracted nationwide attention. Ultimately, GM adopted several of the CSR proposals, and the media attention surrounding the Project for Corporate Responsibility increased shareholder initiatives in the years that followed.

Distinguishing shareholder proposals that involve important social policy questions from those that involve ordinary corporate operations is not easy.

---

116   SEC Rule 14a-8(i)(7).

117   432 F.2d 659 (D.C. Cir. 1970).

Recently, in *Trinity Wall Street v. Wal-Mart Stores, Inc.*,[118] a federal court in Delaware held that a shareholder proposal that asked for a board of directors' resolution restricting gun sales at Walmart should have been included in the company's annual meeting materials. The court rejected the SEC's determination that the shareholder proposal infringed on Walmart's ordinary business discretion, and found that the proposal raised a significant social policy issue and therefore could not be rejected. Walmart appealed the decision to the Third Circuit Court of Appeals.

Supply chain CSR issues are often raised through shareholder proposals. In February 2015, for example, the SEC rejected a request on behalf of Yum! Brands to exclude a shareholder proposal from Yum!'s annual meeting materials. The proposal in question asked Yum!'s board of directors to provide information concerning Yum!'s supply chain's deforestation and human rights practices.[119] In recent years, Nordstrom and other retailers have entertained shareholder proposals requesting information or the adoption of new policies concerning supplier environmental practices. The 2012 annual meeting season alone resulted in votes by shareholders of Apple, Dell, HP, and Intel—more than 50 percent of the personal computer market—to issue sustainability reports on environmental and social issues.

It is important to note, however, that even if a shareholder proposal is submitted at an annual meeting, is voted on, and wins, a corporation is not bound by the result of the shareholder vote. SEC Rule 14a-8 shareholder resolutions are advisory only, although they do provide a strong incentive for management to adjust their practices.

### *Using Supply Chain Contracts to Ensure Supply Chain CSR Practices*

Once a company has determined that it wants to encourage CSR practices in its supply chain, it must convince suppliers to cooperate. The best way to get suppliers to agree to follow CSR measures is to write them into supply chain contracts.

The first step for achieving CSR compliance in a company's supply chain is enacting a robust CSR supplier policy. CSR supplier policies have become

118  Case No. 14-405-LPS, Docket No. 65 (D. Del. Nov. 26, 2014).
119  SEC letter dated February 12, 2015, http://www.sec.gov/divisions/corpfin/cf-noaction/14a-8/2015/trilliumassets021215-14a8.pdf.

widespread, and are used to set forth what is expected of suppliers in terms of their CSR efforts. Of course, to implement an effective CSR supplier policy, companies need to establish what their own CSR priorities are. For a furniture manufacturer, it could be ensuring that supplier operations do not contribute to deforestation. For a clothing manufacturer, it could be ensuring that suppliers' textile workers receive fair wages and are protected from unsafe working conditions. For a high-tech company, it could be ensuring the proper management of chemicals and environmental waste.

Once a company has adopted a CSR supplier policy, the next step is to incorporate that policy into its supplier agreements. Buyers may be able to require first-tier suppliers to make their suppliers comply with buyers' CSR supplier policy as well. If this is possible, we recommend it as a best practice that will increase the impact of CSR efforts. Buyers should also ensure that they have the right to audit suppliers' CSR practices. Where CSR supply chain efforts often fail is in supplier compliance. Trust, but verify.

A sample CSR supplier contract clause is as follows:

**Compliance with Supplier Code of Conduct**

(1) Supplier represents and warrants that it does comply and will comply with Buyer's Supplier Code of Conduct, which may be amended from time to time, for as long as this Agreement shall be in effect. Supplier further represents and warrants that it will ensure compliance with Buyer's Supplier Code of Conduct from its major sub-suppliers [the best practice is to list them]. Should Supplier discover deviations or violations in its practices or in the practices of its major sub-suppliers from the Supplier Code of Conduct, Supplier shall report such violations in writing to Buyer's Head of Global Procurement within seven (7) days of discovery.

(2) Supplier shall, at the request of Buyer, allow unrestricted access to its corporate books and records and operations for the purpose of verifying Supplier's compliance with Buyer's Supplier Code of Conduct. Buyer may conduct this audit itself, or it may hire an independent third party or parties to conduct the audit, at Buyer's preference. Buyer must give Supplier seven (7) days' notice of any Supplier Code of Conduct audit.

Companies should also measure CSR successes, if at all possible, using quantifiable metrics. The example of IKEA translating its CSR measures into a reduction in its carbon footprint is a prime example of a company turning quantifiable CSR results into good marketing. Before marketing CSR successes, however, be sure to verify them, and verify them again. The loss of public trust that will follow a wrongful boast will likely be worse than not engaging in CSR practices at all. One recent result of companies' alleged failure to ensure compliance with supplier codes of conduct has been the recent spate of putative consumer class action lawsuits against companies like Costco and Whole Foods, which allege that those companies failed to enforce their supplier codes of conduct.

### CSR Laws Affecting Supply Chains

CSR issues are not only often matters of supply chain management and investor or consumer pressure, they are sometimes also legally mandated. Different countries have adopted a variety of CSR laws and regulations in recent years, and more CSR laws are being promulgated every day. CSR priorities vary widely among cultures. In the United States, CSR initiatives are often focused on sustainability and what we consider "human rights" issues. In China, on the other hand, where product safety laws are not as aggressive as they are in the United States or Europe, CSR is sometimes framed as simply making products that are safe for human use.

### US Conflict Minerals Law

Section 1502 of the Dodd-Frank Wall Street Reform and Consumer Protection Act, enacted in 2010, created the conflict minerals law that exists now in the United States.[120] Responding to what the US Congress interpreted as an "emergency humanitarian situation" in Central Africa, the purpose of the conflict minerals law was to identify companies whose products used four so-called "conflict minerals"—tin, tungsten, tantalite, and gold—mined in the war-torn region of eastern Congo. Conflict minerals became an international issue beginning in 1996, when armed rebels from Rwanda crossed

---

120    15 U.S.C. § 78a et seq.

the border into the Congo and perpetrated a campaign of unprecedented violence and destruction. These rebel groups took over many of the mines in eastern Congo, and funded their activities from those mines using forced labor. Conflict minerals are routinely used to make electronics, automotive parts, aerospace products, and jewelry. Conflict minerals can be found in less obvious places too, such as in shoes and composites.

The US conflict minerals law requires companies to state whether they use conflict minerals to make any of their products. Under the law, US public companies are required to assess and disclose every year whether their products use conflict minerals from rebel-controlled mines in their supply chains. By publicly identifying companies that use conflict minerals, Congress believed public pressure would cause these companies to seek alternative sources.

Compliance with the conflict minerals law requires unprecedented visibility into supply chains. A company whose products use any of the four minerals at issue must conduct a comprehensive supply chain investigation. First, it must perform a reasonable country of origin inquiry (RCOI) to determine whether the conflict minerals originated in the territory covered by the conflict minerals law. If so, the company must then conduct due diligence to determine whether the minerals are "Conflict Free," "Not Found to be Conflict Free," or "DRC Conflict Undeterminable."[121] If a company makes either of the latter two findings, it must document its due diligence in a conflict minerals report filed with the SEC.

Performing a conflict minerals investigation requires considerable cooperation from supply chain partners. Unfortunately, suppliers have any number of reasons not to want to comply. The process is cumbersome and expensive. Their supplier contracts may be confidential or proprietary. There may be a competitive or price advantage in not disclosing supplier information. And, of course, suppliers may know or suspect that their components use conflict minerals and that there will be negative business consequences once this becomes known.

Therefore, as with other CSR measures, it is best to compel suppliers' cooperation with conflict minerals laws through their supply chain contracts. Conflict minerals contract provisions should require suppliers to pledge not to use conflict minerals in their products. These contract provisions should

---

121    This designation is available only for the 2014-2015 reporting periods for most companies and from 2014-2017 for smaller companies.

also require suppliers to investigate their operations regularly to ensure that no conflict minerals are used. And the contract language should grant buyers the right to audit suppliers to ensure compliance with the law.

Sample contract language providing for conflict minerals visibility is as follows:

**Conflict Minerals**

(1) Supplier represents and warrants that it complies with the US conflict mineral legislation set forth in the Dodd-Frank Wall Street Reform and Consumer Protection Act (the "Conflict Minerals Law") and associated rulemaking. Supplier further represents and warrants that it will ensure continued compliance with the Conflict Minerals Law, as well as any laws governing the use of conflict minerals in any other countries in which it operates or does business.

(2) Supplier represents and warrants that it has conducted a full and unrestricted investigation of the suppliers whose components are used in the Buyer's Product to determine whether these components are made using conflict minerals. Supplier will conduct such an investigation of its suppliers at least annually and will maintain the books and records documenting its audits, which will be available to Buyer upon request.

(3) Supplier shall, at the request of Buyer, allow unrestricted access to its corporate books and records for the purpose of verifying compliance with the Conflict Minerals Law.

## *The California Transparency in Supply Chains Act of 2010*

In 2010, California enacted its Transparency in Supply Chains Act. This groundbreaking legislation requires companies doing business in California to report the efforts they are making to eliminate human trafficking and slavery in their supply chains in a "prominent statement" on their website homepages. Under the California Act, corporate disclosures must conspicuously describe: (1) the extent to which companies verify that human trafficking and slavery are not taking place in their supply chains, including whether verification is done by third parties; (2) whether companies conduct supplier compliance audits; (3) whether companies require their suppliers to certify that their products comply with all applicable laws regarding slavery and human trafficking; (4) whether companies maintain accountability standards for employees or contractors that fail to comply with anti-slavery policies; and (4) whether supply chain employees and management are provided training on slavery and human trafficking issues.

### United Kingdom Legislation

The UK has also enacted a number of important CSR measures. The UK's Social Value Act of 2013 requires public procurement authorities to take CSR issues "into account" when awarding government contracts for services, rather than awarding services contracts based on price alone. This law has required companies that provide services to the UK government to map their supply chains to determine compliance with desirable social programs.

In 2015, the UK enacted the Modern Slavery Act 2015, which requires companies with revenues of £36 million and greater to disclose whether they are making efforts to eliminate slavery in supply chains. Similar to the California Transparency in Supply Chains Act, companies must report their efforts on their websites. Although at the time of this writing, the UK government has yet to issue expected guidance as to what companies' disclosures should include, the law contains several suggested disclosures including (1) corporate structure information; (2) information concerning corporate polices in relation to slavery and human trafficking; (3) information concerning corporate due diligence regarding slavery and human trafficking; (4) information concerning corporate risks for slavery and human trafficking; (5) information concerning the effectiveness of anti-slavery and human trafficking policies; and (6) information concerning employee training on slavery and human trafficking. Disclosures must be approved by companies' board of directors and must be signed by at least one director.

### Data Privacy Laws

Data privacy laws have been enacted by a number of countries to ensure that personal information collected by companies is not improperly used and does not fall into the wrong hands. Data privacy legislation requires companies to consider social issues relating to individual privacy ahead of bottom-line profits. Data privacy laws require companies to be more careful in how they distribute and protect the personal information of customers, employees, and other individuals.

To date, over 80 countries have adopted data privacy laws that limit the information that companies can collect about individuals and that protect personal information that companies do collect from disclosure. The EU has adopted the most rigorous data privacy laws in the world. EU data privacy laws require notice to individuals when their data is collected, an explanation as to why the data was collected, and an opportunity to opt out of the collection. EU data protection laws also allow data collection only for specified and legitimate purposes. In addition, all personal data that is collected must be accurate, and individuals must be able to correct any information that is inaccurate. The EU data protection laws also require that data collected about individuals be kept secure. Violations of EU data protection laws entail penalties and fines.

Significantly, the EU forbids the transfer of personal data to countries without robust data protection laws, which includes the United States. This restriction presents issues for supply chains that have both EU and US members, since supply chain relationships often entail sharing customer data. Fortunately, US companies may gain access to EU data by using "safe harbor provisions," which allow US companies to access EU personal data if US companies can establish that their data protection measures are as strong as the EU legislation requires. To qualify as a safe harbor, a US company must adopt a privacy policy and certify that it will treat the data at issue as though it were still in the EU by following EU data privacy laws. The scope of the EU's data privacy laws is often startling to US companies, which may not at first realize that these laws apply to them if they do business with EU supply chain partners.

Mexico's data protection laws are similar to those adopted in the EU, with the exception that they do not prohibit cross-border data transfers in the same way. Under Mexican law, the company making a data transfer must ensure that the party receiving the data implements robust security measures and those individuals whose data is transferred have consented to the transfer.

Supply chain partners must be cognizant of whether data privacy concerns exist in their supply chain relationships and, if so, they must ensure appropriate protections so as to avoid disputes between them. To avoid liability, supply chain parties should include mutual representations in their supply chain contracts that each supply chain partner will comply with all applicable data protection laws.

———

### Lessons Learned

To ensure that supply chain partners follow CSR priorities, companies should:

- Establish robust and comprehensive CSR policies
- Apply those CSR policies to their suppliers, and, where possible, to sub-suppliers
- Ensure that all supply chain contracts include the right to audit suppliers to ensure CSR compliance
- Ensure compliance with all CSR laws in the jurisdiction in which the company is operating
- Allow shareholders and consumers a meaningful way to express CSR concerns and priorities

# CHAPTER 17

# SUPPLY CHAIN RISK

## Overview

Over the past 25 years, globalization, lean manufacturing, improved inventory control, and customer service have revolutionized supply chains. But as supply chains have become global and more tightly stretched, the consequences of supply chain failure are greater. Consequently, managing the risk of failure in supply chains has become a hot topic. With events like 9/11, the Japanese tsunami of 2011, the Icelandic volcano of 2014, and others, supply chain managers have taken a hard look at supply chain vulnerabilities and how to mitigate risk.

Supply chain risk is not limited to acts of terrorism or natural disasters. Risk comes in many forms, including customs compliance issues, supplier vulnerabilities, labor strikes, market downturns, and just about anything else you can think of. In 2014 and 2015, the big supply chain disruption story involved labor strikes at US West Coast ports, which left goods stranded within sight of shore and without any way to deliver them to their destinations. Supply chain executives may also associate supplier ethics and sustainability issues with risk management, as these issues may damage brand reputation.

There are new supply chain risk management software solutions that help supply chain professionals identify vulnerabilities and assess risk. This software allows supply chain personnel to identify weak links in their supply chains and to identify mitigating strategies and alternatives. The software can characterize the risk associated with individual suppliers by analyzing factors such as geographic location, experience, and past performance. The software can also assess risk for specific shipments or sometimes by product serial number.

Forward-thinking companies have created new roles for "supply chain risk managers" in their organizations whose responsibility it is to identify risks and develop ways to address them. These new risk management roles show that risk awareness has moved beyond insurance and has expanded to a holistic need to assess and manage risk in supply chains. Risk managers identify weak links and develop mitigation plans, including by rehearsing disaster scenarios and emergency responses.

### Effective Disaster Planning

A well-known Silicon Valley company conducts an annual "emergency day," in which the supply chain organization reacts to a fictitious emergency. These emergency exercises have allowed the company to identify and improve on its weaknesses. For example, the company discovered that although its employees were expected to react quickly to emergencies, they had no authority to spend money for emergency supplies or services. In addition, the company's call centers were jammed with customer calls, but no one had clear authority to address their concerns. Once these problems were exposed through the emergency-day exercises, the company could design new processes to improve its emergency responses.

Similarly, the September 11, 2001 terrorist attacks required emergency responders to save lives, but they also required Cisco, Lucent, and other communication companies to reestablish communications and networking equipment as quickly as possible. The communication companies that planned for disaster were able to reestablish communications in a matter of hours. Communication companies that did not plan for disaster struggled.

Disaster planning often requires companies to identify alternative suppliers in case primary suppliers fail. The 2011 Japanese tsunami, for instance, required companies that sourced from the affected area to find alternative suppliers quickly, but not all companies were prepared for this. Lexus was a notable loser. Lexus dealers across the United States were short of new car inventory within weeks of the tsunami because Lexus could not get production components from its Japanese suppliers for many weeks, and did not have alternative sourcing plans in place. Backlogs for new cars grew exponentially, resulting in lost revenue, brand impact, and poor customer experience.

Sometimes, disaster planning requires increased supplier monitoring and management before disaster strikes. The 2013 Rana Plaza factory fire in Bangladesh, for example, caused apparel brands to rethink how they oversee garment factories. The poor working conditions that contributed to the catastrophe made retailers realize that there was significant CSR (corporate social responsibility) and other public relations risks in how they dealt with these factories, even though the retailers did not own the factories. The fire was tragic and it forced the apparel industry to impose greater controls on suppliers to ensure humane working conditions.

The key to managing risk is to make global supply chains resilient by training people to handle emergencies, by developing alternative and creative approaches to supply chain disruptions, and by planning ahead. A natural disaster or other business crisis should not shut down a company or shut off revenue. When supply chain risks materialize, they should cause only a temporary adjustment while alternatives are found and primary supply chains are repaired and reestablished.

### Identifying Risks

In many areas, supply chain risks are known and can be anticipated. These include financial, operational, geographic, CSR, and regulatory/economic risks. For each known risk, a documented risk assessment plan can be helpful to identify mitigating strategies. Well-developed risk assessment plans identify the most likely risks, as well as two or more mitigation strategies. They provide a map for companies to follow in the event disaster strikes.

Creating a risk assessment plan includes the following actions:

- Identifying and documenting a company's vulnerabilities
- Developing two or more responses for each vulnerability identified, including immediate steps to strengthen the vulnerable area before disaster strikes and mid- to long-term planning in the event an identified risk materializes
- Implementing improvements to mitigate each risk and establishing contingency plans
- Reevaluating risk periodically (quarterly for high-risk issues and at least annually for other risks)

The principal categories of supply chain risks and the most common risk events in each category are identified in the chart below. An essential part of identifying and mitigating risk involves talking to employees about what they think the company's operational vulnerabilities are. In addition, experienced risk consultants can help ensure that mitigation strategies are up to industry standards.

## Categories of Supply Chain Risks

| Financial Impact | Operational | Geographic | Corporate Social Responsibility | Regulatory/ Economic |
|---|---|---|---|---|
| Supplier Financials | Supplier Contract Non-perform. | Natural Disasters | Poor Factory Conditions | Foreign Corrupt Practices Act |
| Supplier Fraud | Material Shortages/ Obsolescence | Concentration of suppliers in one region | Factory Labor Conditions and Law Violations | Banking Regulations |
| Supplier Ineptitude | | Geo-political Instability | | Environmental Regulations |
| IP Protection | Transportation Disruptions and Logistic Costs | | Environmental Health & Safety | |
| Market Demand or Supply Changes | IT System Failures | Cultural Values and Norms, Holidays | Product Quality | SOX Violations |
| | | | Product Safety | OSHA |
| | Labor Disputes | Health Issues- Pandemics | Ethics Violations | Export and Import Regulations |
| Inventory Theft | Goods Damaged In Transit | Trade Route Disruption | Counterfeits | |
| Counterfeit or Gray Market Goods | Production Delays | Insufficient Infrastructure | | Commodity Anti-trust |
| | | | | UCC Violations |

## *Classifying Risks: Controllable and Uncontrollable*

We classify risks into two camps: controllable and uncontrollable, although some situations include both. Generally, controllable risks can be identified and addressed through business planning and policies. For example, if a company is worried about its suppliers' financial viability, a financial review process for new suppliers and an annual review for existing suppliers can help mitigate that risk. Or, if IT system failure is a concern, IT improvements and redundancies can be used as a mitigating solution. For controllable risks, the key is to determine the severity and magnitude of each risk, and implement cost-appropriate measures to address them.

Collaborating with finance and other departments in establishing risk-mitigation programs is essential, but not always easy within an organization. Cross-functional solutions can be fraught with corporate politics and legacy processes. No one department may want to take responsibility, and executive pressure may be needed to come to workable solutions. In such cases, we conduct business-process reengineering workshops to address new ideas and requirements and to work across functional boundaries to find the best solutions.

Uncontrollable risks can occur anywhere in a supply chain and include such things as natural disasters, unplanned strikes, factory fires, and other events that give few, if any, indications in advance that they might happen. To mitigate the risk of uncontrollable events, supply chain professionals need to build emergency responses and capabilities that are resilient and flexible, and that can be enabled immediately. Resilient and flexible emergency responses are different from normal business processes in that emergency responses establish merely a framework for making decisions rather than specific protocols. A framework for an emergency response should include guidelines to establish the following tasks:

- Check on your people first. Is everyone accounted for? Are they safe? Do they need assistance? Companies often establish emergency communication plans in case the primary communication system goes down.
- Activate a command center and an emergency plan to manage the emergency response. (The plan for the command center is developed in advance and includes spending and decision authority for emergencies.)
- Determine who will have authority to assess the situation quickly, respond, and report to management. How will others communicate with them (email, phone, meetings)?
- Determine how customers will be affected and if/how they should be notified. How will customers contact you? How will you contact them?

- Coordinate with local, state, and federal government agencies as appropriate.
- Determine how quickly you can return to business by using alternative operations. Determine if you need to engage emergency partners such as contractors or temporary help.

We have developed a risk assessment model to help you identify risks and set priorities for addressing them. On the vertical axis, you should assign the financial-loss level associated with risks you might face, and on the horizontal axis, assess the probability of each of these risks materializing. This exercise helps to clarify your most pressing priorities, which will be found in the top right quadrant. Of course, the map will change depending on industry and location. For example, if your factory is located in America's "Tornado Alley," the risk of natural disaster will be more prominent than other types of risks.

## The Risk Assessment Model

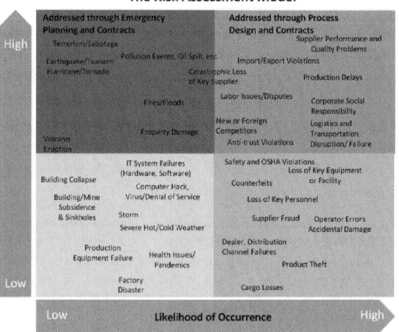

*Note: These quadrants and issues may vary by industry and geo-location.*

Once you evaluate your risk factors by quadrant, your priorities will become more evident. Most companies have limited resources and must prepare a prioritized roadmap for addressing risk, starting with the most urgent needs. Risks with the greatest chance of occurrence and the highest potential financial loss (in the upper right quadrant) should be addressed first. But risk management should not stop there. The best practice is to place day-to-day responsibility for lower-priority risks on your supply chain managers. A formal "supply chain risk management team," whether permanent or ad-hoc, can oversee risk mitigation efforts and provide guidance and feedback.

### *Lean Manufacturing, Outsourcing, and Other Process Risks*

In addition to the obvious categories, today's supply chain may also be infused with "process risk" from lean manufacturing and outsourcing. Lean manufacturing and outsourcing are designed to drive out costs and make organizations more productive and efficient. In streamlining operations, however, they also reduce inventory and place greater responsibility on suppliers. This creates risks that should be evaluated and addressed.

Lean manufacturing is the latest approach to an evolution of process simplification techniques developed over the past 50 years. These techniques are designed to improve process flows through streamlining, reducing inventory, and improving quality and efficiency. (See Chapter 8: Manufacturing.) Streamlined processes, however, can stress the supply chain almost to the breaking point. What is often left is a slimmed-down supply chain with little margin for error, few contingent inventories, and no redundancies. Financially and operationally, lean is a beautiful thing, but lean manufacturing can also expose a company to risk if any part of the supply chain breaks.

Outsourcing enables companies to delegate business tasks and processes to third parties that perform them more efficiently, leaving the delegating company free to focus on core competencies. Although outsourcing can be advantageous and cost-saving, it also introduces new risks. Outsourcing risks vary from the financial risk of associating with outsourcing service providers to physical disruptions that may affect these service providers. To avoid these risks, outsourcing contracts must be carefully drafted so that failure points and expected responses are identified and enumerated. Before deciding whether to outsource, consider the following:

- **The financial health of the outsourcing company:** Does the outsourcing company have the financial stability to deliver as promised? What is the outsourcing company's financial backing and history?
- **Cultural risks:** Are the differences in corporate cultures between you and the outsourcing company likely to create conflict or failure? How should regional cultures and norms be considered?
- **Political risks:** Is the outsourcing company in a region prone to political instability?
- **Natural risks**: Is the outsourcing company in a region prone to natural disasters?
- **Logistics risks:** Are shipping routes prone to delays and strikes? Will the country infrastructure (e.g., electricity, roads, and ports) cause disruptions?

There are certainly more risks to consider depending on the outsourcing evaluation and, ultimately, the contract you write for services. It is always a good idea to try to identify and address all of the potential risks before a contract is finalized.

### Risk Management Costs

When considering potential supply chain disruptions and alternatives, supply chain executives must also consider cost. Companies must find the proper balance between the cost of risk management versus the cost of likely disasters. How much is a company willing to pay to mitigate a specific risk? How much is too much? How do you know? These are difficult questions.

Mary Barra, the CEO of General Motors, struggled with these questions during her first year in the job. She found that in the past, certain trade-offs had been made between the cost of fixing GM's ignition switch problems and the cost associated with the potential accidents. Product recalls have huge ramifications and costs through the supply chain, and include costs for consumers. In addition to the re-manufacturing and logistics costs associated with recalling a product, brand reputation may be permanently damaged. And of course, the price may be astronomical if someone is injured or dies because risks materialize. (See Chapter 13: Recalls.) Mary Barra, like other CEOs, inherited the risk assessments and decisions of her predecessors and the associated costs.

Risk decisions are complicated and may require the assistance of a variety of professionals and legal staff to evaluate alternatives. In addition, executives must consider the total cost of risk management programs, including staff, travel to supplier sites, training, maintaining alternative networks, communications, legal fees, and so forth. When all of the costs are considered, best practices tend to focus on addressing the most urgent and highest risk needs (the top 20 percent), with a more pragmatic approach to additional risk management programs. These decisions should be carefully documented in case the company's actions need to be defended in the future.

### Failure Alert: Ignoring Early Risk Indicators

Risk exists in all kinds of processes and events.

In the 1990s, Emery Worldwide was one of the leading cargo airlines worldwide. Emery started in 1946 and was the first freight forwarder to receive a carrier certificate from the US government. For 40 years, Emery was the largest freight forwarder/integrated air carrier in the United States.

Hewlett-Packard (HP) at that time had a logistics organization that was responsible for moving products around the world. In doing so, HP engaged with many transportation carriers, including Emery. Rosemary Coates (author) was a regional logistics manager at HP and was called into a meeting with the head of HP Logistics and Emery. Emery executives explained that they were having financial difficulties and needed HP's freight traffic revenue over several additional routes to keep them operating. Because there was very little freight carrier competition in the market at the time, HP's executives felt it was important to help Emery stay in business, and as a result, gave Emery additional freight routes.

But Emery continued to lose money and started cutting corners on aircraft maintenance and repairs. In spite of HP's trust and support, information about Emery's maintenance issues was not shared with HP. Emery's service continued to deteriorate with grounded planes and poor performance that often left HP scrambling to reroute freight to other carriers. Finally, the FAA (Federal Aviation Administration) grounded all of Emery's planes on August 13, 2001, due to poor aircraft fleet maintenance. Emery officially ceased operating on December 5, 2001.

The lesson learned here is that risk takes many forms, and it is best not to ignore risks when they present themselves. Identifying controllable risks before engaging with a partner or supplier will help you to think about ways to mitigate potential loss before it happens. In this case, HP knew in advance there were significant financial risks at Emery and even received warning signs about failure of services over time. The trade-off between the risk of service failure and the loss of a service competitor in the marketplace should have been weighed at regular intervals, perhaps monthly.

In situations in which risks are staring you in the face, it is imperative that supply chain professionals take action to address and minimize these known risks. If a high-level business strategy requires a company to continue to work with a risky partner, this decision should be made consciously with knowledge of the potential consequences. The process of addressing risk creates opportunities to plan what to do when disaster strikes and to develop alternatives.

## Legal Overview

Disasters, catastrophes, and damage from risk provide fertile ground for supply chain disputes. Therefore, supply chain contracts should address what each supply chain partner's responsibilities are in the event disaster strikes. Supply chain contracts should require that critical suppliers engage in robust disaster planning, and that these supplier's own critical suppliers do the same. If disaster readiness is not ensured all the way down the supply chain, it is often not until disaster strikes that companies realize where their true vulnerabilities are.

### *Requiring Disaster Planning in Supply Chain Contracts*

There are ordinary suppliers, and then there are critical suppliers. Ordinary suppliers may be replaced without much trouble. They provide non-customized products in manageable quantities and generally do not have exclusive relationships with buyers. Critical suppliers are different. They are the ones which, if they go down, the end product cannot be made. To minimize the impact of disasters, companies must identify their critical suppliers, and should require that they engage in disaster planning through their supplier contracts with those critical suppliers. If critical suppliers themselves have key relationships with sub-suppliers without which the end product cannot be made, disaster-planning requirements should be "flowed down" to the end of the supply chain to minimize the likelihood of supply chain disruptions.

A model clause requiring a disaster plan is below:

### Disaster Planning

Supplier shall adopt and enact a Disaster Plan providing for weather, labor unrest, terrorism, state of war, and other contingencies. The Disaster Plan must ensure that adequate disaster protection is in place for any and all key sub-components purchased by Supplier for use in the Products purchased by Buyer. The Disaster Plan shall be reviewed and approved by Buyer prior to the start of production, and shall be audited by an independent third party specializing in disaster planning. Supplier must review its Disaster Plan at least annually to ensure its continued suitability.

### *"Force Majeure" Clauses*

Supply chain partners should also consider whether to excuse or delay the performance of one or both parties in case of a catastrophic event. This is typically accomplished through *force majeure* clauses, derived from the French term meaning "superior force." Essentially, a force majeure clause allows parties (usually suppliers, but it could be buyers as well) to excuse or delay performance in the event a specified risk materializes. Sometimes the force majeure events that excuse performance are weather disasters, but sometimes they extend to labor issues, political disruptions, and even sub-supplier nonperformance as well.

Not surprisingly, buyers generally do not like broad force majeure clauses that excuse supplier performance, and suppliers often want them. What is surprising, however, is that when force majeure clauses are included in supply chain contracts, they are often treated as mere boilerplate and are not the result of thoughtful examination of potential supply chain risks. It makes sense to apply thought and analysis to force majeure clauses, since disaster-related disputes can turn into high-stakes, high-dollar fights.

Drafting appropriately tailored force majeure clauses requires planning and forethought. The events that constitute force majeure events in a supply chain contract that excuse or delay performance can be broad and diverse.

There is no "standard" force majeure clause. Supply chain parties negotiating a force majeure clause should consider three issues: (1) what events excuse performance, (2) to what degree is performance excused, and (3) what communication is required with the other party.

**What Events Excuse Performance:** Force majeure events tend to fall into one of four categories: (a) weather catastrophes, (b) non-weather environmental catastrophes, (c) political/civil unrest, or (d) unforeseen commercial events. Supply chain partners may include items in any, all, or none of these categories. The best practice is to include as many specific force majeure events in the contract as the parties think might apply, followed by a catchall phrase such as "and other exceptional weather or climate-related events."

It is common to excuse or delay supply chain performance for weather and environmental catastrophes. It is less common to excuse or delay performance for political and civil disruptions. It is not common to excuse or delay performance for unexpected commercial events such as failed sub-suppliers because these risks are generally understood to be within a supplier's control. What is appropriate in each supply chain contract depends on the potential risks, the products being supplied, and other circumstances.

A list of specific force majeure events that could be included in a supply chain contract is as follows:

## Specific Force Majeure Events

| | |
|---|---|
| **Weather Catastrophes** | atmospheric disturbances, cyclones, draught, earthquakes, erosion, explosions, fire, flood, hurricanes, landslides, lightning, monsoons, storms, tempests, tidal waves, tornados, tsunamis, typhoons, volcanic eruptions |
| **Non-Weather Environmental Catastrophes** | asteroid hit, environmental contamination, epidemic, explosion, industrial disaster, nuclear disaster, pollution of air or water sources, radiation, radioactivity, UFOs |

| Political/Civil Disruptions | acts of enemies of the state, acts of foreign enemies, acts or threats of terrorism, arbitrary governmental action, armed conflict, civil disorder, civil war, confiscation, embargo, export/import restrictions, expropriation, failure of communications systems, failure of transportation, failure of utilities, hostilities, invasion, lockouts, material change in the applicable law or regulations, military force, nationalization, political insurrection, strikes, rebellion, revolt, revolution, riots, UFOs (again), union action, war |
|---|---|
| Unforeseen Commercial Events | accidents, currency fluctuation, failure or loss of facilities or equipment, failure of a supplier, loss of communications, loss of electrical supply, material change in contract price conditions, structural collapse, supply shortages, transportation failure or stoppages |

Finally, choosing the right "catchall phrase" at the end of a force majeure clause is also important. Supply chain force majeure clauses often use the phrases, "other acts of God," or "other events beyond the parties' control" to designate generically the types of events that excuse performance beyond those that are individually listed in the contract. The problem with these phrases is that they are ambiguous (what does "act of God" really mean?), and often generate more disputes than they resolve. We recommend a more precise catchall force majeure phrase, such as "… or any other weather, climate, or environmental events the supplier could not have avoided, prevented, or taken precautions to prevent, using best efforts."

**To What Degree Is Performance Excused:** Defining the extent to which a force majeure event excludes a supplier's performance amounts to choosing between delaying or completely excusing performance. Many parties choose a hybrid approach, allowing for performance to be delayed as long as necessary, with performance being totally excused if the disaster becomes so catastrophic as to render performance impossible. Sample force majeure language is below:

### Consequences of Force Majeure Event

… In the event a Force Majeure Event occurs, neither party shall be liable for any damages or losses for so long as the Force Majeure Event continues to prevent performance. After a Force Majeure Event ends, the parties must resume performance as soon as practicable, but in any event no longer than ninety (90) days following the end of the Force Majeure Event. If either party is unable to continue performance under this Agreement after the expiration of such ninety (90) day period, the parties shall endeavor to modify to their obligations under this Agreement to make performance possible notwithstanding the Force Majeure Event. If these efforts are not successful or the parties are unable to agree on modified obligations under this Agreement, this Agreement will be terminated and all further performance under this Agreement shall be excused.

**What Notice of Force Majeure Must Be Provided:** The final component of a force majeure clause specifies any communication that must be provided by a supplier claiming force majeure. In drafting this part of a force majeure clause, supply chain parties should take into account any possible communications difficulties they may have in the event of a disaster. An example is as follows:

### Force Majeure Notice

If either party believes it needs to delay, suspend, or terminate performance as a result of a Force Majeure Event, it shall as soon as possible after the Force Majeure Event becomes foreseeable, but in any event no later than seven (7) days after the Force Majeure Event commences, notify the other party in writing of the nature and anticipated duration of the Force Majeure Event. The party providing a notice of Force Majeure Event under this provision shall make regular updates to the other party no less frequently than one time per every twenty-four (24) hour period.

If the primary supplier is an exclusive provider, buyers may want to include a contract provision allowing the buyer to purchase goods from alternative suppliers in the event a force majeure event occurs.

### Force Majeure Clauses as Best Practices

Sometimes disaster strikes a supply chain, and there is no force majeure clause in a supply chain contract. What happens then? Although buyers may assume that without a force majeure clause, suppliers cannot excuse or delay performance, this is generally not the case.

For US supply chain contracts, UCC 2-615 states that unless the parties have agreed otherwise, a supplier's performance will be excused if it has been made "impracticable" by the "occurrence of a contingency the non-occurrence of which was a basic assumption on which the contract was made." Comment 4 to UCC 2-615 clarifies that "[i]ncreased cost alone does not excuse performance" absent special circumstances, "because that is exactly the type of business risk which business contracts made at fixed prices are intended to cover." Weather disasters or externally-caused factory disruptions, on the other hand, can excuse performance, unless supply chain partners provide otherwise. In *Raw Materials Inc. v. Manfred Forberich GmbH & Co.*, for instance, an Illinois court held that a railroad rail supplier could assert an impracticability defense to the buyer's contract action for failure to deliver products when a port that the products had to go through unexpectedly froze.[122]

Internationally, force majeure law varies widely. Under English law, performance must be "impossible," not merely impracticable, to be excused, absent a controlling force majeure contract clause. On the other hand, the CISG (which generally applies to international supply chain contracts unless the parties choose otherwise) states that a party is excused from performance if it encounters "an impediment beyond his control and that he could not reasonably be expected to have taken the impediment into account at the time of the conclusion of the contract or to have avoided or overcome it, or its consequences."[123] A contractual force majeure clause will override this provision as well.

---

122    2004 U.S. Dist. LEXIS 12510, 53 U.C.C. Rep. Serv.2d (Callaghan) 878 (N.D. Ill. July 7, 2004).
123    CISG, Art. 79(1).

### Case Study: Force Majeure Notice Provisions Are Not Technicalities

Sometimes supply chain partners believe that contract provisions requiring them to give notice to the other side concerning force majeure events are merely technicalities, and are lax about following them. This is a mistake, as the case of *Aquila, Inc. v. C. W. Mining*,[124] illustrates.

In the fall of 2003, coal mining company C.W. Mining and electrical utility Aquila entered into a contract in which C.W. Mining agreed to supply coal to Aquila. Shortly after the contract was signed, a labor dispute broke out at the coal mine. Simultaneously, the mine began to experience serious geological problems. Both labor issues and geological problems would have constituted grounds for excused performance under the contract's force majeure clause.

In December 2003, C.W. Mining notified Aquila that the labor dispute was a force majeure event that impacted its ability to make coal shipments, but the coal supplier did not inform the buyer of its geological problems. The geological problems worsened, and the federal Mine Safety and Health Administration shut down several of the supplier's mines. The coal supplier still did not notify its buyer about the geological issues, and in fact represented that the geological issues would soon be resolved.

In 2005, the coal supplier cancelled the contract, claiming force majeure as a result of the labor dispute, and the buyer filed suit. At trial, the court determined that the geological problems, and not the labor dispute, were the true cause of the supplier's inability to perform. The trial court further held that the coal supplier was not entitled to terminate the contract due to this force majeure because the supplier did not notify the buyer that the geological issues were a force majeure event, as the parties' contract required.

Although the supplier argued that the buyer had "actual knowledge" of the geological issues and therefore did not need formal notice, the court disagreed, holding that the buyer's mere awareness was "materially and consequentially different from notice that a party has a serious and potentially enduring problem qualifying as a force majeure event." To compensate the buyer for the increased price it had to pay other suppliers to get the coal it needed, the trial court awarded it $24 million in damages. The US Tenth Circuit Court of Appeals affirmed the judgment.

---

124    545 F.3d 1258 (10th Cir. 2008).

### *Contingent Business Interruption Insurance*

Another option for mitigating disaster-related damage is insurance. Standard commercial property insurance policies often insure direct disaster damage to the insured entity, but not financial damage caused by disasters impacting suppliers. However, many carriers offer contingent business interruption (CBI) coverage, which often does cover losses from at least some supplier business interruptions.

Not all CBI policies are the same, and chances are that off-the-shelf CBI policies will not provide the kind of protection that a company with a complex supply chain needs. CBI policies generally cover business interruptions by direct suppliers, but not indirect suppliers. CBI policies also often cover only physical damage, but not other business interruption losses. For instance, damage caused by flood at a supplier's operations would be covered, but damages caused by a supplier's loss of electricity would not be covered if there are no physical damages to the supplier's products.

CBI policies can be negotiated, however. Comprehensive coverage will usually require a company to examine its supply chain from end to end to locate all of the risks associated with critical components and sub-components. This may be an exercise worth doing, particularly since scientists warn that with climate change, we can expect more frequent natural disasters in the future.

---

### Lessons Learned:

To manage risk in supply chain relationships, supply chain partners should:

- Rehearse emergencies to find supply chain weak points, and empower employees to address problems that arise
- Conduct an honest and thorough assessment to identify the biggest risks, assign responsibility for addressing them, and adopt measures to mitigate unacceptable risks; reevaluate regularly
- Direct the greatest resources to the top 20 percent most significant risks, and address other risks pragmatically
- Pay attention to the potential consequences of working with risky supply chain partners

- Include clauses in supplier contracts that require key suppliers to have disaster plans in place
- Decide when and under what circumstances disaster will excuse or delay contract performance

# CHAPTER 18

# CHANGING THE SUPPLY CHAIN AGREEMENT

## Overview

As every program and supply chain manager knows, properly negotiated and well-administered supply chain agreements are not always perfectly suited to the entire duration of a supply chain relationship. When business conditions change, it may be necessary to revise the supply chain agreement to reflect evolving requirements, technologies, capabilities, and supply and demand. Sometimes, supply chain partners are able to work through this process seamlessly. However, sometimes the process of amending supply chain agreements becomes contentious or drawn out. And sometimes, supply chain partners make changes to their agreement informally—"on the factory floor"—without memorializing those changes in their contracts.

What many supply chain partners do not know is that informal conversations and even non-verbal conduct can modify the terms of supply chain agreements. Even if a supply chain contract says that it cannot be modified orally, courts routinely disregard these provisions. In fact, despite lawyers' best efforts, in the United States, there is no airtight contract language that will prevent inadvertent supply chain contract modifications.

### *When Supply Chain Contract Modifications Arise*

Typically, supply chain contract modifications occur in one of three settings. The first is a commercial setting in which one of the supply chain partners requests an adjustment to the contract price, a delivery date, or another commercial term. These proposed modifications generally go through the purchasing or procurement departments and are typically understood and treated by both parties as formal contract modifications. The supply chain parties either agree to modify the contract or they do not, and business continues.

The second setting in which contract modifications arise involves technical, engineering, or design changes that occur during product development or production. These changes can be precipitated by product integration issues or testing, or they can arise simply as a result of the normal product development process. Technical changes are often documented through specification deviations or formal engineering documents such as engineering change orders. In highly regulated industries like automotive and aerospace, engineering changes may need to be approved by a regulating body, such as NHTSA or the FDA. However, some technical or engineering changes occur less formally. Sometimes supply chain partners agree to engineering changes verbally, via email, or in some other informal fashion. Sometimes modifications are discussed or debated without resolution, but one or both parties will act as though the change was approved. Sometimes one supply chain partner announces a technical modification, but the other party fails to respond. Informal, unconfirmed modifications are fertile ground for supply chain disputes and are not a best practice.

The third setting in which supply chain contract modifications occur is covertly, when one supply chain partner has stopped following the contract, but the other supply chain partner fails to enforce its rights. Sometimes suppliers do not comply with warranty, quality, testing, or performance requirements, and the buyer fails to object. Sometimes delivery dates slip, and the buyer tolerates late shipments. Scenarios like these result in supply chain disputes if the party who once looked the other way later tries to enforce the contract as written, which is also not a best practice.

### How to Negotiate Supply Chain Contract Modifications

If you find yourself in a situation where your company needs to negotiate a change to a supply chain contract, it is generally best to confront and respond to the issue directly. Simply ignoring the problem, procrastinating, or hoping that it will go away will often just make matters worse.

Photos courtesy Tex Texin

The first step is to get your ducks in a row internally. Assemble the key stakeholders in your company—engineering, procurement, project management, finance, and perhaps others—and work through a clear definition of the issue. It is generally best not to let any single constituency within your company determine the strategy without the input of others. For example, Engineering might have the best grasp on what the problem is if it is technical in nature, but the engineering staff may not be aware of the commercial ramifications of a potential fix. More perspectives are better than one. Determine the two or three best solutions, and consider what your company is willing to concede to get the necessary changes implemented. Not all

239

contract modifications need to be paid for with money. Sometimes adjusting non-monetary contract provisions will satisfy a supply chain partner. Look expansively at each supply chain partner's contract obligations and interests when determining strategy.

The second step is to take the modification proposal to your supply chain partner. Like your internal discussions, your discussions with your supply chain partner should include all of your partner's key stakeholders, including personnel who are authorized to make a decision about the proposed contract modification. When you are making your pitch, understand where you stand in the commercial relationship. If you are working together on a program that is generally successful and valuable to your supply chain partner, your partner will be more prepared to hear what you have to say. If your performance has not always been good, or if the program you are working on has not been successful or is not a priority for your supply chain partner, the path will be more difficult.

Be prepared when you go into these discussions with your supply chain partner. All too often, companies do not adequately prepare for contract modification negotiations. Do your homework to understand the challenges your supply chain partner faces. What are its industry issues? Does your supply chain partner have a corporate parent or investors who are looking critically at its programs or have corporate priorities that may be at odds with your proposed changes? How profitable is your program in your supply chain partner's portfolio? What questions and objections is your partner likely to have regarding your proposed change? These are overarching issues that you need to understand as you approach your supply chain partner to negotiate a contract change.

Be sure to signal to your supply chain partner that you take the negotiations and the proposed contract changes seriously. If you are corresponding in writing, try to do so by formal letter (even if as a PDF attachment to an email), rather than simply by email. Or if you do correspond via email, at least be sure to do so in a formal manner. Avoid misspellings, incomplete sentences, and typos that have become commonplace in email communications. If you visit in person (generally a good approach), have a polished presentation fortified with facts and a solid plan for moving forward.

If you need to be critical about something that your supply chain partner has done, come to the negotiation armed with the technical, testing, and other data that will show why your contract change is justified. It is best to discuss the issue in a factual, non-accusatory way. If a proposed modification is necessary because of your company's mistake, be honest. Trying to "spin the facts" will generate mistrust and will harm the long-term relationship. If you are negotiating in a foreign country, be aware of cultural considerations. For example, you may need to give negative feedback in a very indirect way in some cultures so as not to offend the receiver. Get coaching from consultants and HR specialists who can help you prepare for cultural differences and foreign business approaches.

The third step in negotiating a supply chain contract modification is memorializing any changes that are agreed on in writing. Even if your supply chain contract does not require modifications to be in writing (although it should), having a formal, written record of the parties' agreement is always the best practice and helps avoid costly and distracting supply chain disputes. Memorializing contract changes in writing also ensures that the parties truly agree on a contract change. Even if you think you have come to an agreement with your supply chain partner orally, the devil is often in the details, and until all of the particulars of the contract modification are discussed, you can never really be sure that you and your supply chain partner are on the same page. Also be clear about when a contract change will go into effect. Ensure that both supply chain partners have the time they need to prepare for the change.

The final step in negotiating a supply chain contract change is to make sure a signed copy of the contract modification circulates to all personnel involved in the program, and is filed in the program's central contract file. Do not assume that all employees will find out about a contract change on their own. Advise all impacted personnel on the planned implementation date as well.

### *Periodic Renegotiation of Supply Chain Agreements*

Some supply chain agreements require periodic renegotiation as a matter of course. Some long-term agreements, for example, contemplate occasional price renegotiations to adjust for changes in the market or commercial landscape. Supply chain contracts with distinct development and production phases will often leave terms in the production phase open, to be negotiated pending the completion of product development. (See Chapter 3: New Product Design and Development Contracts.)

It is also common for supply chain contracts to be renewable at the option of the parties after an initial term. These term contracts provide an opportunity at regular intervals for the parties to address provisions that they do not like or are no longer relevant. Ordinary course renegotiations should be approached in the same formal and serious ways as other contract modifications.

### Case Study: Unexpected Benefits of an Airline Bankruptcy

A large airline declared bankruptcy after many years of struggling with heavy debt and mounting operating costs. Once the bankruptcy was filed, the airline's purchasing department was charged with renegotiating thousands of PO (purchase order) contracts with suppliers. The airline's overall goal was to get 20-percent price reductions from every supplier, and over a one-year period, the airline was relatively successful. In addition to price reductions, the airline traded 45-day payment terms for longer-term contracts.

The airline's suppliers didn't have much choice in these renegotiations. If suppliers resisted the forced price concessions, their contracts would not be renewed or would be rejected in bankruptcy. However, many of the suppliers traded price concessions for other things of value that they wanted, such as contract extensions, co-development projects, and free travel on the airline. The lesson is that contract modifications, even if compelled, can be opportunities for both supply chain partners to expand the value of the relationship.

## Legal Overview

Modifications to US supply chain contracts are governed by UCC 2-209, which contains some of the most difficult to understand provisions in the UCC. UCC 2-209 applies to modifications, rescission, and waivers of contract. One difficulty with UCC 2-209 is that it appears to support the enforcement of so-called "no oral modification clauses," which state that all contract modifications must be in writing to be enforceable. But on the other hand, UCC 2-209 dictates that, at least in some circumstances, contract terms can be waived or modified verbally or by conduct, even if the contract has a no oral modification clause. A second difficulty with UCC 2-209 is that it dictates that at least some contract modifications must be in writing to satisfy the UCC's statute of frauds (the UCC provision that requires contracts over $500 to be in writing to be enforceable). However, UCC 2-209 is not clear as to which contract modifications require such a writing.

In short, the law governing supply chain modifications in the United States is uncertain. Therefore, supply chain partners need to police their contract rights and any contemplated contract modifications vigorously to avoid uncertainty, controversy, and disputes.

### Inadvertent Waiver in the United States

It has become commonplace for supply chain partners to include "no oral modification clauses" in supply chain agreements to prevent inadvertent modifications or waivers of contract rights. An example of a typical no oral modification clause is below:

#### No Oral Modification or Waiver

This Agreement may not be modified, waived, or rescinded other than by a writing executed by both parties. No verbal communication, representation, conduct, course of performance, course of dealing, usage of trade, or purported waiver or estoppel shall modify or alter the terms of this Agreement.

At first blush, UCC 2-209 appears to affirm the enforceability of no oral modification clauses, since UCC 2-209(2) states, "A signed agreement which excludes modification or rescission except by a signed writing cannot be otherwise modified or rescinded"—a rule that seems very sensible to us. However, the force and clarity of UCC 2-209(2) is undermined almost completely by another subsection of UCC 2-209: Subsection (4). UCC 2-209(4) provides that even if an "attempt at modification or rescission" is not in writing, it can nevertheless "operate as a waiver" of contract rights, thus modifying the contract, even if the contract has a no oral modification clause.

The juxtaposition of UCC 2-209(2) and 2-209(4) has bedeviled supply chain executives and attorneys since its creation. Courts are not consistent in how they reconcile the enforceability of no oral modification clauses under UCC 2-209(2) with the UCC 2-209(4) waiver exception. Some courts give more deference to no oral modification clauses. Other courts are more willing to find contract waivers.

*Exxon Corporation v. Crosby-Mississippi Resources, Ltd.*[125] provides an example of a court more willing to find that contract rights were waived by informal conduct. *Exxon* involved a natural gas supply contract. After the contract was executed, the buyer asked the supplier to amend the contract to lower the price, but the supplier refused. However, over the life of the contract, the buyer consistently paid the supplier less than the contract price. The supplier accepted the payments, but placed a reservation of rights on the buyer's checks, stating that the supplier's acceptance did not "waive any rights to correct monies due payee." The contract also contained a no oral modification clause.

Even though the supplier refused to agree to the requested modification, the court held that by accepting the buyer's payments at less than the full contract price, the supplier waived its right to full payment. The court also held that enforcing the original contract price would unfairly harm the buyer—if the buyer had known it had to pay in full, it could have gone to other suppliers.

Similarly, in *Weyerhaeuser Company, Inc. v. Accurate Recycling Corporation,*[126] a recycling company entered into two written contracts with the buyer to sell recycled materials for use in two of the buyer's plants—one contract for each plant. When the buyer closed one of the plants, it stopped making purchases under the associated contract, and the supplier sued. Both contracts contained no oral modification clauses. Even so, the court held that under UCC 2-209(4), the supplier waived its right to enforce the contract that the buyer abandoned. Although the supplier promptly objected to the buyer's failure to make purchases, and although the supplier sued to enforce the contract, the court held that the supplier's attempts to find a substitute buyer waived its contract rights.

These decisions underscore that no supply chain contract is safe from inadvertent modification.

Of course, many courts do enforce no oral modification clauses and are reluctant to find that contract rights have been waived. In *The Marley Cooling Tower Company v. Caldwell Energy & Environmental, Inc.,*[127] for example, a cooling system buyer argued that the supplier waived a contract provision barring consequential damages by informally agreeing to pay a late charge (a consequential damages item). Although the supplier's project manager orally

---

125    40 F.3d 1474, 25 U.C.C. Rep. Serv. 2d (Callaghan) 1103 (5th Cir. 1995).
126    2007 U.S. Dist. LEXIS 86149 (W.D. Wash. Nov. 21, 2007).
127    280 F.Supp.2d 651, 51 U.C.C. Rep. Serv. 2d (Callaghan) 376 (W.D. Ky. 2003).

agreed to accept the late charge and the supplier's vice president stated internally that he would authorize it, the supplier ultimately changed its position and refused to accept the penalty. The contract had a no oral modification clause. The court therefore held that the supplier's verbal statements did not waive the contract's bar on consequential damages. Many other cases are in accord.[128]

Not satisfied with picking one approach over the other, the US Seventh Circuit Court of Appeals has created a third path for reconciling UCC 2-209(2) and 2-209(4), holding that it is possible to waive a no oral modification clause, but only if the other party "reasonably relies" on the waiver. Writing for the court in *Wisconsin Knife Works v. National Metal Crafters*,[129] Judge Richard Posner acknowledged that UCC 2-209 "could be clearer; but the draftsmen were making a big break with the common law … and naturally failed to foresee all the ramifications of the break." The "path to reconciliation," the court held, was to require "reasonable reliance" on a purported contract waiver, "in part because it adds something in the way of credibility to the mere say-so" of the party claiming waiver.

Complicating the modification/waiver issue is the final subsection of UCC 2-209, subsection (5). UCC 2-209(5) states that a party that has waived a contract provision that has not yet been performed "may retract the waiver by reasonable notification," unless the other party has made "a material change of position in reliance on the waiver."[130] How a party is supposed to "retract" a contract waiver that it did not realize it made is, of course, unexplained.

Even though the law governing inadvertent contract modifications is unclear, we advise supply chain partners to include no oral modification clauses in their contracts. But because courts do not always honor no oral modification clauses, we also advise supply chain partners to enforce their contract rights strictly to avoid inadvertent waivers. If supply chain partners establish a practice of rigorously policing contract compliance, courts are more likely to enforce no oral modification clauses.

---

128  *See, e.g., TWB Distribution, LLC v. BBL, Inc.*, 2009 U.S. Dist. LEXIS 117467 (W.D. Ky. Dec. 17, 2009) (granting motion to dismiss against supplier claiming waiver of contract termination date pursuant to no oral modification clause); *ePresence, Inc. v. Evolve Software, Inc.*, 190 F.Supp. 2d 159, 47 U.C.C. Rep. Serv. 2d (Callaghan) 132 (D. Mass. 2002) (granting motion to dismiss against buyer claiming waiver of software contract pursuant to no oral modification clause).

129  781 F.2d 1280, 42 U.C.C. Rep. Serv. (Callaghan) 830 (7th Cir. 1986).

130  UCC § 2-209(5).

## Contract Modifications and the Statute of Frauds

The second difficult issue posed by UCC 2-209 is whether and when contract modifications must comply with the statute of frauds. The statute of frauds is the UCC provision that requires contracts over $500 to be memorialized in writing to be enforceable.[131] UCC 2-209(3) states, "The requirements of the statute of frauds ... must be satisfied if the contract as modified is within its provisions." It is not clear (1) whether 2-209(3) requires modifications to contracts that originally fell within the statute of frauds to be in writing, (2) whether it requires modifications that bring a contract into the statute of frauds to be in writing, or (3) whether it requires modifications that would by themselves be governed by the statute of frauds to be in writing. Courts are not consistent in their approach.

Therefore, to ensure compliance with the statute of frauds, supply chain partners have one more reason to memorialize all contract modifications in writing. Formally recording all contract modifications also ensures that supply chain partners reach agreement on all terms, provides a record when memories fade, and lessens the chance of supply chain disputes.

## International Law Governing Contract Modifications and the UCC

The CISG is similar to the UCC on contract modification and waiver of contract rights. Article 29(2) of the CISG states that if there is a no oral modification clause in a written contract, the contract "may not be otherwise modified or terminated." But the CISG also states that "a party may be precluded by his conduct from asserting" a no oral modification clause "to the extent that the other party has relied on that conduct."[132] In other words, under the CISG, no oral modification clauses can be waived if the other party reasonably relies on the waiving party's conduct. Recall that this is the same as the Seventh Circuit's approach to no oral modification clauses.

Unlike the UCC, the CISG does not contain a statute of frauds, so statute of frauds concerns are not present with international supply chain contract modifications. Nevertheless, we recommend that all modifications to international supply chain contracts be made in writing for the same reasons that apply to US supply chain contracts.

---

131   UCC § 2-201(1).

132   CISG Art. 29(2).

## *Ambiguous Conduct and Contract Waivers*

Anytime supply chain partners engage in behavior that could be construed as a contract modification or waiver, and anytime supply chain partners discuss a possible contract modification or waiver, the best practice is to create a clear written record memorializing what the parties ultimately agreed to do. Even if supply chain partners decide ultimately not to proceed with a proposed contract change, their decision should be memorialized in writing. Similarly, if one supply chain partner grants a one-time concession without intending any further waiver of its contract rights, it should insist that the other party sign an acknowledgment stating that no further contract modification or waiver has occurred. Formally recording the intent of supply chain partners will help prevent unintended waivers and supply chain disputes.

―――

## Lessons Learned

Supply chain partners who are contemplating modifying their supply chain contract should:

- Treat contract modifications seriously by fully analyzing the ramifications of a possible supply chain contract change and evaluating the best path forward
- Engage all key constituencies within the company in discussions about possible contract changes
- Memorialize all contract changes in writing and inform all personnel involved with the program about contract changes
- Include a no oral modification clause in all supply chain contracts, even though not all courts consistently enforce them
- Create a written record of all discussions concerning potential contract changes, including whether or not they were implemented

# CHAPTER 19

# Dispute Resolution Clauses in US Supply Chain Contracts

## Overview

The previous chapters of this book focused on managing the operational aspects of supply chain relationships to avoid supply chain disputes. This chapter focuses on how parties in a supply chain can use dispute resolution clauses in their supply chain agreements to structure and manage disputes that arise between them.

Because dispute resolution clauses in international supply chain contracts (those involving non-US entities) involve special considerations, they will be discussed separately in the next chapter. This chapter will discuss dispute resolution provisions in supply chain relationships in which both parties are US companies.

### *Understanding Dispute Resolution Clauses*

A dispute resolution clause is a contract provision that describes how the parties will resolve disputes that arise between them. Dispute resolution clauses are found in all kinds of contracts, not just supply chain contracts. They are sometimes referred to as "arbitration clauses" when arbitration rather than litigation is chosen as the means for resolving disputes. When litigation rather than arbitration is chosen, these clauses are sometimes referred to as "forum selection clauses." Arbitration clauses and forum selection clauses are two aspects of the broader subject of how parties agree to resolve disputes through dispute resolution clauses.

Dispute resolution clauses are common in supply chain contracts, although not universal. Even POs for commodity and small-volume purchases often include dispute resolution clauses. A dispute resolution clause typically describes (a) the mechanism through which disputes will be resolved (generally litigation or arbitration), (b) the geographic location in which legal proceedings will take place, and (c) the law that will apply. Sometimes, a dispute resolution clause also specifies (d) any steps the parties must take prior to initiating a dispute, typically a negotiating protocol or mediation; (e) confidentiality; (f) any limitation on damages that may be awarded; (g) any special rules governing the presentation of evidence or discovery; (h) time limits; (i) whether "expedited relief" is available in case of emergencies; and (j) whether appellate review is allowed.

A model dispute resolution clause that covers many of the issues identified above is as follows:

### Model Dispute Resolution Clause

Any controversy, claim, or dispute arising out of or relating to this Contract, its validity, its enforcement, or the breach thereof shall be settled by binding arbitration administered by the American Arbitration Association (AAA) in accordance with the Commercial Rules then in force. The arbitration shall be presided over by a sole arbitrator. The seat and place of the arbitration shall be New York, New York. The governing law will be the law of the State of New York without regard for conflict or choice of law principles. The parties shall consult and negotiate with each other in good faith in an attempt to reach a settlement for at least sixty (60) days prior to initiating arbitration. Neither party shall be liable to the other for any punitive, exemplary, special, indirect, incidental, or consequential damages, including damages for lost profits, whether based on contract, tort, or otherwise. Any dispute, negotiation, or arbitration occurring in connection with this provision shall be strictly confidential and cannot be disclosed to any third party unless required by law or governmental or statutory authority.

If a supply chain contract does not include a dispute resolution clause, either party may file a lawsuit in any court with jurisdiction, which will generally be the hometown courts where each supply chain partner operates. The responding party is then at the mercy of a legal process that has not been considered or agreed to and that may be extremely inconvenient. Litigation in unexpected or inconvenient locations is precisely what dispute resolution clauses are designed to avoid.

### How to Draft Dispute Resolution Clauses

Dispute resolution clauses are almost always negotiated before a dispute has arisen and are generally part of the original supply chain contract. The document that contains the dispute resolution clause could be a long-term agreement, PO, acknowledgment, or terms and conditions. Supply chain parties are free to negotiate dispute resolution clauses at any time during their relationship, but in practice it is almost impossible to negotiate a dispute resolution clause once a dispute has arisen. Usually, by that point, the relationship is too contentious.

Unfortunately, dispute resolution clauses tend to be "midnight provisions"—meaning that they are negotiated, or often simply inserted, into the contract as last-minute boilerplate. Often, parties give little thought to dispute resolution during negotiations because the focus tends to be on finalizing the business deal. This is understandable, but some thought should be given to the dispute resolution at the outset of the relationship. Also, a particular dispute resolution mechanism will not be equally well suited to all of a company's supply chain relationships. Therefore, the best practice is to consider dispute resolution clauses on a relationship-by-relationship basis. Smaller-dollar supply chain contracts or those that can easily be moved to another vendor may be able to be addressed in a more formulaic way. But long-term supply chain agreements or those with strategic importance merit individual assessment.

### Why Dispute Resolution Clauses Are Important

A well-considered dispute resolution clause can minimize the cost and contentiousness associated with supply chain disputes. A well-considered dispute resolution clause can also work strongly to the benefit of the party who has taken the time to consider dispute resolution if the other party has not. Finally, a well-considered dispute resolution clause can sometimes act as a strong deterrent to a party that is considering initiating a dispute. It is important, therefore, for supply chain and procurement professionals negotiating a supply chain contract to consult with in-house counsel concerning the terms of any dispute resolution provision that is used.

## Legal Overview

Despite often being regarded as boilerplate, dispute resolution clauses have many nuances that should be considered. The principal questions are usually whether the parties prefer litigation to arbitration and where any legal proceedings should take place. In the case of arbitration, additional relevant questions include which arbitration institution should administer the case, how many arbitrators should be used, and what law should govern.

### *Ensuring That the Dispute Resolution Clause Is Enforceable*

From both a business and a legal point of view, the worst nightmare involving a dispute resolution clause is litigation *about* the dispute resolution clause. Dispute resolution clauses are supposed to simplify and expedite disputes, not complicate them and make them more expensive. But a dispute resolution clause that is ambiguous or that cannot be implemented will complicate rather than simplify the dispute resolution process. The scholarly term for dispute resolution clauses that for one reason or another are unworkable is "pathological."

The first way a dispute resolution clause can be pathological is by failing to specify that it is the "exclusive" means of resolving disputes. Sometimes, this happens when a supply chain contract specifies that a particular dispute resolution mechanism is available, but does not make clear that it is mandatory. Contract language that states that supply chain partners agree to "submit to the jurisdiction" of a specified court, or that a specified court "shall have jurisdiction," is permissive and not mandatory and therefore should be avoided. If a permissive clause is used, the parties are still free to litigate disputes in any other forum with jurisdiction.

To be considered a "mandatory" dispute resolution clause, courts have required language stating that all disputes "shall" be litigated in a given forum, or—better yet—that the specified forum has "exclusive" jurisdiction over all disputes.

### Permissive versus Mandatory Dispute Resolution Clauses

Permissive:   The courts of New York shall have jurisdiction over all disputes arising out of or in connection with the Agreement. **BAD.**

Permissive:   The Parties agree to submit to the jurisdiction of the courts of New York for all disputes arising out of or in connection with the Agreement. **BAD.**

Mandatory:  All disputes arising out of or in connection with the Agreement shall be decided solely and exclusively by the courts of New York and in no other forum. **GOOD!**

If a contractual dispute resolution clause selects arbitration as the means for resolving disputes, as opposed to litigation, it also must be clear that no other dispute resolution mechanisms are allowed. Sometimes, supply chain partners get this wrong by using ambiguous contract language that makes it seem as though arbitration is one dispute resolution option available to the parties, among others. An example is as follows:

### Bad Arbitration Clause

The parties shall submit all disputes arising out of or in connection with this Agreement to arbitration as administered by the American Arbitration Association (AAA). However, in the case of litigation, all disputes shall be submitted to the courts of the state of New York.

The first sentence appears to select arbitration as the exclusive means of resolving disputes. But the second sentence referencing "litigation" introduces ambiguity. When do the parties intend arbitration and when do they intend litigation? The second sentence should be eliminated.

Another way dispute resolution clauses can make disputes more complicated than necessary is by referencing procedures or entities that do not exist or that are not legally available. For instance, parties cannot select a court that would otherwise lack jurisdiction. Absent special circumstances, supply chain partners from New York and Illinois cannot select "the courts of the State of Missouri" to resolve disputes if Missouri does not have any connection to the transaction or contract. The parties should choose between New York or Illinois courts. Also, two parties from the same state cannot elect to a federal court to resolve disputes because when both parties are from the same state, federal courts generally lack jurisdiction. A state court must be selected.

Supply chain partners also sometimes mistakenly specify rules or arbitration institutions that do not exist. For instance, we have seen a commercial contract that specified arbitration under the AAA's "Rules for Commercial Financing." The problem, unfortunately, is that there is no such thing as the AAA Rules for Commercial Financing. Most arbitration panels ignore nonsensical procedural references. (In this case, the AAA applied its "Commercial Rules.") But again, disputes concerning incomprehensible procedural references often generate needless peripheral litigation and expense.

### *Choosing between Litigation or Arbitration*

A major decision in drafting a dispute resolution clause is whether supply chain partners prefer litigation or arbitration. "Litigation" in this context means court. There is a judge who presides over the case until the trial and, for most supply chain disputes, a jury will be empanelled to decide issues presented at trial. The proceedings will be open to and accessible by the public with few, if any, confidentiality protections.

"Arbitration" means private dispute resolution, typically administered by an arbitration institution. There is no judge or jury, but rather one or three arbitrators, hired and paid by the parties. The arbitrators set the procedure for adjudicating the dispute and will ultimately decide the case. Arbitration proceedings are not open to the public and generally are confidential. Arbitration fees can, however, be very expensive.

There are many considerations involved in choosing litigation or arbitration. Arbitration is often marketed as being faster, cheaper, and better for complex disputes, and sometimes it is. But, in our opinion, not always. For complex disputes, arbitration may not be materially cheaper than litigation. The most expensive part of litigation is usually the discovery process, and discovery in US arbitrations is often similar to discovery in US litigation, although many US arbitration institutions have taken measures recently to limit the scope of arbitration discovery. Arbitrations also require hefty filing fees and hourly compensation for the arbitrators, not required in litigation. Moreover,

US litigation has several mechanisms for resolving a dispute through pre-trial motions, rather than requiring a full-blown trial or hearing. Dispositive pre-trial motions are often appropriate in breach of contract actions, but are not procedurally available under most arbitration rules. In 2013, the AAA modified its Commercial Rules to allow dispositive motions if one party is "likely to succeed" on a claim or issue. But the AAA has offered little guidance on what "likely to succeed" means or what procedures are to be used to pursue a dispositive motion.

Some lawyers believe that, for truly complex disputes, having a case decided by experienced arbitrators is more reliable than trial by jury, but in our experience this is also not always accurate. While we think three-member arbitrator panels are fairly reliable when given a set of complex facts, single arbitrators can be prone to arbitrariness and bias. Three-member arbitration panels, of course, entail three times the arbitrator fees.

Arbitration does enjoy an advantage over litigation in that arbitration decisions can almost always be enforced outside of the United States, while court judgments often cannot be. This is because most countries that are meaningfully involved in international commerce are parties to a 1958 treaty called the Convention on the Recognition and Enforcement of Foreign Arbitral Awards, also known as the "New York Convention." Under the New York Convention, the member states agree that arbitration judgments obtained overseas are enforceable in local courts. There is no similar treaty that provides for the enforceability of foreign court judgments. We will discuss this in more detail in the next chapter on international arbitrations.

Similarly, if confidentiality truly is an issue, arbitrations can be kept confidential. Litigation in US courts may protect sensitive trade secret information during the pre-trial stage, but that information most likely will be disclosed once a case proceeds to trial.

In summary, the choice of litigation or arbitration requires the parties to consider:

- Whether a dispute is likely to be resolved more cheaply or more quickly by litigation or by arbitration;
- Whether the availability of pre-trial dispositive motions in US courts favors litigation rather than arbitration;
- Whether the case is too complex for reliable determination by jury;

- Whether a judgment may need to be enforced outside the United States; and
- Whether confidentiality is a concern.

### *Choosing the Arbitration Institution*

Arbitration institutions administer arbitration proceedings. They have procedural rules that govern the proceedings, they administer disputes, and they often assist the parties in appointing arbitrators. In the United States, there are hundreds, if not thousands, of arbitration institutions. For medium to large commercial disputes, the three most prominent are the American Arbitration Association (AAA), JAMS, Inc. (formerly known as the Judicial Arbitration and Mediation Services, but now known exclusively by its acronym), and the International Institute for Conflict Prevention and Resolution (CPR).

These institutions have similar rules, procedures, and fee structures, and in general they are responsive to competition from each other. But there are some differences. The AAA is somewhat less transparent about the identity of its arbitrators than JAMS or CPR. The JAMS arbitrator roster is composed mostly of retired judges, which we think is an advantage. JAMS and the CPR allow only trained attorneys to serve as arbitrators, but the AAA also allows non-lawyers to be arbitrators, which sometimes is an advantage.

All three major US arbitration institutions are relatively liberal in allowing document discovery. There is some difference in practice between them, however, on deposition practice. Historically, the AAA has been the most liberal in allowing depositions, with previous versions of the AAA rules allowing depositions under a number of different circumstances, particularly in complex cases. The CPR and JAMS, on the other hand, have been more restrictive. Sensitive to criticism that the AAA rules were too much like litigation, the AAA has tightened its rules and now provides that depositions in complex matters are available only in "exceptional cases."

The three major US arbitration institutions have also increased the availability of internal "appellate review" of arbitration awards. Although the Federal Arbitration Act[133] (a US statute) and many state statutes forbid courts from reviewing arbitration awards except in limited circumstances, there is

---

133   9 U.S.C. § 9, et seq.

no US policy against an arbitration institution reviewing its own awards. Consequently, the AAA, JAMS, and the CPR have adopted provisions that allow them to review their awards to ensure correctness. Appellate review is not available as a matter of course, however. All parties must consent to appellate review, either in their dispute resolution clause or separately, after a dispute arises. To agree to arbitration appellate review, supply chain parties can use the following contract language:

**Model Provision for Appellate Review of Arbitration Award**
"… Either Party may appeal from any final award of an arbitration panel, in accordance with the [AAA Optional Appellate Arbitration Rules, or the rules of any other arbitration institution that has appellate provisions]."

## *Choosing the Number of Arbitrators*

Typically, arbitrations are decided either by a single arbitrator or by a panel of three arbitrators. Each approach has advantages and disadvantages. Using a single arbitrator is cheaper and may be appropriate to supply chain contracts of smaller value. But using a single arbitrator exposes supply chain parties to the increased risk of arbitrator error. Unless the parties' original contract provides for arbitration appellate review—and so far, this has not become common practice—the single arbitrator is the sole and final decision-maker. Three arbitrators are less likely to reach a wrong decision in our view, but using three arbitrators entails three times the cost. And sometimes, if a case is straightforward, three arbitrators can be overkill.

Most US arbitration rules default to a single arbitrator unless the parties agree otherwise. Therefore, if disputes in a supply chain relationship are likely to be complex, if a supply chain relationship is strategically important, or if disputes will likely involve a lot of money, the dispute resolution clause should provide for a three-member arbitration panel.

## *Choosing the Applicable Law*

In the United States, supply chain disputes are likely to involve a breach of a contract for the "sale of goods" (e.g., the sale of tangible things, as distinguished from the sale of services). Nearly every state in the union (Louisiana being the sole exception) has adopted Article 2 of the UCC, which governs contracts for the sale of goods. Therefore, US contract law is mostly uniform as between the states, although there are instances in which state courts vary as to how they interpret certain provisions of the UCC. That said, certain states—those with high volumes of commercial activity—often have more developed UCC case law, and therefore their courts are more predictable in comparison to courts in states with less commercial activity.

### *Failure Alert: The Problem of Inconsistent Dispute Resolution Clauses*

One problem that we sometimes see in complex supply chain relationships occurs when a supply chain agreement is composed of multiple documents that contain inconsistent dispute resolution clauses. Sometimes, there is a main supplier or long-term agreement that contains a dispute resolution clause, and also a secondary contract document—perhaps one party's terms and conditions—that has a different dispute resolution clause. Or, sometimes, parties' terms and conditions contain differing dispute resolution clauses, but the parties fail to make clear which one prevails.

In *Summa Humma Enterprises, LLC v. Fisher Engineering*,[134] a buyer and supplier entered into a contract for the purchase of snow plows. The business relationship between the parties consisted of a purchase and security agreement and the supplier's terms of sale. The purchase and security agreement provided that the parties would "consent[] to personal jurisdiction in the State of Maine, and voluntarily submit[] to the jurisdiction of the courts of Maine in any action or proceeding relating to or in connection with this Agreement"—a permissive (non-binding) dispute resolution clause. The terms of sale, on the other hand, contained a mandatory dispute resolution clause that provided that the parties "irrevocably consent and submit to the exclusive jurisdiction of the state and federal courts located in the State of Maine." The purchase and security agreement, which contained the permissive dispute resolution clause, provided that it "shall control" in the event of "any inconsistency between" the two documents.

---

134    2013 U.S. Dist. LEXIS 856 (D. N.H. Jan. 3, 2013).

The inconsistent dispute resolution clauses led to litigation. The court held that the mandatory dispute resolution clause in the terms of sale controlled, and dismissed the case in favor of litigation in Maine. The court's reasoning was that the two clauses could be "construed together," and since the mandatory dispute resolution clause was more restrictive than the permissive dispute resolution clause, by enforcing the mandatory clause, the parties could comply with both.

Similarly, in *Spartech CMD, LLC, v. International Automotive Components Group North America, Inc.*,[135] a buyer and supplier entered into a contract for the sale of chemical compounds. The contract was made up of five purchase orders issued by the buyer, each of which incorporated terms and conditions from the buyer's website. These terms and conditions provided for binding arbitration in Michigan. However, one of the purchase orders was never sent to the supplier. For each of the five orders, the supplier responded with an "acknowledgement." The supplier's acknowledgment contained a dispute resolution clause requiring litigation in Pennsylvania courts. The buyer initiated arbitration in Michigan. The seller filed a federal court action in Michigan to stay the arbitration in favor of litigation in Pennsylvania.

The Michigan court held that for the four transactions in which the buyer issued POs, the supplier was bound by the arbitration clause referenced on the buyer's website. The supplier's acknowledgment did not change this outcome because it could be read narrowly to apply to any post-arbitration litigation that arose. For the PO that had never been sent to the supplier, the court held that there was no agreement to arbitrate, and that the parties must litigate in Pennsylvania.

Both of these cases involve dispute resolution clauses that caused significant confusion, and ultimately litigation, and thus, represent failure in the supply chain relationship. This type of failure can be avoided by reading all supply chain contract documents carefully to ensure that dispute resolution clauses are clear, consistent, and accurately reflect the parties' intent.

––––––

135   2009 U.S. Dist. LEXIS 13662 (E.D. Mich. Feb. 23, 2009).

**Lessons Learned**

US supply chain partners contemplating dispute resolution clauses in their contracts should:

- Pay particular attention to dispute resolution provisions in complex, long-term, strategic, or high-dollar value supply chain relationships
- Evaluate whether arbitration or litigation is the best option
- Consult with in-house counsel before agreeing to a dispute resolution clause
- If arbitration is chosen, determine whether to include appellate review by the arbitration institution
- Ensure that dispute resolution clauses are enforceable and that they do not contradict other terms in supply chain agreements

# CHAPTER 20

# DISPUTE RESOLUTION CLAUSES IN NON-US SUPPLY CHAIN CONTRACTS

## Overview

Dispute resolution clauses in supply chain contracts with non-US partners involve special considerations. Rather than choosing between competing US state laws, which are usually more or less the same, foreign jurisdictions often have very different laws from what US companies expect. The judicial structure and procedures abroad are also often different, making the notion of resolving disputes on foreign territory intimidating. How do you protect your rights when you do not understand the legal system?

Consequently, it is especially important to think about dispute resolution clauses in contracts with non-US supply chain partners. However, choosing the right forum and dispute resolution mechanism can be tricky given the cultural differences between supply chain partners in different countries with different legal systems.

### Litigation in the United States

US companies often assume that, when they can get away with it, requiring non-US supply chain partners to litigate in US courts in the event of a dispute is the best solution. US companies may also presume that they will have an advantage in US courts when their adversary is a non-US entity. Most likely, however, this thinking is wrong.

There are many reasons that pressuring non-US supply chain partners into US litigation is not the best solution. For one thing, non-US companies may not be willing to do business if it requires them to litigate in the United States, or they may simply not participate in US court proceedings. Internationally, there is deep distrust of the US jury system that has been fueled by high verdicts, discovery costs, and suspected anti-foreign bias.

A 2003 North American Free Trade Agreement (NAFTA) arbitration decision illustrates the low regard with which at least some in the international community regard the US legal system. In *Loewen v. United States*,[136] the claimant, the Loewen Group, was a Canadian funeral home company that expanded its operations into the Mississippi Gulf Coast in the United States. Loewen then entered into an insurance contract with a Mississippi insurer. The Mississippi insurer sued Loewen in Mississippi court for breach of contract, claiming $5 million in damages. At trial, counsel for the Mississippi insurance company attempted to provoke jury bias against the Canadian Loewen, which ultimately proved successful. The result was a $500 million jury verdict against Loewen, $400 million of which was punitive damages. Ultimately, Loewen settled with the Mississippi insurance company for $125 million.

Following the settlement, Loewen initiated a NAFTA arbitration against the United States, claiming that it was denied justice by the Mississippi trial court. Under the NAFTA treaty between the United States, Canada, and Mexico, investors of one country are permitted to sue the governments of the other countries directly for unfair and inequitable treatment, denial of justice, or expropriation. The NAFTA arbitration panel held that the Mississippi court denied justice to Loewen by allowing the plaintiff to incite anti-Canadian jury bias, although the arbitration panel dismissed the case on technical grounds. The *Loewen* case demonstrates that the US justice system is not universally believed to be fair, particularly to non-US companies.

Indeed, many, if not most, countries outside the United States do not enforce US court judgments in their own courts, and do not allow execution on assets in their territories to satisfy US court judgments. While this may not matter if a non-US supply chain partner has assets in the United States that can be used to satisfy a US court judgment, if not, resolving disputes in US courts may not be the best option.

---

136   ICSID Case No. ARB(AF)/98/3, Award dated June 26, 2003.

### Arbitration in the United States

The distrust that non-US companies have for US courts generally does not extend to US arbitrations. Virtually all countries enforce arbitration awards rendered in the United States and will aid in the collection of US arbitration awards. This is because of the New York Convention (the Convention on the Recognition and Enforcement of Foreign Arbitral Awards). (See Chapter 7: International Procurement.) Signed by over 140 countries, the New York Convention provides that signatory countries must enforce arbitration awards, including those rendered in the United States, through their courts and in their territories, except in limited circumstances. Only the world's most outlier nations (Iraq, North Korea, and Chad, for example) have not signed the New York Convention. Therefore, arbitration in the United States has many advantages for US supply chain parties in disputes with non-US supply chain parties, such as convenience and familiarity, without the disadvantage of being difficult to enforce.

That said, there may be reasons that non-US supply chain partners are unwilling to agree to arbitration in the United States. The United States may be seen as a non-neutral location for disputes with US companies, and non-US companies may prefer arbitration in their own country or in a neutral location.

### Litigation in Non-US Courts

Some sophisticated supply chain organizations in the United States and the companies they support may not mind litigating abroad. The legal departments of sophisticated corporations may have legal personnel abroad and close relationships with foreign law firms, and may be sufficiently versed in foreign law to be comfortable in at least some foreign courts. The majority of US companies, however, even sometimes large, multinational corporations, do not have this level of sophistication or experience with judicial systems outside the United States. When a company's legal department consists solely or principally of US attorneys and when foreign proceedings are likely to be conducted in a language other than English, most US companies will not be comfortable litigating in non-US courts.

In addition, and not surprisingly, not every country's courts are equally reliable or fair. Nevertheless, the United States will generally enforce judgments rendered by foreign courts so long as basic standards of fairness are met. Therefore, US companies may be at a disadvantage in foreign courts, and will have no way to contest foreign judgments after the fact.

There are many differences between US litigation and litigation elsewhere in the world. First, discovery is almost unheard of in non-US courts. The general rule outside the United States is that each party must find and introduce the evidence it needs to support its claims. Non-US courts generally do not compel the cooperation of the opposing party or third parties in disclosing information, or do so to a far lesser extent than US courts do. Although this approach may save legal fees, it often precludes access to evidence in a legal dispute.

In the United States, the presentation of evidence and the determination of a case occurs almost exclusively during trial or during a tightly controlled pre-trial procedure such as summary judgment, after discovery has been completed. In many other parts of the world, by contrast, evidence is taken at various points during the proceedings, which can last years, and is presented to a judge, rather than a jury. Unless you are familiar with the protocols surrounding the production and introduction of evidence in foreign courts, to US companies, these procedures can seem byzantine and confusing. In addition, outside of the United States and Canada, most foreign countries do not use juries in civil matters at all. Judges decide civil cases, but, in many countries, judges do not have advanced legal training and are indistinguishable from other civil servants. Finally, in courts outside the United States, the losing party is often compelled to pay the winning party's attorney's fees, which US companies may not anticipate. In short, US companies considering whether to agree to litigation in non-US courts need to carefully investigate the selected law, court rules and procedures, and any local idiosyncrasies.

### Non-US Arbitration

For many US companies that have supply chain relationships with international partners, a forum selection clause that provides for arbitration outside of the United States may be the best option. Non-US entities may be more willing to agree to arbitration outside the United States, and as we discussed earlier in this chapter, arbitration awards are generally enforceable in all countries where international commerce takes place. Dispute resolution clauses that choose arbitration outside the United States should specify the location the arbitration will take place, the applicable law, and the language in which the arbitration will be conducted. English is the most commonly used language in international arbitrations.

International arbitration has some unique characteristics. In most respected international arbitration institutions, discovery is significantly more limited than it is in US courts. Parties are generally compelled to produce only the documents they intend to rely on at the arbitration hearing and any relevant documents that a requesting party cannot get from any other source. Depositions are virtually unheard of in international arbitrations, and evidence at arbitration hearings is generally presented through written witness statements rather than through oral direct testimony, although most international arbitration rules allow for verbal cross-examination.

Many of the procedural rules used in international arbitrations are codified in the International Bar Association's (IBA) Rules on the Taking of Evidence in International Arbitration,[137] although each arbitration institution also has its own rules. Foresightful parties can incorporate the IBA Rules into their dispute resolution clauses, although usually international supply chain partners can also agree to use them after a dispute arises. Even if not expressly adopted by the parties, international arbitration tribunals often use the IBA Rules as the default procedural rules of international commercial arbitrations.

Still, not all countries' arbitrations are equal. There are better and worse places in the world to conduct international supply chain arbitrations. Below, we discuss the most commonly used or most commonly considered arbitration locations for US supply chain partners.

### (a) Mexico

Mexico's proximity to the United States and its relatively inexpensive labor makes it a popular choice for US companies looking for low-cost suppliers. The Mexican work force is relatively sophisticated, allowing for more complex products to be made in Mexico than in many other locations. NAFTA

---

137 International Bar Association, "IBA Rules on the Taking of Evidence in International Arbitration" (London, May 29, 2010), http://www.ibanet.org/Publications/publications_IBA_guides_and_free_materials.aspx.

and other treaties have created favorable tax treatment for goods crossing the US-Mexican border, and Mexico affords relatively strong protection to intellectual property rights, which can be important for supply chain relationships in which intellectual property is shared.

On its face, Mexican law respects the arbitration process. Mexico has been a signatory to the New York Convention (providing for the enforcement of arbitration awards) since 1971. In practice, however, the story is different. The process in Mexico for getting an arbitration award recognized by the courts and enforcing it (whether the award was rendered in or out of Mexico) can be lengthy and tortuous, and may involve byzantine constitutional procedures unique to Latin American countries. Because of this, it is commonplace for Mexican companies to resist the enforcement of arbitration awards. Retribution against Mexican judges or attorneys who try to enforce arbitration awards happens sometimes.

Although Mexico boasts a number of institutions that administer domestic arbitrations, the most prominent international arbitration institution in Mexico is the International Chamber of Commerce (ICC), an international body that administers arbitrations all over the world.

### (b) Europe

Europe is an extremely reliable place to arbitrate disputes. Although many supply chain relationships that US companies have in Europe are with suppliers from relatively low-cost Central and Eastern European countries, this is not where arbitration in Europe generally takes place. The most common international arbitration institutions in Europe are the ICC, the London Court of Arbitration (LCIA), the International Centre for Dispute Resolution (ICDR),[138] and the Arbitration Institute of the Stockholm Chamber of Commerce (SCC). The Vienna International Arbitral Centre (VIAC) is also an up-and-coming arbitration institution for disputes involving Central European parties.

Of these institutions, the ICC provides the most extensive administrative services, including formally reviewing awards before they are issued to the parties. The LCIA is a popular institution for arbitrations involving Russian

---

138   The ICDR is the international branch of the AAA.

parties. All of these institutions are reputed to be competent and fair, and their procedural rules are similar.

### (c) Asia

Because many US supply chain relationships involve Asian companies, arbitration in Asia is on the rise. Arbitration in Asia is generally considered to be preferable to litigation in most Asian courts because courts in many Asian countries do not adequately protect private contract rights. Indeed, commercial litigation in most Asian countries is rare, and there is little precedent for protecting or enforcing contract rights in supply chain relationships.

However, most Asian countries that transact supply chain business with US companies are signatories to the New York Convention and therefore, at least in theory, enforce arbitration awards. China, India, Indonesia, Korea, Malaysia, the Philippines, Singapore, Thailand, and Vietnam are all New York Convention signatories. That is not to suggest, however, that each country administers arbitrations equally well, protects the arbitration process equally, or provides equal assistance in enforcing arbitration awards. They do not.

_China_. Although China is home to literally hundreds of arbitration institutions, US companies should avoid arbitration in China if at all possible. The Chinese International Economic and Trade Arbitration Commission (CIETAC) is by volume the largest arbitration institution in the world, and the most popular arbitration institution in China. It has been subject to complaints about bias against non-Chinese parties incompetence, however. The Beijing Arbitration Institute (BAC) is the second most popular arbitration institution in China, and some non-Chinese companies view it as less biased. Ad hoc arbitration (meaning arbitration outside of the auspices of an arbitration institution) is illegal in China, and the Chinese government does not allow foreign arbitration institutions to operate in mainland China.

In _general_, few arbitrators in China have the training or experience to adjudicate complex disputes, although foreigners are increasingly being approved to serve as arbitrators in Chinese arbitration proceedings.

Chinese arbitrations are procedurally more perfunctory than international arbitrations in other countries. The evidence-gathering that takes place in Chinese arbitrations is often minimal, unless the parties specify otherwise in their dispute resolution clause. Notably, there is no established procedure under the CIETAC rules for discovery. "Hearings" consist principally of the arbitrator's review of documentary evidence. Oral testimony is generally not used in Chinese arbitrations. Cross-examination therefore is generally impossible.

China has also been the subject of international criticism for poor enforcement of arbitration awards, although China is a signatory to the New York Convention. In reality, however, Chinese courts often lack the power to enforce arbitration awards effectively or quickly, and Chinese defendants are notorious for transferring assets to other entities to make themselves judgment-proof. Chinese law also lacks any means to allow a prevailing party in an arbitration to discover where a defendant's assets are located, to aid in the collection of any award.

If a US company must arbitrate in China, the best practice is to negotiate a dispute resolution clause that (1) selects English as the language of the arbitration, (2) mandates a three-arbitrator panel rather than a single arbitrator, (3) allows non-Chinese citizens to be chosen as arbitrators, and (4) adopts the IBA Rules of Evidence. Importantly, under Chinese law, to be enforceable, an arbitration clause must specify the arbitration institute that will administer the dispute. A model forum selection clause that provides for arbitration in China is below:

### Model Forum Selection Clause for Arbitration in China

Any controversy, claim, or dispute arising out of or relating to the Agreement, its validity, its enforcement, or the breach thereof, shall be settled by binding arbitration administered by the Beijing Arbitration Commission (BAC), with the International Bar Association Rules on the Taking of Evidence in International Arbitration to govern the arbitration proceedings. The language of the arbitration shall be English. The arbitration shall be presided over by three arbitrators, with each Party to select and appoint one arbitrator and the party-appointed arbitrators jointly to select and appoint the chair. Any Party may select a non-foreign national to be its party-appointed arbitrator, and the chair of the panel must not be the same nationality as either of the Parties. The seat and place of the arbitration shall be Beijing, China. The governing law will be that set forth by the United Nations Convention on Contracts for the International Sale of Goods (CISG), without regard to any conflict or choice of law principles. Neither Party shall be liable to the other Party for any punitive, exemplary, special, indirect, incidental, or consequential damages, including damages for lost profits whether based on contract, tort, or otherwise. Any dispute, negotiation, or arbitration occurring in connection with this provision shall be strictly confidential and cannot be disclosed to any third party unless required by law or governmental or statutory authority.

In short, it is generally not advisable to agree to arbitrate in China. Often, Chinese supply chain partners are comfortable arbitrating disputes in Hong Kong or Singapore, so these locations provide a good compromise.

**Hong Kong:** Although Hong Kong has been reunited with China since 1997 as a "Special Administrative Region" and although the vast majority of its population is ethnically Chinese, its business and legal structures are very different than in mainland China. Because Hong Kong became a British colony after the Opium Wars in 1842, Hong Kong inherited the British common law legal system, which it retains to this day. Even after its "return" to China in 1997, the law gives Hong Kong considerable legal autonomy from China. As a result, Hong Kong is hospitable to arbitration and has become a reliable choice for arbitration in Asia.

The premier Hong Kong arbitration institution is the Hong Kong International Arbitration Centre (HKIAC). The ICC also has an office in Hong Kong, and ICC arbitration is popular as well. Both institutions are highly respected and experienced, probably more than any other arbitration institutions in Asia. Ad hoc arbitration is also permitted and popular in Hong Kong. The business community and the judiciary both have pledged to ensure the integrity and autonomy of arbitration, and enforcement of arbitration awards in Hong Kong is relatively good.

**Singapore:** Recently, Singapore has begun to challenge Hong Kong as the premier country for arbitration in Asia. Singapore's government has enacted laws to protect the arbitration process, and the judiciary has crafted an impressive body of precedent supporting the independence of arbitration and the enforcement of arbitration awards. The judiciary is also reliable and competent in enforcing the rule of law and protecting arbitration awards and proceedings. Moreover, confidentiality is the default for arbitrations under Singapore law.

Because some non-Asian parties are wary of arbitration in Hong Kong due to its relationship and proximity to China, Singapore provides an attractive and viable alternative. Until recently, Singapore was the preferred Asian arbitration location for non-Asian entities doing business in India because, prior to 2012, India did not allow enforcement of arbitration awards from China or Hong Kong. (That has now changed.) The premier Singapore arbitration institution is the Singapore International Arbitration Centre (SIAC).

The Singapore government has also taken steps to increase the convenience and attractiveness of arbitration in Singapore. In 2009, Singapore's government sponsored and built the Maxwell Chambers facility that houses several arbitration institutions (including the LCIA, ICC, ICDR, and others).

**Elsewhere in Asia:** Other Asian countries are emerging as reliable places for arbitration. In Malaysia, although there is no national arbitration institution, the Kuala Lumpur Regional Centre for Arbitration is a prominent arbitration institution that affirmatively markets itself outside Malaysia to attract foreign interest. The Malaysian government supports arbitration, and as a former common-law country and a current New York Convention signatory, enforcement of arbitration awards in Malaysia is reliable. The same can be said for arbitration in the Philippines, South Korea, and Thailand, although those systems are not as well developed as Malaysia's. Although not an Asian country, Australia is also a popular location for arbitrations arising out of Asian commercial relationships.

India is idiosyncratic. Arbitration has been slow to take hold in India, and India's government has a spotty history with respecting the integrity of arbitration proceedings. Traditionally, arbitrations in India have been ad hoc, although in 2009, the LCIA established an arbitration center in New Dehli.

Indonesia and Taiwan should be avoided as international arbitration locations. The Indonesian government has a known history of interfering with arbitrations. Taiwan is not a signatory to the New York Convention, so arbitration awards cannot be reliably enforced within Taiwan.

## Failure Alert: Problems Enforcing an Arbitration Award

The following case illustrates how difficult it can be to enforce an arbitration award if a country's laws do not support enforcement.

In 2004, Corporation Mexicana de Mantenimiento Integral S. de R.L. de C.V. (COMMISA), a Mexican subsidiary of a US company, initiated an ICC arbitration in Mexico City against a subsidiary of a Mexican state-owned company, Pemex-Excploracion y Produccion (PEP), pursuant to the parties' commercial agreement. In response to COMMISA's arbitration demand, PEP administratively rescinded the parties' contract, which COMMISA could challenge only in Mexican court via a special constitutional procedural called an *amparo*. The lower-level Mexican court held that the *amparo* proceeding was not the proper way to challenge the rescission, however. An appellate court reversed the *amparo* judgment and referred the matter to the Mexican Supreme Court to determine the constitutionality of the rescission. The Mexican Supreme Court upheld the rescission.

The ICC arbitration meanwhile proceeded simultaneously with these constitutional procedures. In 2009, COMMISA prevailed in a majority (2-1) decision, winning a nearly $300 million judgment. COMMISSA then petitioned a US court in New York to confirm the award because PEP had assets in the United States, and the New York court granted COMMISA's petition in 2010. PEP appealed the confirmation to the US Second Circuit Court of Appeals, and initiated litigation in the Mexican courts to nullify the arbitration award. The US courts stayed the execution proceedings, pending resolution of the case in Mexico.

PEP lost in the lower court in Mexico, which upheld COMMISA's arbitration victory. PEP refiled its challenge in a second court, which also upheld the award. PEP then filed an *amparo* proceeding to challenge the second court's decision—and again lost. Finally, PEP appealed to a separate appellate court in Mexico, which held that COMMISA's arbitration award was invalid. The basis for the annulment was that a new law enacted in Mexico prohibited arbitration against government-owned entities. The case was then sent back to a Mexican lower court, which also nullified the arbitration award. PEP filed two ancillary actions in Mexican court, and COMMISA also filed a separate Mexican court action.

The US Second Circuit Court of Appeals remanded COMMISA's petition to confirm its favorable award in the United States to the New York

District Court to determine whether the Mexican court's annulment of the arbitration award had any effect on its confirmation in US courts. The US district court confirmed the award, holding that the Mexican court's nullification "violated basic notions of justice." This decision was issued in 2013—nearly 10 years after the arbitration commenced.[139]

Confused yet? The exact details of what happened in the COMMISA case are not as important as the fundamental lesson: be wary of agreeing to arbitrate supply chain disputes in countries that do not support arbitration.

----

**Lessons Learned**

US companies that enter into supply chain contracts with non-US supply chain partners should:

- Always address dispute resolution in their contracts
- Assess whether arbitration or litigation is best, considering that arbitration judgments are more uniformly enforced
- Conduct research on any dispute resolution forum that is chosen to determine the forum's willingness to respect arbitration proceedings, and to enforce arbitration judgments

---

139   *Corporacion Mexicana de Mantenimiento Integral, S. de R.L. de C.V. v. Pemex-Exploracion y Produccion*, 962 F.Supp.2d 642 (S.D.N.Y. 2013).

# CHAPTER 21

# BEST PRACTICES IN CONTRACTING

## Overview

In previous chapters, we have discussed many of the issues that give rise to supply chain disputes and how to avoid them. We turn now to the content of supply chain agreements.

Although supply chain relationships are now regarded as an integral part of business, supply chain agreements are nevertheless often given insufficient attention. Supply chain contracts still tend to over-rely on templates and boilerplate clauses with little thought to whether they are appropriate for the particular circumstances. Often, supply chain contracts receive insufficient legal review, and few resources are dedicated to administering supply chain contracts in a thoughtful way. Particularly for high-value or strategic relationships, supply chain contracts are not one-size-fits-all transactions and should not be treated as such.

### Purchase Orders (POs)

POs are the most common form that contracts take in manufacturing supply chain organizations. Unfortunately, since they are so common, POs often use the same terms and conditions, no matter what the purchasing relationship is, or what the supply chain needs are. In addition, most buyers and commodity managers focus primarily on cost because this is their primary performance measure, which means that the non-cost aspects of POs are often neglected. Often, buyers are also so overwhelmed with work that boilerplate POs are essential to get orders placed quickly and efficiently. It is not until the value of a PO exceeds some threshold (typically $500,000-$1 million) that senior management gets involved.

There are many options and approaches that should be considered before a PO is executed, especially for high-value or strategic purchases. POs should be carefully constructed, particularly if there are unique aspects to the agreement or supply chain relationship.

Best-practices companies identify the unique items of value in their supply chain relationships early in their discussions with potential partners. These unique items of value are sometimes called "trades" because they can be used as negotiating items. For example, a software supplier may agree to trade an additional price reduction if the customer agrees to provide a beta test site and feedback for new software the supplier is developing. Trades can be valuable exchanges, but they need to be clearly documented in the contract so that both parties understand their commitments and responsibilities.

Buyers and suppliers tend to think of a PO as establishing the terms that will govern the supply chain relationship long term. In fact, trades can be raised and considered throughout a supply chain relationship, and POs can be modified as the relationship progresses. Legal staff should provide continual guidance and review as to what terms are legally possible and should help draft appropriate contract provisions. Rushed supply chain contracts, or those that are not reviewed at appropriate intervals, may omit important terms or fail to capture opportunities for both supply chain partners.

Some companies conduct cross-functional reviews of their supply chain contracts throughout their procurement cycles, especially on large deals, but the vast majority of companies do not. Most supply chain agreements are not reviewed regularly. Therefore, terms and trades that were once reflective of a great business deal between partners, deteriorate over time as business conditions change.

The best way to avoid contracting mistakes and omissions is for a company's legal staff to work closely with its buying staff from the beginning of the contracting process throughout the supply chain relationship. Another way to avoid mistakes is to provide training to buyers about contract drafting, management, and pitfalls.

### Contract Manufacturing, Third-Party Logistics Providers (3PLs), and Other Outsourcing Contracts

Contract manufacturing, 3PLs (third-party logistics providers), and other outsourced services in supply chains present more complex procurement challenges. These services agreements typically include multi-year projects that are made up of complex tasks and performance metrics. Outsourced service providers are also likely to operate globally, which increases risk.

Contract manufacturers such as Foxconn, Flextronics, Jabil, Sanmina, Celestica and others, set up manufacturing lines to build products for other companies, such as Apple and Dell. The contracts that cover these services specify price, performance, detailed manufacturing instructions, and quality standards. In addition, contract manufacturing relationships usually involve IT systems integration points between buyers and contract manufacturers. Contract manufacturers typically rely on their customers' systems to determine production levels, serialization, quality control, and fulfilment data. (See Chapter 8: Manufacturing.) So, in addition to price and delivery, agreements with contract manufacturers need to consider a host of production requirements and must also provide protection for the buyers' IT systems.

Relationships with 3PLs are similar. These companies typically provide warehousing and distribution services and sometimes light assembly. Again, it is common for buyers' IT systems to be integrated with 3PLs, so 3PL contracts must ensure IT protection. The details of the fulfilment process, inventory control, and response times are important components of most 3PL contracts. (See Chapter 9: Warehousing and Logistics.)

Other outsourced service relationships, such as with call centers and consulting contracts, are complex and require special attention. Consequently, outsourcing contracts typically require more time and effort to develop and negotiate. Legal staff should be intimately involved throughout these projects, not just at the end when the contract is being written.

### International Considerations

International supply chain relationships have unique characteristics. For example, in international contract manufacturing, the decision whether to forbid or allow contract manufacturers to use subcontractors is extremely important and should be expressly stated in the contract. If subcontractors are allowed, the contract should also include provisions that allow the buyer to monitor subcontractor use and performance. (See Chapter 7: International Procurement.)

Different cultures view contracts differently. For example, Chinese businesspeople consider the contract to be the beginning of the negotiating process, while Westerners view the contract as a final expression of the terms governing a relationship. Just as college commencement may feel like the end of a process to a student, but the beginning of an independent life to the student's parents, so too do we view the ending and beginning of business differently in different cultures. Other cultures may not scrupulously honor contract terms and conditions as written, but rather view contract terms and conditions as a jumping-off point to begin doing business. To many Chinese contract manufacturers and suppliers, for example, a contract simply marks the beginning of production and the basis for figuring out how to do business profitably. Once a contract is signed, Chinese contract manufacturers and suppliers typically try to figure out ways to produce less expensively in order to improve their margins, regardless of what the contract says. Contract drafting in these circumstances must be even more careful.

### Failure Alert: Mattel Toys' Contract Manufacturing Fiasco

You may remember Mattel Toys' lead paint issues a few years ago. One of Mattel's Chinese contract manufacturers subcontracted toy painting to another Chinese factory. The subcontractor substituted lead paint for the paint that Mattel specified in the contract with its primary contractor. The results were injuries to children, massive recalls, and damage to the Mattel brand. Mattel's contract allowed Mattel to monitor its contract manufacturer's factories and subcontractors, but Mattel did not effectively exercise these contract rights. The lesson learned is that active monitoring and oversight are important parts of supply chain relationships.

## Legal Overview

Here, we will discuss some common supply chain contract provisions and considerations. Supply chain partners have many options in structuring their agreements. This section is intended as a drafting aid for legal and procurement departments that deal with supply chain contracts.

## *Commercial Terms*

First, we will discuss the commercial terms that commonly appear in supply chain agreements, meaning terms that relate to price, order quantity, delivery, and payment terms.

### *(a) Price*

Most supply chain agreements establish a product price. The easiest type of price term is a fixed price that applies to a product over the entire term of the agreement; however, there are other options. Some supply chain partners may not agree to a fixed product price if the underlying costs are uncertain. Some supply chain partners also may not agree to a fixed price if a product's market value fluctuates. Any number of factors could cause supply chain partners to consider pricing options other than a fixed price. Some of the options are as follows:

- **Price that varies by order quantity:** Sometimes suppliers, to incentivize higher purchase volumes, set lower prices for higher-volume purchases.
- **Price re-opener:** In supply chain contracts with price re-opener provisions, price is renegotiated if an agreed-upon event occurs. Price re-opener provisions are often used in natural resource supply agreements, for example.
- **Price formula or cost-plus pricing:** For supply chain contracts that set price according to a formula, price is usually a function of a supplier's costs plus a set profit margin. Cost-plus pricing is sometimes found in supply chain contracts that have a substantial research and development component to ensure that the supplier recoups its costs. Cost-plus pricing is also sometimes used in government contracts.
- **Take-or-pay pricing:** In take-or-pay contracts, the buyer must purchase a minimum quantity of goods, and if the buyer does not, the buyer must pay a penalty to cover the shortfall. Take-or-pay contracts are common in natural resources contracts, but if the take-or-pay penalty does not approximate the supplier's actual damages, in the United States, these provisions may be held to be unenforceable "penalties" under UCC 2-718(1).

- Most favored customer pricing: Under most favored customer pricing, a supplier pledges not to charge the buyer a higher price than it charges any other customer. A related type of price term is one in which the supplier agrees to match any competing offer that the buyer secures.
- Non-recurring cost recovery: Sometimes, buyers agree to cover a portion of a supplier's up-front engineering expenses or other non-recurring costs. Non-recurring cost recovery provisions are sometimes used in development supply chain contracts as a means of sharing responsibility for research and development costs.

In some supply chain contracts, the parties expect that inflation will cause product costs to increase over time. In others, however, supply chain partners expect that costs will decrease over time. This is often true with contracts for electronic products. In such cases, supply chain partners may provide for price increases or decreases in their contracts. A sample contract provision setting forth a decreasing price is as follows:

**Expected Cost Reductions**
Supplier acknowledges that Buyer competes in a highly competitive market and that Buyer's customers impose cost-reduction obligations on Buyer. Supplier agrees to use its best efforts to supply Products to Buyer at the lowest price possible. On January 1 and June 1 of each year of this Agreement, Supplier will submit a cost-reduction plan to Buyer, as well as a full accounting of its costs in making the Products. Buyer will then establish pricing for the following six (6)-month period.

Finally, all supply chain contracts should be clear as to which party is responsible for paying any applicable sales, excise, or any other taxes.

### (b) Quantity

Recall that order quantity is the only term that the UCC requires to be in writing for a contract to be enforceable.[140] (See Chapter 6: Procurement.) The

---

140 UCC 2-201(1).

only exception is for "requirements" contracts, in which a supplier agrees to supply all of a buyer's requirements for a product.[141] The order-quantity rule may be badly suited to supply chain relationships in which it is often more convenient to establish framework terms and conditions with specific order quantities to be determined later.

Additional considerations for supply chain contract quantity terms include:

- Whether forecasts provided by either party are binding or informational;
- Whether to include minimum and/or maximum order quantities;
- Whether the buyer is allowed to modify order quantities, and if so, whether notice is required to the supplier, whether the supplier is required to agree to the modification, and whether the supplier can petition for a price increase in the event that order quantity changes; and
- Whether the supplier must manufacture a minimum quantity of products, even if the buyer is not obligated to purchase the entire amount.

### (c)  Contract Duration and Termination

Provisions governing the duration of supply chain agreements and contract terminations are also important. Critical supply chain relationships should not be easily terminable. Relationships for commodity parts may allow terminations more liberally.

If a supply chain contract does not state otherwise, it is presumed to be terminable at will by either party. Importantly, if a supply chain contract provides grounds for one party to terminate the contract, but no grounds for the other party to terminate, this does not mean that the second party is not allowed to terminate the agreement. To the contrary, under these circumstances, the supply chain contract is terminable at will by the second party without restriction.[142]

---

141   UCC 2-306.

142   *See, e.g., Advanced Plastic Corp. v. White Consolidated Industrial, Inc.*, 828 F. Supp. 484 (S.D. Mich. 1993); *Riverside Marketing, LLC v. Signaturecard, Inc.*, 425 F. Supp. 2d 523 (S.D.N.Y. 2006).

Supply chain contracts sometimes begin with an initial "term" and then include renewal provisions by which these contracts may be extended. There are two types of renewals: contracts that renew automatically unless one party provides notice that it does not wish to renew, and contracts that renew only if a party provides notice that it does wish to renew.

Most supply chain contracts allow either party to terminate in the event that the other party declares bankruptcy. Supply chain partners should be aware that, often, these provisions are not enforceable in the United States due to bankruptcy rules that prohibit creditors from terminating contractual relationships with debtors in certain circumstances. Supply chain contracts often allow for termination in the event of a party's material breach. Some also contain provisions allowing one or both parties to terminate if a specific type of breach occurs. Many supply chain contracts contain provisions that require the supplier to continue to supply product for a certain period of time to allow the buyer to find a substitute supplier. Similarly, some supply chain contracts require the buyer, upon termination, to purchase the supplier's remaining raw materials and work in progress.

### (d) Payment Terms

Most supply chain contracts include provisions that govern payment. Relevant considerations when drafting payment terms include:

- Whether payment is due a set time after order, after delivery, after inspection, or after the buyer's final approval of the product;
- Whether there are time limits for the buyer to conduct its inspection or give approval if payment is due after inspection or after the buyer approves the product;
- Whether payment must be made in cash or whether credit will be extended or accepted;
- Whether payments must be secured by letters of credit or other means (for international or first-time customers especially);
- Whether interest applies in the event of a late payment;
- Whether late payment entitles the supplier to suspend performance or suspend future deliveries;
- Whether the buyer is obliged to pay for non-conforming products;

- Whether the buyer has the right to set off any amounts owed to it from the supplier against amounts the buyer owes the supplier; and
- The currency of payment or how currency conversion is determined.

## (e) Delivery Terms

Supply chain contracts also usually contain provisions that govern product delivery. Delivery terms typically establish which party is responsible for delivery and which party is liable in the event of loss or damage during delivery. Delivery schedules are usually set forth in POs. In Chapter 10, we discussed the delivery aspects of supply chain contracts, including terminology that is commonly used to describe these delivery obligations.

Typically, risk of damage or loss passes from the supplier to the buyer when title to the product changes hands. Other delivery terms that should be considered are as follows:

- Whether either party must purchase insurance to cover damage that occurs during delivery;
- The means of transportation;
- In the event that the primary transportation plan becomes unavailable, what the secondary options are, and which party bears any increased cost if the primary transportation plan becomes unavailable;
- Whether and to what extent the buyer should be charged if it does not take immediate delivery of products, requiring them to be placed into storage;
- Whether there are special labelling, packaging, or tracking requirements (often the case in the medical, pharmaceutical, and food industries);
- Whether particular shipping documentation is required, such as certificates of conformance or analysis;
- Whether time is of the essence; and
- Which party is responsible for paying customs duties.

## Boilerplate Terms

Supply chain contracts involve many terms that are considered boilerplate because they are not central to the commercial relationship between the parties.

While we do not want to give the impression that these terms are unimportant—because as soon as a dispute arises, they often become very important—they are often less thoroughly negotiated. Some boilerplate terms that bear particular consideration are:

- **Order of precedence**: As we discussed in Chapter 3, many supply chain contracts consist of multiple documents. An order of precedence provision identifies the documents that compose the supply chain agreement and establishes priority among them.

- **Assignment or delegation:** Many buyers prefer not to allow suppliers to assign or delegate their duties. Often, buyers select suppliers based on their unique capabilities. Similarly, a change in control within a supplier is also sometimes a concern for buyers, and may be treated as an "assignment." Suppliers are also sometimes concerned about assignments by buyers, especially in requirements contracts because requirements may vary widely between different buyers. A sample provision barring assignment and change of control is below:

  ### No Assignment or Delegation
  Supplier may not assign or delegate its rights and duties under this Agreement without the prior written consent of Buyer, which consent may not be unreasonably withheld. A sale in which Supplier sells or otherwise disposes of more than twenty-five percent (25%) of its assets or shares shall constitute an assignment and delegation under this Agreement that requires the prior written consent of Buyer.

- **Confidentiality:** Many supply chain contracts involve sensitive, proprietary, or trade secret information that needs to be protected.

- **Subcontractors or sub-supplier provisions:** Often, supply chain parties state whether suppliers may use subcontractors. Relatedly, some supply chain agreements state whether suppliers must disclose material providers or sub-component suppliers, and whether the buyer must approve any change in sub-suppliers. In some industries, such as aerospace, federal regulation prohibits changes in suppliers, processes, or materials without the approval of the regulator.

- **No oral modification and anti-waiver clauses:** Many supply chain contracts prohibit modifications that are not in writing and executed by the parties. Under the UCC, however, courts may not consistently enforce these provisions. (See Chapter 18: Changing the Supply Chain Agreement.)
- **Integration clauses:** An integration clause generally states that the written agreement comprises the entire agreement between the parties, and that no other representations or promises are included. A sample integration clause can be found in Chapter 3.
- **Insurance:** Sometimes buyers demand that suppliers show proof of general commercial liability, product liability, or other insurance. Special insurance can sometimes be secured to cover things like recall expenses.
- **Intellectual property:** Often supply chain agreements state which party is the owner of any intellectual property associated with a product, manufacturing technique, or tooling. These provisions often also state whether there is a licensing agreement between supply chain partners.
- **Force majeure and excuse:** Some supply chain contracts contain provisions that excuse performance in the event of a catastrophic event. (See Chapter 17: Supply Chain Risk.)
- **Survival:** Supply chain contracts often provide that the parties' indemnification and confidentiality obligations survive the termination of the agreement.
- **Record retention:** Supply chain agreements sometimes include provisions requiring one or both parties to retain all records relating to the program until such time as the program ends, notice is provided by the other party, or some other event occurs.
- **Independent contractor:** Many supply chain contracts include a paragraph stipulating that the supplier is an independent contractor to the buyer, which allows the buyer to avoid liability associated with the supplier's employees and other duties. This can be especially valuable if employees of the supplier work onsite at the buyer's facility. A sample clause is below:

### Independent Contractor Relationship
The Parties expressly acknowledge, recognize, and agree that Supplier is and undertakes its performance under this

Agreement as an independent contractor with sole liability and responsibility for the payment of all federal, state, and foreign unemployment insurance, social security, and/or other similar taxes and benefits.

- **Dispute resolution provisions:** Supply chain partners often choose the forum in which any disputes that arise between them will be resolved. Ideally, this is a forum convenient to both parties, although this may not be possible. Supply chain partners should consider whether they prefer arbitration to litigation. For international supply chain contracts, arbitration is usually the better option, because arbitration awards are more readily enforced abroad than US court judgments. Some supply chain contracts include a duty to mediate and/or negotiate prior to instituting legal action. (See Chapter 19: Dispute Resolution Clauses in US Supply Chain Contracts and Chapter 20: Dispute Resolution Clauses in Non-US Supply Chain Contracts.)
- **Choice of law:** If a dispute arises, parties often prefer to identify the law that will govern the dispute. For US contracts, the law is very similar, if not identical, between states. For international contracts, the law of the non-US supply chain partner may differ greatly from US law. If no choice of law clause is provided, the law will be supplied by the CISG for most international supply chain contracts. Parties to international supply chain contracts also sometimes augment the CISG with the UNIDROIT Principles, which state additional rules of law.
- **Construction**: Supply chain partners sometimes state that the supply chain agreement was negotiated by sophisticated commercial parties, each of which was advised by counsel, and that in the event of a dispute, the agreement is not to be construed against either party.

### *Commonly Considered Quality, Warranty, and Reliability Terms*

Supply chain partners often include quality, warranty, and reliability terms in their supply chain agreements. These terms often describe any inspection that a buyer must perform when it receives product, product performance requirements, and the buyer's remedies in case performance standards are not met.

### (a) Inspection Provisions

Under the UCC, buyers generally have the right to inspect "at any reasonable place and time and in any reasonable manner" before payment or acceptance.[143] A buyer is required to reject non-conforming products within a "reasonable time" after delivery, and must "seasonably" notify the supplier of its rejection.[144] The buyer bears all expenses related to product inspections unless products are non-conforming. In this case, inspection expenses are paid by the supplier.[145]

These are the default rules governing receipt, inspection, and rejection of goods in US supply chain contracts, but supply chain partners may adopt different rules in their supply chain agreements. Supply chain contracts often include the following provisions and considerations relating to product receipt and rejection:

- Some supply chain contracts include a mechanism through which supply chain partners can initiate and resolve disputes about whether goods are non-conforming. Some supply chain contracts leave this determination to the sole discretion of the buyer. Others provide that products that the buyer claims are non-conforming must be submitted to an independent third party for testing.
- The default rule under the UCC is that a buyer can withhold payment for non-conforming goods, but some supply chain contracts provide otherwise.
- Where appropriate, some supply chain contracts dictate when non-conforming products may be reworked by the supplier and redelivered to the buyer.

Buyers with extensive inspection and intake procedures also sometimes allow suppliers with proven track records to qualify as "preferred suppliers," which entitles them to expedite some intake procedures.

### (b) Warranty and Reliability Provisions

Most supply chain contracts contain provisions that govern product performance. These can be warranty terms, or they may dictate reliability

---

143   UCC § 2-513(1).
144   UCC § 2-602(1).
145   UCC § 2-513(2).

requirements on a broader production-wide or "fleetwide" basis. Other agreements, on the other hand, disclaim warranty and reliability coverage.

Product warranties typically guarantee that products will perform as intended for a specified period of time. Fleetwide reliability guarantees, on the other hand, provide that the failure rate for products as a group will be no greater than a specified value (for example, one failure per every thousand products supplied). In the aerospace industry, it is common for suppliers to guarantee a "mean time between failure" (MTBF) rate that guarantees no more than a specified number of failures per hour of fleetwide operation.

Under the UCC, unless parties provide otherwise, all products are presumed to have two "implied warranties"— an "implied warranty of merchantability" and an "implied warranty of fitness for a particular purpose." But these implied warranties can also be disclaimed. Under the UCC, express warranties can be created by conduct, sales talk, samples, or drawings. (See Chapter 12: Warranties.)

It is also common to include a "warranty of title" guaranteeing that the supplier has good title to the products and may sell them to the buyer, and a "warranty of non-infringement" guaranteeing that products are not the subject of any intellectual property claims by third parties. Other warranty and reliability considerations include:

- Whether to include a warranty that products will conform to technical specifications.
- Whether to include a standard express warranty that products will "be merchantable and free of defects in workmanship and materials."
- Whether to guarantee that products will conform to representations made in a supplier's RFX documents.
- Whether to set forth warranty and reliability requirements in a stand-alone product support agreement. This is common practice in the automotive and aerospace industries and can be helpful if maintenance or reliability obligations are extensive or complex. In the medical and pharmaceutical industries, it is also typical to negotiate separate quality agreements.
- Whether a warranty is invalidated for misuse of a product.
- Whether to include provisions governing how warranty complaints will be investigated. For complex products, buyers and suppliers

sometimes agree to form a joint quality committee to ensure proper responsibility for quality issues. For products where safety is a concern, investigations may need to be conducted in conjunction with government agencies.

- Whether to include warranty requirements that incorporate industry standards.
- Whether to include warranties governing component integration activities or functions. Integrating multiple components into an end product can be precarious. Supply chain partners need to consider who bears responsibility for integration activities and to what extent. (See Chapter 4: Product Integration.)
- Which party pays shipping and delivery expenses for returned and replacement goods. This can be a big issue in supply chain agreements for components that are critical to safety or product functioning and where expedited (and expensive) delivery is required.
- Whether to allocate responsibility for recall expenses. In some industries, recalls are expected and recall expenses are built into the cost of doing business. In other industries, recalls are unexpected catastrophic events. When supply chain contracts do address recalls, they often specify which party will provide notice of a recall to consumers, which party will administer a recall, which party will pay recall costs, and which party will coordinate with regulators. (See Chapter 13: Recalls.)
- Whether to require independent testing to verify compliance with quality standards. In some supply chain agreements, products or samples may be subjected to independent testing to ensure conformity with material, purity, quality, or technical standards.
- Whether to impose a time limit for warranty claims. The default statute of limitations under the UCC (as enacted in most states) is four years, but supply chain partners may shorten this period by agreement, although generally not to less than one year.
- Whether to limit available remedies for breach of warranty. Many supply chain contracts limit the remedies available in the event of a breach of warranty to "repair or replacement" of defective products. Some (a minority) of courts hold that this limitation "fails of its essential purpose" if a defect cannot be fixed completely or quickly. To

avoid this, suppliers can include refund of the purchase price as an alternate remedy. (See Chapter 12: Warranties.)

- Whether attorneys' fees may be recovered in the event of a warranty dispute. Many supply chain contracts include provisions awarding attorneys' fees to the prevailing party, but we discourage this practice. Many courts do not fully enforce these provisions, and they sometimes encourage unduly aggressive and inefficient litigation tactics.

Agreements with warranty and reliability obligations often also include indemnity provisions that govern responsibility for third-party claims. Indemnity clauses can cover intellectual property infringement claims, liability for recalls, and liability for warranty claims by the end customer.

### *Technical Specifications*

Technical specifications are unique to each product. Some technical specifications set forth design parameters, such as engineering dimensions, material requirements, product integration parameters, and so forth. Other technical specifications set forth performance requirements and are thus similar to warranty provisions. It is common for technical specifications to include testing requirements and protocols. If testing requirements are included, it is common to require the party that administers the test to warrant that all test equipment is in good working order and in compliance with all required maintenance. Supplier testing may be required to be approved by the buyer.

Some technical specifications also set forth procedures through which supply chain partners can agree to "deviations" from the specifications. In supply chain contracts that involve highly engineered products, there may be some technical specifications that are not critical to the success or performance of the product. When this is the case, suppliers may be allowed to petition buyers to "deviate" from the technical specifications. This is a good practice, but we would caution supply chain parties to ensure that all deviations are memorialized formally in writing. (See Chapter 18: Changing the Supply Chain Agreement.)

Supply chain contracts for less complex components often allow buyers to modify technical specifications without suppliers' agreement. For more complex or highly engineered products, on the other hand, supplier approval is often required.

### "Visibility" Terms

Often, buyers need "visibility" into the practices of their suppliers, and sometimes buyers need visibility into sub-supplier practices, all the way to the end of the supply chain. Buyers often use supply chain contracts to ensure that they have the right to inspect supplier operations and to monitor corporate social responsibility issues. The following is a non-exclusive list of items for which buyers may want to ensure supply chain visibility:

- Compliance with anti-bribery legislation
- Use of conflict minerals
- Data privacy protections
- Access to adequate supply of essential components
- Non-use of child or slave labor
- Hazardous waste disposal and other environmental compliance matters
- Non-use of suspect or illegal chemicals or substances
- Insurance coverage
- Existence of government investigations or other regulatory actions
- Prudent disaster planning
- Compliance with required certifications

Supply chain contracts may also provide buyers with the right to audit suppliers and sub-suppliers to verify supplier compliance. (See Chapter 16: Corporate Social Responsibility and the Supply Chain.)

### Special Consideration for Development Contracts

Development contracts involving new products, processes, and technologies pose special challenges. (See Chapter 3: New Product Design and Development Contracts.) If supply chain partners intend to put a newly developed product into production, they need to structure the commercial terms of their post-development relationship. This can be difficult to do before supply chain partners fully determine the quality, technical, and cost parameters of a new product. Things like the amount of rework necessary to produce a product that meets specifications will also impact profitability.

Supply chain contracts that govern the product development process often include timing milestones, such as for preliminary design review, critical design review, testing deadlines, and first-article production. Development parts and early production parts may have less expansive warranty and reliability guarantees than parts made later in production. Development contracts may also have flexibility provisions that allow one or both parties to make or request design or other engineering changes or revisions to product price.

---

### Lessons Learned

Supply chain partners engaged in the process of drafting contract terms should:

- Understand that boilerplate supply chain contracts are usually not optimal, particularly for high-value or strategically important purchases
- Take special care in drafting complex services agreements
- Take special care in drafting international supply chain contracts, and in monitoring compliance
- Give due consideration to the many commercial, warranty, visibility, and other contract options available to supply chain partners

# CHAPTER 22

# BEST PRACTICES ONCE A DISPUTE HAS ARISEN

## Overview

Not every supply chain dispute can be avoided. Whether it is because one or both supply chain partners are behaving unreasonably, a dispute has become intractable, a program suffers unexpected financial losses, or executive management is demanding action, parties to supply chain contracts sometimes end up in a formal legal dispute.

Anytime this happens, it means there has been a supply chain failure. However, there are ways to minimize the business disruption, pain, and cost of supply chain litigation. This chapter will give you some idea of what to expect during the litigation process, how to work to achieve the best possible outcome, and how to minimize the impact to your business.

The primary rule with any business conflict is, do not ignore it. Ignoring a percolating dispute is the worst way to manage it. Furthermore, understand that until a dispute is fully resolved, it will require a great deal of your time and attention. Even if you have skilled in-house and outside counsel, your work is not done. Among other tasks, you will have to organize your business records, coordinate your legal strategy, and address all employee concerns relating to the dispute. If you are a public company or if you work with regulators, you may also have disclosure or reporting requirements.

Attorneys and expert witnesses will certainly help you work through supply chain legal disputes. However, because they were not personally involved when the supply chain partnership was created or when the dispute arose, you will need to help them. Working with your legal team will be an ongoing process until the dispute ends. Even attorneys and experts that specialize in supply chain disputes will need to learn how your organization works and gather information about the supply chain relationship at issue. Often, supply chain disputes involve communications and conduct that take place over many years. It takes time to master that history, and your counsel and experts can only do it with the help of the employees who lived through the relationship, along with access to the relevant business records.

Without casting blame, we find that communication between technical people (such as engineers) and attorneys is often challenging. Engineers and other technical professionals think and speak in precise and quantifiable ways. Attorneys and the experts who assist them, on the other hand, deal with more ambiguous legal concepts, like "reasonableness," whether damages are "material," and whether losses are sufficiently "proximate" to be recoverable. Engineers and technical people often want precise answers about what will happen in a supply chain dispute. Attorneys and experts cannot always provide precise answers.

### Selecting Attorneys and Expert Witnesses

If you are involved in your company's efforts to select legal counsel in a supply chain dispute, there are some things you should know. First, experience matters. A novice attorney is not the best candidate for a complex or multi-million-dollar supplier dispute. A family law attorney, no matter how experienced, is also probably not the best choice for a supply chain dispute. You should choose attorneys experienced in technical business litigation.

Personality fit is also important. You may be spending a year or more working with the attorneys you hire. A common perception is that it is good to hire a "bulldog." We agree to the extent this means you should hire experienced legal counsel who presents well and is persuasive. We do not agree, however, that you should hire someone who will pick unreasonable battles, who does not follow the ethical and procedural rules that govern attorney conduct, who refuses to work cooperatively with the opposing party's attorneys, or who does not communicate well. Aggressive and nasty lawyers sometimes get their way, but not usually on issues that truly matter. Most likely, they will just make the process miserable for all involved, often including their own clients.

Consult with colleagues and other professionals you know about potential legal counsel. Often, people who have gone through supply chain disputes in the past provide the best recommendations.

Hiring expert witnesses is another area in which experience and skill should be your guiding principle. Expert witnesses are professionals who have subject-matter expertise that is relevant to a legal dispute. For instance, in a dispute about a product's quality or performance, you would likely hire one or more engineering experts. In a dispute about supplier performance, you might hire an expert in supply chain management/procurement. In a dispute over a contract with a Chinese supplier, you might hire an expert in global supply chain management and Chinese manufacturing. A company's attorneys, with the advice and feedback of the company, typically guide expert-witness hiring decisions. If your counsel is experienced in supply chain litigation, they no doubt have contacts with qualified experts. In addition to being experienced, experts must also have excellent credentials and communication skills. Like your attorneys, experts typically bill by the hour. However, they are often invaluable.

Supply chain experts can play a key role in supply chain legal disputes. Based on their years of experience, they can explain to whoever is deciding your case the best practices that buyers and suppliers should follow. Becoming an expert in legal cases requires having the right background and experience, which does not happen overnight. Look for experts who have 25 or more years of hands-on supply chain experience, preferably in your industry. Good experts are able to focus in on the issues most relevant in the dispute. Experts who go off on tangents or who introduce ideas that do not fit with the rest of the case do more harm than good.

Experts are often asked to write "expert reports" that state their opinions and support your position in the lawsuit. In matters requiring expert reports, look for experts who have writing experience, either though published books, articles, white papers, or legal reports in other cases. Expert reports require a specific style of writing, and experts with experience in this area will save you time and money.

Experts in almost any subject matter can be found through agencies and referral organizations that act like agents for expert talent. These agencies charge a mark-up on experts' hourly rates. Experts can also be found in national and local catalogues available online and in print. An advanced keyword search online, such as "Chinese manufacturing expert witness," will produce experts that you can contact directly. Hiring attorneys and experts is much like hiring employees. You should carefully interview the candidates and check their references.

## Legal Overview

Supply chain disputes can be complex, since they often involve highly technical subjects, international business transactions, and extensive documentary evidence. Managing a legal dispute is difficult even if the parties no longer have a business relationship. It is even more difficult if the parties are still doing business together. "Business as usual" is almost always disrupted, and gamesmanship inevitably takes over.

Even though emotions typically run high after litigation starts, supply chain partners who are still working together need to find a way to get business done. We recommend finding employees from each side of the relationship that get along well, and channeling communications through them as much as possible. Sometimes, functioning breaks down because employees are afraid that anything they say will be held against them in the legal proceedings. In such cases, counsel can often negotiate a deal in which business communications made through this special channel cannot be used in the legal proceedings.

### Before Litigation Begins

Typically, if a supply chain relationship becomes the subject of a legal dispute, the relationship will have deteriorated well before legal proceedings began. Often, new management, increased management oversight, or unanticipated financial losses precipitate litigation. Prior to litigation, communications often become tense. The start of this tension may signal the last chance to resolve differences between supply chain partners without legal action, however. If the relationship is truly beneficial to both parties, a meaningful attempt to air grievances and implement change at this time may save the time and expense of litigation.

Be cautious if you detect signs that your supply chain partner intends to initiate legal action. This is not the time to be lax or cavalier about responding to communications or to allow emotions to influence how you communicate.

### *The Complaint or Demand for Arbitration*

Legal action is initiated by filing a complaint in the case of US litigation or a demand for arbitration in the case of arbitration. Complaints and demands for arbitration are stylistically similar in that they both set forth the legal claims of the complaining party and the facts upon which those legal claims are based.

If you are the party initiating a legal dispute, you should ensure that the employees at your company most involved in the dispute thoroughly review the complaint or demand for arbitration before it is filed. Typically, complaints and arbitration demands are drafted by attorneys before they have reviewed all of the underlying evidence (which often consists of several million documents), so they need help to ensure that every statement made in these initial legal documents is scrupulously accurate.

Ensuring accuracy is doubly important if you are seeking any sort of "emergency" or "expedited" relief, sometimes called a "temporary restraining order" or "preliminary injunction" in US litigation, or "interim measures" or "emergency measures" in arbitration. If a supply chain partner's breach of contract will cause immediate and irreparable harm, the judge or arbitrator may enter a short-term order to prevent it, pending the outcome of the litigation. Companies that overstate their case and successfully obtain emergency relief when they do not truly merit it often find that they lose the trust of the judge or arbitrator during later stages of the proceedings.

If you are the party initiating legal action, you may have a choice of several different forums in which to file your case if your supply chain agreement does not contain a forum selection clause. In US litigation, one choice may be deciding between state or federal court. Most supply chain litigants prefer federal court (although there are exceptions) because it is more uniformly administered and because federal judges tend to have more experience with sophisticated commercial disputes than state court judges (although there are many exceptions, and this decision needs to be evaluated on a case-by-case basis). The downside to being a plaintiff in federal court is that, to prevail, the jury must be unanimous, whereas in many state courts, the plaintiff can prevail with less than a unanimous verdict.

If your supply chain contract requires arbitration, you probably do not have much choice as to where or how the case must be filed. Arbitration clauses generally dictate the arbitration institution that will administrate the case and the location where the arbitration will be held.

If a complaint or demand for arbitration is filed against your company, it is critical to give the complaint or demand the same detailed attention as you would if you were the party initiating legal proceedings. The complaint or arbitration demand should be transmitted to your legal counsel as soon as possible, and legal counsel should be given unfettered access to the employees at your company who know the most about the dispute, even if they are relatively low-level employees. The employees with the most knowledge about the underlying facts should all be asked to review the complaint or arbitration demand. If your employees identify any inaccuracies, the inaccuracies should be pointed out as soon as possible to your counsel, along with any business records that relate to the claims being made.

### *Responding to the Complaint or Demand for Arbitration*

If you are responding to a complaint or demand for arbitration, you have several choices. First, in US litigation, you may be able to file a motion to dismiss. A motion to dismiss asks the judge to dismiss the case on the grounds that even if all the allegations in the complaint are true, they do not state a viable legal claim. In some supply chain disputes, the parties' contract contains language that on its face negates claims being made. For instance, if a complaint asserts that components that the plaintiff purchased from a supplier were defective, but the supply chain agreement disclaims all warranties, a motion to dismiss would be appropriate. Motions to dismiss are generally not available in arbitrations, which is one of the reasons supply chain partners might prefer litigation to arbitration. (See Chapter 19: Dispute Resolution Clauses in US Supply Chain Contracts.)

If a motion to dismiss is not an available strategy, a defendant will generally file an answer to the complaint or a response to a demand for arbitration. Answers and responses are paragraph-by-paragraph rejoinders to each of the plaintiff's allegations, drafted by your attorneys with the help of the company's most knowledgeable employees. In answering, your attorneys will need to thoroughly investigate each of the plaintiff's allegations, and determine how best to respond to them.

The other consideration in responding to a complaint or demand will be whether to file a "counterclaim," which is a statement of any legal claims you as a named defendant may have against the plaintiff—kind of like a complaint in reverse. In supply chain disputes, parties often assert claims against each other, and counterclaims are typical. To assert a counterclaim, you need to work closely with your counsel to ensure that your allegations are accurate and well supported, just as you would if you were filing a complaint or arbitration demand.

### Discovery

The most costly and time-consuming part of litigation in the United States is "discovery." Discovery is the process by which the parties gather evidence from each other and sometimes from third parties. Discovery is time-consuming, expensive, and burdensome—but incredibly important. Often, discovery is where cases are won or lost. Litigants often despair the cost of discovery, and there are cases in which discovery becomes more burdensome and expensive than it should be. However, even reasonably conducted discovery requires a lot of time and money. To understand the likely costs up-front, you may want to ask your counsel to prepare a case budget, and to update it as the litigation proceeds.

The biggest cost component of discovery is usually the production and review of documents. This consists of exchanging the business records held by both litigants. The rule in US litigation is that parties must produce all relevant business records in discovery that are requested by the opposing party, which includes emails, paper documents, network files, engineering models, text messages, ERP data, and any other business records stored in any way by the company or its employees. Finding all of the relevant materials is a labor-intensive process. If you have not done it before (and even if you have), be sure to work closely with your attorneys to ensure compliance with all discovery rules.

In US courts, litigants are generally required to respond fully to all document requests that are "reasonably calculated to lead to the discovery of admissible evidence," which could amount to millions of documents—easily—in a supply chain dispute. Arbitrations in the United States also usually involve extensive document discovery. Litigation and arbitration outside the United States may involve less expansive discovery, but usually some is allowed. Companies (especially non-US companies) that do not have much experience with litigation are often surprised by the scope of document discovery involved in commercial disputes. Altogether, document discovery can take a year or more.

While responding to document requests seems (and is) burdensome, it is best to do it right the first time. Failure to produce requested evidence risks penalties and sanctions from the court or arbitrator. Experienced legal counsel will tell you that resisting discovery is often not worth the time and expense.

### Litigation Holds

Finding and preserving all of your business records usually involves issuing a "litigation hold." A litigation hold is a document your attorneys will draft that will be distributed to all of the employees in your company involved in the supply chain relationship in dispute. These employees likely will include engineers, quality personnel, finance people, management, and anyone in the supply chain function who interfaced with the opposing party. In supply chain disputes, litigation holds often go to a large number of employees because supply chain disputes typically touch many areas of a company's operations.

A litigation hold instructs company employees to locate and preserve all evidence relevant to the dispute. Your attorneys will also likely involve your company's IT department in the litigation hold process. Besides being able to search your company's IT systems to find relevant business records, your tech people may also be asked to suspend any automatic destruction functions ordinarily in place for email, ERP, or network storage to prevent the destruction of relevant evidence. To the extent that your company stores documents in off-site locations, these documents will have to be retrieved.

Expect your lawyers to want to follow up individually with your employees, including your IT staff, to ensure compliance with a litigation hold (be concerned if they do not). Your lawyers will probably work with an electronic discovery vendor to store and manage the business records you produce. When the other side produces its documents and other evidence, those too will be sent to the vendor who can make locating particular documents by using search terms much easier. This is a relatively new phenomenon in litigation. 10 years ago, document discovery generally consisted of exchanging hard-copy documents only, and productions rarely exceeded one million pages. Now, with the proliferation of email and other electronic communications, most document discovery in commercial disputes is produced and stored electronically.

Your attorneys will need to review all of the business records that are produced to prepare your case. Attorneys have different ways of handling document review, but generally, they work with the discovery vendor and perhaps with lower-cost "contract lawyers" to conduct an initial review of documents that are produced. Through this initial review, your attorneys will identify a smaller set of materials that are most relevant to the dispute. Your attorneys will then need to review and discuss these documents with your employees.

In US litigation, parties can also serve "interrogatories," which are written questions directed to the opposing party, and "requests for admission," which require the answering party to admit or deny the inquiring party's contentions. Both interrogatories and requests for admission must be answered carefully. Expect to go through several drafts of interrogatory answers and responses to requests for admission with your attorneys. Interrogatories and requests for admission are generally not allowed in arbitration or in any other legal proceedings outside the United States.

### Subpoenas to Third Parties

In US litigation, parties may send subpoenas to third parties to obtain documents or to command a third party to give deposition or trial testimony. Just like document requests between parties, subpoenas can generate thousands of responsive documents. In the United States, subpoenas are also increasingly used in arbitrations, although there is currently a split between courts as to whether arbitration panels have the authority to compel third parties to comply with subpoenas.

### Depositions

Depositions are a normal part of US litigation and sometimes occur in US arbitrations as well. Depositions generally do occur outside the United States. In a deposition, the attorneys for one party will question a witness associated with the opposing party (typically, an employee or expert witness). Sometimes, attorneys will request the deposition of an individual by name. Other times, attorneys will identify a deposition subject (e.g., product testing), and the responding company will designate an appropriate witness to be deposed on that subject. Either way, when your company's employees are being deposed, you can expect that your attorneys will want to prepare them thoroughly.

Some attorneys videotape deposition practice sessions to help witnesses become less nervous and to improve their testifying skills.

Depositions are typically conducted in an attorney's or a court reporter's office. Deposition testimony is transcribed by a court reporter, and depositions are sometimes also videotaped. Depositions can take from an hour to multiple days, although federal courts in the United States impose a seven-hour limit on each deposition. Some attorneys are very aggressive in deposition. Others are more conversational. Either way, employees who are deposed have to be careful to give correct and precise answers.

It is common for witnesses to become fatigued during their depositions, especially if they have never been deposed before or if a deposition has taken more than half a day. Attorneys and witnesses must be vigilant to ensure that fatigue does not cause careless answers. Sometimes tired witnesses will lose focus and become more agreeable to the opposing attorney's questions in the hope that this will make the deposition go faster. This never works and in fact almost always has the opposite effect.

### What Happens with the Evidence

After you have exchanged documents, asked and answered interrogatories and requests for admission, allowed your employees to be deposed, and hired expert witnesses, what happens next?

There are several possibilities. The first and most common is that as discovery has progressed, the parties and their attorneys take a critical look at merits of their case. They will assess the cost to continue with the litigation versus the likelihood of prevailing at trial. It is common for supply chain litigants to begin seriously discussing settlement at this point.

Alternatively, at the end of the discovery process in US litigation, one or both parties may move for "summary judgment" if a case does not settle. Summary judgment allows the court to decide all or part of a case without trial if the "undisputed facts" show that one party is entitled to prevail. For example, summary judgment would be appropriate if a buyer alleged that the supplier's components were defective, but in deposition, the buyer's engineers admitted that the components performed as required under the contract specifications. Summary judgment is generally not available in arbitration. Non-US courts each have their own rules and procedures.

If settlement or summary judgment does not occur, a supply chain dispute will proceed to trial or to an arbitration hearing. Trials and arbitration hearings in the United States involve the presentation of evidence through witnesses and company documents. Your attorneys will need to prepare your witnesses extensively for trial—even more than for deposition. You can expect that any of your employees who testify at trial or in an arbitration will be unavailable for real work for substantial periods of time. You can also expect that your legal team—attorneys and experts—will be preparing almost constantly during the weeks leading up to the trial or arbitration. This preparation is essential, although expensive.

Testifying at trial or in arbitration can be stressful for employees, so you should remember to be understanding during this time. Supply chain disputes often require the testimony of low- to mid-level company employees, like engineers and supply chain personnel. While corporate executives understand that they are required to deal with the company's legal issues, for lower-level employees, this can be burdensome and difficult.

---

## Lessons Learned

If supply chain partners find themselves in litigation, they should:

- Retain experienced and skilled legal counsel
- Take measures to ensure that normal business can still take place during the dispute
- Work cooperatively with counsel
- Exercise extreme care in reviewing all pleadings and other documents prepared by counsel
- Be aware that discovery is burdensome but important, and comply with all discovery obligations
- Hire competent and qualified expert witnesses
- Ensure that counsel has access to the business records and employees necessary to work through the dispute

# CHAPTER 23

# IN CLOSING...

These are our opinions and thoughts about supply chain management and how to avoid and defend the disputes that are going to arise between supply chain partners. Our purpose in writing this book was to give a fundamental overview of common processes and relationships that exist in global businesses. We hope you found the process descriptions to be informative and the case studies to be helpful.

We are sure, as you read this book, you will agree and also disagree with some things we have written. It would not surprise us if the industry you are in or the client you are representing has somewhat different issues and processes. Supply chains and partners vary by company and circumstance, and we did not attempt to cover every possibility. What we tried to do was describe the basics and the approaches to consider to keep your company or client out of legal trouble.

We also wanted to describe some areas where we have found companies to be vulnerable, such as supplier negotiations and oversight, third-party logistics, and engineering language and agreements. These vulnerabilities can be mitigated by following our recommendations in agreements, contracts, and in pursuing and defending legal cases.

We have led you through the most common supply chain processes, including forecasting, engineering design, planning, procurement, importing/exporting, manufacturing, warehousing, order fulfilment, logistics, and delivery. We have discussed executive oversight of the supply chain, product recalls, corporate social responsibility, and risk in the supply chain. Finally, we have discussed what to do once a dispute has arisen.

We shared our knowledge and experience based on many years serving clients, helping them avoid trouble, and defending them when trouble was unavoidable. We hope you have learned from our experience and writing.

We want to end with a few final recommendations:

- Avoid disputes by planning ahead for contracts and relationships.
- Draft contracts with supply chain partners that are flexible, but include specific language that can be followed during the contract term.
- Remember that your job is not done when the contract is signed. Supply chain partner relationships should be actively managed over the life of the contract.
- Consider the differences in culture and practice when doing business internationally. Involve legal resources in the local country to assist with contracts and business practices.
- Take responsibility at an executive level for oversight of the supply chain, including global corporate social responsibility and managing risk.
- Know what to do should a dispute arise; do not ignore conflict, and expect to spend a significant amount of time and money to get a dispute resolved. Carefully select a good attorney and expert witnesses.

# MODEL CONTRACT PROVISIONS

# TABLE OF AUTHORITIES

# INDEX

## ~Q~

## ~R~